ADVANCE PRAISE FOR "THE NEW YORK TIM BUSINESS AND ECONOMICS"

"This is an inspired piece of work. A must-read for all aspiring journalists, it's also a handy backgrounder for those in the field who try to explain the economy's Rube Goldberg–like workings to their readers or viewers. My students will benefit mightily from it."

—Joseph Weber, University of Nebraska-Lincoln and Former Chief of Correspondents for Business Week

"Looking for examples of high-quality business writing? Look no further than Mark Tatge's New York Times Reader."

—Linda Austin, Executive Director, Donald W. Reynolds National Center for Business Journalism, Walter Cronkite School of Journalism and Mass Communication, Arizona State University

The New York Times Reader

business
AND
economics

Mark W. Tatge
and the Writers of
The New York Times

CQ PRESS

A Division of SAGE
Washington, D.C.

CQ Press
2300 N Street, NW, Suite 800
Washington, DC 20037

Phone: 202-729-1900; toll-free, 1-866-4CQ-PRESS (1-866-427-7737)

Web: www.cqpress.com

Cover design: Matthew Simmons, www.myselfincluded.com
Cover photo: ©iStockphoto.com/pavlen
Composition: C&M Digitals (P) Ltd.

∞ The paper used in this publication exceeds the requirements of the
American National Standard for Information Sciences—Permanence of
Paper for Printed Library Materials, ANSI Z39.48–1992.

Printed and bound in the United States of America

14   13   12   11   10   1   2   3   4   5

Library of Congress Cataloging-in-Publication Data

The New York times reader : business and economics / Mark W. Tatge and
the writers of The New York times.
     p. cm. — (TimesCollege from CQ Press)
Includes bibliographical references.
ISBN 978-1-60426-483-8 (pbk. : alk. paper)
  1. Journalism, Commercial—Authorship—Vocational guidance.
2. Business writing—Vocational guidance. I. Tatge, Mark W.
II. New York times. III. Title. IV. Series.

PN4784.C7N37 2010
070.4'86—dc21

                                                    2009053538

To my love, Julie.

*With you by my side,
anything seems possible.*

about Mark W. Tatge

Mark W. Tatge spent three decades as an investigative editor and reporter before joining Ohio University's E.W. Scripps School of Journalism, where he teaches business, communications law, online reporting and media management courses. He formerly worked as senior editor at Forbes Magazine and as an investigative reporter at the Wall Street Journal, the Cleveland Plain Dealer, the Dallas Morning News and the Denver Post. He is a frequent financial commentator on ABC, CNBC, MSNBC, CNN, FOX and PBS. Tatge has won the Peter Lisagor Award for Exemplary Journalism, The Ohio Society of Professional Journalists' First Amendment Award and the Morton Margolin Prize for Distinguished Business Reporting. He was also named the Best Business Writer in Texas by The Associated Press Managing Editors. He is a past Kiplinger Fellow in Public Affairs Reporting at Ohio State University, where he completed his master's degree in journalism, and in 2010 he will receive his MBA from Ohio University.

contents

foreword

LAWRENCE INGRASSIA

editor, business and finance

© The New York Times

FOR THE PAST YEAR, business reporters have been writing the first draft of history. Decades from now, economists will pore over what we covered at the time of the great financial meltdown of 2008 to help figure out what happened: what went wrong, how it might have been avoided, who should be held accountable—in business and in government—and how the global economy pulled back from the abyss.

One of the first places they will turn, I'm confident, will be The New York Times—to writers like Peter Goodman, Diana Henriques, David Leonhardt, Gretchen Morgenson, Joe Nocera, Floyd Norris, Andrew Ross Sorkin, Louis Uchitelle and their many colleagues, who have been real-time chroniclers and commentators of the most convulsive economic period of our times.

If you aspire to be a great business and economic journalist, you can learn a lot by reading what Times reporters have written in the stories that follow on these pages. What you will find, largely, are stories that revolve around people. Sure, some are about economic policies, or financial products, or business strategies, or corporate competition. But, in the end, the stories are really about people: Company CEOs. Federal government regulators. Washington politicians. Mid-level managers. Assembly line laborers. Tapped-out consumers. Unemployed and underemployed workers.

That's the lens we look through at The New York Times when writing about business and the economy. What does it mean to people? To the way we live and work, to our financial and social well-being? Policies in the abstract can be mind-numbing and wonkish. But they matter, and our job—our mission—is to bring them to life, to explain and illuminate, to put them in perspective.

That's what distinguishes Times business reporting. Yes, we report on corporate developments, new products, economic trends, management changes. But we strive to make our coverage relevant by focusing on the big issues in the world of business and economics that affect people's lives, for better and for worse. What is the proper role of Wall Street in the economy? How do tax policies shape society? What are the advantages, and disadvantages, of free trade? How is technology making our lives easier—but also, to what extent does it endanger privacy?

We also understand that just about every important issue that The Times covers is related, one way or another, to the economy. Health care is a public policy issue, yes, but it is also a huge economic issue, for individuals, for companies and for the government. The politics of the Middle East can't be covered without recognizing the importance of oil to the global economy. China's emergence as a superpower is an economic story first and foremost. Global warming isn't just a science story; it is a business story as well. I could go on. That's something that I think makes business journalism so unusual, so interesting and different. Or, as I like to say, it's almost always about money.

How important is economic coverage for Times readers? Well, a few decades ago, the business desk was—let's be honest—not exactly the place where top reporters aspired to work. Today, it is among the biggest departments, with more than 100 staffers overall, including editors and reporters, and boasts some of the best-known bylines at The Times. Rarely a day goes by without a business or economics story on the front page, and often there are more than one. In the 2008 presidential campaign, one of the most historic elections in U.S. history, economic news dominated the political debate and the headlines. As I repeated many times to my colleagues in Washington on the national desk, the metro desk and the foreign desk, "We're all business reporters now."

What it takes to be a great business journalist is pretty much the same as what it takes to be a great journalist covering anything: intellectual curiosity, skepticism, persistence, passion—and patience. Few topics are truly mastered in a short period. Developing knowledge, and building sources who really know what is going on and are willing to lift the veil, takes time.

Gretchen Morgenson, Joe Nocera and Floyd Norris are three of the best in the business, and they all have been business reporters for a long time. They take complex subjects and make them simple. The best stories—and you will find many in this collection—are sophisticated enough to be illuminating to experts while also being clear enough to be understandable to the average reader. They tell you something that you don't know, or make you think in different ways about things that you do know, or help you understand something that was mystifying, or prompt companies or policymakers to examine the implications of what they are doing.

If you write stories that do this, you'll have a great career. Even better, you'll have a lot of fun.

preface

AS EXPERIENCED TEACHERS KNOW, teaching journalism students to write about technical subjects like business, medicine or science can be a tortuous task. Do you focus more on teaching writing or teaching the topic? You try to cover both, and at semester's end you're left wondering whether you've done justice to either goal.

One sensible way to bring students up to speed is to use examples to examine how top journalists approach the topic. But finding a good collection of stories for a specialized reporting class is a struggle. The examples in many books are either too technical or not technical enough, and trying to compile your own collection takes forever. That's where this business reader comes in. It draws from the resources of The New York Times to come up with a starting lineup of business experts and stories that will help you teach students about reporting business and economics.

In these pages you will find interviews with six Times writers who share their insights about a diverse selection of topics ranging from taxes to con games to Twitter. You'll hear from economics writer David Leonhardt, financial correspondent Floyd Norris, investigative reporter Diana Henriques, business columnist Joe Nocera, tax writer David Cay Johnston and economics writer Louis Uchitelle. These six journalists represent a wide range of skills and experiences but share one essential talent: they are very good at breaking down complex topics and explaining things simply, providing analysis and context.

As all journalism teachers know, students have a better chance of grasping a complex topic when it's broken into easily digested chunks. That's especially true when it comes to understanding—and writing about—the world of business and the economy. In producing this book, I've attempted to compile an operations manual for aspiring business reporters—one that will give your students the tools to understand how our economy functions so they can talk with titans of industry and translate jargon into language a general audience can easily understand.

STRUCTURE OF THE BOOK

In keeping with my goal to make this a teaching tool, I have grouped the book into two sections—writing about the economy and writing about business. In each section, you will find great stories by New York Times writers.

The first section has stories grouped by topic, such as making sense of the economy, inflation, jobs, wages, taxes and debt. The second section focuses more on hardcore business topics—corporate earnings, markets, mergers and management. The second half of the volume also spotlights the mechanics of writing in some of the most common types of business stories, namely profiles, earnings stories and initial public stock offerings. Throughout the book, stories were selected with the aim of giving students a basic grasp of the topic while exposing them to larger seismic trends occurring in business and the economy—for example, retiring baby boomers, the vanishing middle class, shrinking paychecks, vanishing pensions and growing public discontent with Big Business.

SPECIAL BOOK FEATURES

A note describing what the story is about and pointing readers toward particularly educational aspects of the reporting or writing precedes each story. Six of the 10 chapters include conversations with New York Times writers who talk about how they come up with story ideas, how they report and shape stories and how they overcome the challenges of writing about business. Many were not trained in business or economics before embarking on their career paths. The writers tell about how they got into journalism and offer advice for students wishing to pursue a career in business writing.

Sprinkled throughout the book are story scans, which highlight the building blocks used to assemble basic stories that business journalists are most frequently called upon to write. These glimpses at what make stories work offer a road map that novice writers can easily follow.

Another valuable teaching tool is the list of discussion questions and key concepts—part of an end-of-chapter section called Making Connections. These questions can be reviewed in class or assigned for homework. Both are geared toward building a bridge between the book and the real world where students will be called upon to conceptualize and execute their own story ideas.

Additional Times resources of value for business and economics writing are on a Web site established specifically for this series, including links to interactive graphics and multi-media presentations that accompanied the stories in this reader. Go to college.cqpress.com/nytimes.

USES FOR THIS BOOK

This book is designed so it can be used in a variety of ways. It could be used in business, economics, journalism, public relations and nonfiction writing classes. If you are teaching economics, the book is chock-full of stories and statistics about the U.S. work force, employment, immigration and pay trends. Business teachers will find chapters focusing on taxes, management, corporate restructuring and executive compensation. The annotated stories and interviews with writers will give public relations professionals insights into how reporters conceptualize and tackle stories. Journalists and other nonfiction writers will find a wealth of information here that will help the novice better understand business and come up with better story ideas and nut grafs.

No matter what the use, this book has some of most talented people in the country offering insights into their jobs and how they approach them.

ACKNOWLEDGMENTS

I owe a big debt of gratitude to my editor, Jane Harrigan. Jane calmly guided me through the editing process and helped me polish this volume under a tight deadline. She offered many suggestions that ultimately improved the organization of the volume and hopefully will make it an indispensible tool in the classroom. I also thank CQ Press editorial director Charisse Kiino, who embraced this project and gave it her full support.

I owe special thanks to Ohio University Scripps College of Communication dean Greg Shepherd and director Thomas Hodson for supporting me and business journalism at the E. W. Scripps School of Journalism. Without them, I could not have undertaken this project. I also owe many thanks to all the students at Ohio University for their interest in and support of business journalism. Their curiosity about business writing made it easier to focus this book on its intended audience. And I would like to thank my classmates and professors—including classmate Herbert Blankson, economics professor Khosrow Doroodian, graduate executive education director Ed Yost and marketing professor Jane Sojka—at the OU College of Business, where I am completing my master of business administration. They offered advice, support and inspiration when it was needed most.

This book would not have been possible without the invaluable support of editorial director of book development Alex Ward, business editor Lawrence Ingrassia and many others at The New York Times. I am extremely grateful to New York Times writers Diana Henriques, David Leonhardt, Joe Nocera, Floyd Norris, Louis Uchitelle and former Times writer David Cay Johnston, who recently retired after spending many years covering taxes. Each of them spent hours with me talking about how they do their jobs, offering invaluable insights that will aid students in their quests to be business journalists. I'd also like to express my gratitude to everyone whom I pestered about the book outline and its many incarnations—including University of North Carolina professor Chris Roush, Northwestern University professor Joe Mathewson, Associated Press writer Doug Daniel and author Bob Shook.

My most heartfelt appreciation goes to my wife, Julie, who critiqued my various drafts and offered insights she developed as the Chicago Tribune's financial editor. Without the help, friendship and support of all these people and many others, this book would not have been possible.

introduction

TIMES COULDN'T BE BETTER to write about business and the economy. Two big U.S. automakers—General Motors and Chrysler—filed for bankruptcy in 2009, unemployment reached a 26-year high as many businesses closed their doors, and a once-respected Wall Street financial adviser bilked wealthy individuals of $60 billion before he was caught.

The scam artist is finally in prison and the economy is actually looking better, but the public's appetite for business news remains as strong as ever. People want to know: Will I lose my job? What's going to happen to my health-care benefits? Should I refinance my mortgage or wait? It's the job of the business journalist to help answer such questions and more, giving citizens, public officials and business leaders indispensible information so they can make intelligent decisions.

In today's fast-paced world, business coverage is no longer limited to the financial section of a daily newspaper. "The need for financial knowledge has seeped into every area of reportage," says Diana Henriques, senior financial reporter for The New York Times. "It is almost impossible to cover anything from arts to sciences to criminology to immigration without a grasp of the world of business."

Nor is business coverage limited to print. Flip on any cable or network news show and you'll find stories about business or the economy. Same thing for radio. And need I say more about the plethora of specialized Web sites that allow just about anyone to research specific market interests? No matter what the platform, business is a front-and-center topic.

Reading The New York Times gives beginning journalists a window into how the pros write and report their stories. On a daily basis, The Times can't match the number of words about business produced every day by its neighbor, The Wall Street Journal. So to compete, it differentiates itself by doing a superlative job of explanation and analysis. Times writers excel at breaking down complex subjects and putting them into language a general reader can understand, not to mention adding online components—blogs, interactive graphics, audio slideshows and interviews with key business players. All these options add new ways of looking at subjects in the news and allow people to customize their own business reports.

As a business journalist, you have the power and the opportunity to make a marked difference in the lives—not to mention the pocketbooks—of your readers. It's hard not to get hooked on business writing; there is never a shortage of stories, no matter what the avenue or era.

During the 1980s, it seemed like every company in America was being taken over by high-flying corporate raiders who were financing their takeovers with high-risk junk bonds. A decade later it was the Internet boom. Armed with a hot idea, it was easy for young, tech-savvy entrepreneurs to find financial backers. Investors bid up stock prices like drunken sailors on holiday, making millions for these techie hotshots. It didn't seem to matter that many of these companies were losing money and were in danger of going out of business. Everyone wanted a piece of the pie, a bit of the glamour and glitz.

But that party didn't last. Momentum fizzled in 2000 with the dot-com collapse. Scared investors then sought something safer, something more tangible than a vaporous dot-com—housing. Money began pouring into housing. With values rising, consumers got into the game, too, using the growing equity in their homes to go on an unprecedented spending spree—snapping up everything from new cars and clothes to vacations and fancy electronics. Many traded up to bigger homes. They bought older 1960s ranches, tore them down and built McMansions in their place.

But like the dot-com surge before it, the housing bubble also "popped," touching off a particularly nasty recession in late 2007. It seemed like everybody was in financial trouble. The federal government began bailing out most of corporate America. And people began talking about whether the country might be heading for another Big D, as in Great Depression. Near-panic set in.

Panic comes when people misunderstand what they are up against. Little wonder that many did not know what to do during this latest crisis. Surveys show many people lack even a basic understanding of money, banking and the economy. Forty-one percent of U.S. adults, or more than 92 million Americans, give themselves a C, D or F when it comes to their knowledge of personal finance, according to a 2009 survey conducted by Harris Interactive.[1] The same study found that 28 percent of homeowners said their mortgage payment, the length of the mortgage or the loan's interest rate turned out to be different from what they expected. That may explain why some people lost their homes when their adjustable-rate mortgages kicked upward or their balloon payments came due. They could no longer afford the houses they bought.

Business journalists help make sense of events like the housing mess. They help consumers and policymakers navigate a sea of complex information and make better decisions. But there's an additional perk to being a business journalist: Most media outlets pay up for a business writer, and there's usually no shortage of jobs. Even during the last recession, employers like Bloomberg continued to expand and hire business reporters. Why? Business journalism creates value. Readers see utility in information that helps them save or make money, so they will pay more for it. Employers, in turn, can afford to pay higher salaries.

Journalism schools have come to realize that they need to do a better job training their students to succeed in this complex, demanding field after graduation. Many, including the E. W. Scripps School of Journalism at Ohio University, where I teach, have started business writing programs.

Reading good business stories and studying how they work is an essential part of learning to report on business. This New York Times Reader can help you improve as a writer and reporter. The book is broken into two parts, covering the economy and covering business, each of which is sometimes taught as a separate course. The economy section focuses more on how to cover the mountains of statistical information—items like the gross domestic product, unemployment rate, consumer price index, trade deficit—released by the federal government every month. The financial markets watch these data reports closely and often react. You as a reporter will be asked to write stories about these statistics, making sense of what they mean.

The second section, covering business, reflects what a reporter encounters day to day while covering topics such as the airlines, biotechnology, food, retailing or investment banking. You can't write about something you know nothing about, and the biggest struggle most beginners have is trying to get their arms around big topics like Wall Street or corporate mergers. This section offers examples of stories that can serve as templates, along with an analysis of what makes the story work. You can use these stories as resources and as inspiration when you're assigned to write your first corporate profile, earnings story or article about an initial public stock offering.

A key feature of the book is the interviews with Times writers talking about business writing. You'll learn how these reporters got where they are and what they see as the challenges and rewards of business reporting. Like everybody else, Times writers face insecurities and stress. "I rarely start a week knowing what I am going to write for a column," says financial columnist Floyd Norris, noting that he always feels pressure to come up with something fresh. Norris and many of the other reporters interviewed for this volume started out doing something else before they got hooked on business journalism. Joe Nocera, for example, covered politics—and he likes business better. "I like the human drama of business, the crimes of it, the victories of it, the triumphs of it, the innovation of it," Nocera says. "I just think there are lots of storytelling opportunities in business."

Nocera is a veteran at business reporting. A 2007 Pulitzer Prize finalist, he joins a long list of reporters at The Times who have won international accolades for their stories on topics ranging from dangerous workplaces to deceptive sales of financial products to the sale of medicine laced with toxic industrial solvents. Examples of each are outlined in Chapter 10.

Beyond the basics of business journalism, this volume captures seismic trends that every journalist will face in the coming decade—subjects such as the impact of China's rapid industrialization on the rest of the world, the changing complexion of the U.S. workforce, the mushrooming federal deficit and the growing income gap between America's rich and poor.

Beyond these big themes, keep in mind that what's in this book represents just a small percentage of all the supplementary material The Times offers online. New forms of digital media greatly expand the possibilities for business reporting. On The Times' Web site, you'll also find in-depth interviews with reporters covering the economic crisis; videos detailing the plight of people who lost their jobs and their homes; and interactive graphics and multimedia slideshows explaining economic trends, bankruptcies and business scandals. Finally, there are business blogs on a lengthy list of topics written by Times writers and contributors, where the audience becomes part of the conversation. Many breaking-news events are chronicled and explained in DealBook, a portion of The Times' Web site devoted to mergers, acquisitions, securities sales and regulatory actions. A reporter may write one or two longer stories on a big-fish takeover artist who is on the prowl, but that reporter also would post shorter daily updates to a blog about this same development. These blog posts are then linked to a Webcast or to actual public records filings. The remarkable thing about all this content is that it's searchable and ready for download.

Business journalism is not a destination; it's a journey. What you'll learn here is only one-tenth of what you will learn practicing the skills you acquire over the course of your career. Journalism is about acquiring knowledge, taking that knowledge and information and doing something useful with it. You are a translator who gets to be part of the mix, rubbing elbows with the powerful and the downtrodden. It is a thrilling experience, with something different at every turn. Enjoy the ride, and use the advice in this book as your navigational aid.

making sense
of the economy

THE ECONOMY IS LIKE A TENNIS BALL: It goes up and down, and just how long it keeps bouncing depends on the force behind it. As this book goes to press, Washington and Wall Street are debating how to get the ball bouncing again. The economy is emerging from a long slump and will probably be greatly improved by the time you read these words. That's because the economy operates in cycles, moving up and down.

Nobody likes recessions, but they are inevitable. The excesses of capitalism get worked out during an economic downturn. The big questions are these: When the dust settles, are we better or worse off? And where are we going? These are some of the questions the stories in this chapter attempt to answer.

In measuring the economy's progress, journalists can use the reams of statistics, indexes and reports produced each month by the federal government. But writing stories based solely on "the numbers," important as they are, isn't recommended unless you want to bore your readers to death. You can also find plenty of economists willing to talk your ear off offering theories on what's happening now and giving prognostications about where the economy is headed. These experts, too, are important; they add valuable perspective and context, though they come from many different vantage points and use different philosophies in drawing conclusions about the economy.

Good business journalists need to dig deeper, go behind the numbers and beyond individual experts. What does history show? Can an expert's statement be proven statistically? Or is it just another economic fad? Experts and statistics matter. But in the end, business writing is about people. It is really a study of human behavior and what motivates people to take certain actions. In this case, much of the motivation focuses on money.

This chapter gives a sampling of some of the different approaches journalists can take in writing about the economy. You'll read about people delaying starting a family, how small businesses are struggling and why candy sales do well in a recession, as well as more familiar stories about economic trends. In their own ways, each of these stories offers important economic indicators; they point to the health of the economy and whether we are on the way up or the way down.

A reporter at The Denver Post once wrote a story measuring how full downtown parking lots were on any given day. Could this be a leading indicator of how well the economy is doing? Yes. It was not a very scientific measure, but it is the kind of story you should be on the lookout for. Looking for the impact of the economy on everyday life allows you to take a complicated subject and make it interesting and relevant to the layperson.

There are many ways to write about the economy—but the best reporting offers perspective on where we've been and where we're headed. At chapter's end you'll read a lengthy story by New York Times economics writer David Leonhardt that does an excellent job of examining the challenges that faced the American economy as President Barack Obama took office. A companion story that examined Obama's economic policies during the 2008 presidential campaign won a Gerald Loeb Award for business writing. The United States will be grappling during the coming decade with the issues Leonhardt discusses.

You don't have to be an economist to write interesting stories on the economy. You just need to be able to explain what is happening. This requires lots of reading, reporting and some basic training. "If I got to play journalism dean, I wouldn't let anyone graduate from my school without a statistics class and without being able to use Excel," Leonhardt says.

Selection 1.1

Everyone on the business beat learns to write straight news stories based on the latest government statistics. In this story the news centers on the gross domestic product (GDP), one of the most widely quoted measures of economic output. Notice that Jack Healy looks at not just GDP but also at a host of other indicators that respond to the GDP—the dollar, oil prices and the stock and bond markets. In each case, the writer attempts to explain what the change in each number means and put the change in a broader context for the reader. What makes the story is showing the magnitude of the changes in each item in response to the GDP. Each number cited tells a different story.

STOCKS AND BONDS
Quiet End to a Resurgent Month on Wall Street
By JACK HEALY

Stock markets shrugged off the news on Friday that after a year and a half of recession, the economy finally appeared to be reaching a bottom. But the government's quarterly assessment of economic growth caused big waves in other corners of the investment world.

Oil prices surged higher, gaining $2.51 to settle near $70 a barrel. Prices of metals like gold, silver and copper rose as traders speculated that a recovery would reignite demand for raw materials. The dollar

Published: July 31, 2009.

stumbled to its lowest levels of the year against six major currencies. And yields on government bonds fell sharply, reflecting lingering concerns that consumers were still holding tight onto their wallets.

But the lukewarm day in stock markets capped a stellar July performance for Wall Street.

After drifting lower during the first two weeks of the month, stock markets stormed back as stronger-than-expected corporate profits convinced investors that big banks and other companies could continue to make money despite the recession.

The Standard & Poor's 500-stock index gained 7.4 percent for the month, and the Dow Jones industrial average rose 8.5 percent.

Economists and market-watchers spent much of the day parsing a report from the Commerce Department showing that the gross domestic product fell at a pace of 1 percent from April through June. Although consumer spending fell 1.2 percent after growing during the previous three months, business investment fell at a slower pace, and government spending helped to stem declines in the broader economy.

The report raised expectations that the recession would soon end, and that the economy would grow again late this year. Some optimists, like Philip J. Orlando of Federated Investors, even said that "the Great Recession likely ended in the second quarter."

Investors on Friday did not quite share that optimism.

The Dow Jones industrial average gained 17.15 points, or 0.19 percent, to close at 9,171.61, and the broader Standard & Poor's 500-stock index was up 0.73 points or 0.07 percent, at 987.48. The Nasdaq fell 0.29 percent, to close at 1,978.50.

"The G.D.P. was better than forecast, better than the first quarter, but there was some strong government spending cranked into that mix," said David Dietze, chief investment strategist at Point View Financial Services. "We can't rely on government largess to get us out of this. The consumer's got to get his mojo back, and we didn't see that."

Trading in Treasury markets reflected some of that hesitance, analysts said. While interest rates fluctuated as the government auctioned off a record $115 billion in notes this week, yields fell when bond traders saw few signs of incipient inflation in the government's economic figures.

The price of the benchmark 10-year Treasury note rose 1 1/32, to 97 2/32, while the yield fell to 3.48 percent, from 3.61 percent late Thursday.

Shares of the Ford Motor Company rose 8.25 percent, to $8, as the House of Representatives rushed to extend $2 billion in emergency funds to the "cash for clunkers" program, which offers car owners rebates for junking their old gas-guzzling cars for new fuel-efficient models.

Selection 1.2

Each month a series of leading indicators forecasting the future outlook for the economy is released. Economists and forecasters closely watch these figures for clues on where the economy is headed. Learning how to read the indicators is well worth the effort spent. In this column, Floyd Norris talks about the recent recession, how it compares with earlier downturns and what the indicators tell us about the future. This story, although more technical than some other pieces appearing in this chapter, offers insights as to yet another way to report on the health of the economy. Contrast how Norris reports on the leading indicators with the more straight news approach in the previous story.

OFF THE CHARTS

Leading Indicators Are Signaling the Recession's End

By FLOYD NORRIS

The American recession appears to be nearing an end, but only after it has become the deepest downturn in more than half a century.

The index of leading indicators, which signals turning points in the economy, is rising at a rate that has accurately indicated the end of every recession since the index began to be compiled in 1959.

The index was reported this week to have risen for the third consecutive month in June, and to have risen at a 12.8 percent annual rate over those three months. Such a rise, pointed out Harm Bandholz, an economist with UniCredit Group, "has always marked the end of the contraction."

Mr. Bandholz said he expected that the National Bureau of Economic Research, the official arbiter of American economic cycles, would eventually conclude that the recession bottomed out in August or September of this year.

If that proves to be accurate, the recession that began in December 2007 will have lasted 21 or 22 months, making it the longest downturn since the Great Depression.

There are caveats to the forecast, of course. Somewhat illogically, the index of leading indicators is subject to revision in coming months, which could make the recent gain seem smaller and not necessarily indicative of an approaching recovery.

Only seven of the 10 leading indicators for June have been reported by the government, while the other three were estimated by

Published: July 25, 2009.

the Conference Board, an independent research group that compiles the indicators. Some of the seven indicators that have been reported may be revised.

As can be seen in the accompanying charts, six of the seven recessions since 1960 either ended in the month the indicator first showed a 12 percent annualized gain, or had ended a month or two before the index did so.

The exception was the 1990–'91 recession, which was followed by one of the slowest recoveries ever. The official end of the recession was in March 1991, but the recovery was so tepid that it was not until December 1992 that the economic research bureau made that call. As it happened, December was the same month the indicator first showed such a strong three-month rise.

An end to recession is not, of course, the same thing as the beginning of a boom. The indicator "has an unblemished record on calling the turning point," said another economist, Robert J. Barbera of ITG, "but it is not a particularly good guide to the power of the upturn."

Indeed, one of the strongest moves in the leading indicators came at the end of the brief 1980 recession, as credit controls were removed. But the economy soon fell into another, longer recession.

Mr. Bandholz thinks we may get a "W" recovery, in which early gains are followed by weaker figures. "We do not expect this recovery to be strong and self-sustaining," he said. "What is lacking is support from consumer spending."

During the most recent three months, the strongest indicators have been the financial ones. The Standard & Poor's 500-stock index has risen while the gap has widened between long-term and short-term interest rates. The indicators index was also helped by an increase in consumer expectations and a slowing in deliveries by suppliers. (Slower deliveries are assumed to be caused by rising orders, although such a change could indicate the suppliers simply laid off too many workers.)

Two of the 10 indicators—the money supply and new orders for consumer goods—have shown declines.

Another measure compiled by the Conference Board, the index of coincident indicators, has fallen for eight consecutive months, and dropped in 17 of the last 19 months. That indicator is often used by the economic research bureau in dating decisions, and its failure to stabilize is a reason that Mr. Bandholz says he thinks the downturn is not yet over.

The index of coincident indicators has fallen 6.4 percent from the peak it reached in November 2007, making this the deepest recession since 1960. Before this cycle, its steepest decline was a 5.6 percent slide during the 1973–'75 downturn.

Selection 1.3

Economic booms and busts have an impact on human behavior. Some of the best stories come through understanding business cycles, asking the right questions and then knowing where to look for answers. This story looks at the numbers—health statistics rather than the economic numbers more commonly seen on the business pages. If allowed more time to follow up, a reporter could develop an even larger story by interviewing some couples who had delayed starting a family because of the recession. Numbers are the start of a story and can lead to even broader connections.

Birth Rate Is Said to Fall as a Result of Recession
By SAM ROBERTS

For the first time since the decade began, Americans are having fewer babies, and some experts are blaming the economy.

"It's the recession," said Andrew Hacker, a sociologist at Queens College of the City University of New York. "Children are the most expensive item in every family's budget, especially given all the gear kids expect today. So it's a good place to cut back when you're uncertain about the future."

In 2007, the number of births in the United States broke a 50-year-old record high, set during the baby boom. But last year, births began to decline nationwide, by nearly 2 percent, according to provisional figures released last week.

Those figures from the National Center for Health Statistics, indicate that births declined in all but 10 states in 2008 (most of them in a Northern belt where the recession was generally less severe) compared with the year before. Over all, 4,247,000 births were recorded in 2008, 68,000 fewer than the year before.

California logged 14,500 fewer births than in 2007, a 2.6 percent decline and the first since 2001, when the state struggled with job losses in Silicon Valley that led to layoffs in distribution, construction and other sectors.

Early figures for 2009 appear to confirm the correlation with the recession. As more families were feeling the effects of layoffs and economic uncertainty, births decreased even faster.

In Arizona, births declined about 3 percent in 2008, the first annual decrease since an economic downturn in 1991. In the first six months of 2009, 7 percent fewer babies were born compared with the year before. The state's population bubble burst and the

Published: August 6, 2009.

jobless rate rose from 5.5 percent to 8.7 percent in the 12 months ending in June.

In the first three months of 2009, births also declined 7 percent in Florida, another state where the economy took a tumble.

"It may be that many couples saw it coming," said Carl Haub, senior demographer for the Population Reference Bureau.

Stephanie Coontz, a professor at Evergreen State College in Olympia, Wash., and research director for the Council on Contemporary Families, a research and advocacy group, said, "We probably can't prove it yet, but I agree."

"That's what happened in the Great Depression," Professor Coontz said, "and although in some periods since then, we have sometimes seen women decide to have a baby if they get laid off, that decision is usually only made if the husband is working and his job seems secure.

"More than 80 percent of the job losses in this recession have been borne by men," Professor Coontz added. "There are a lot of families where a maternity leave would mean that no income at all was coming in."

Historically, birth rates have fluctuated with the economy. Record lows were recorded during two economic crises: the Depression in the 1930s and the Arab oil embargo in the 1970s.

By the 1970s, birth rates were also affected by the rise of feminism and easier access to contraceptives and to abortion. But would they have dropped as low as they did, Mr. Haub asked, without "the added impetus of inflation, not to mention long lines at the gas station?"

"While that question can never be definitively answered," he said, "we do know that the economic setting hardly seems conducive to starting families or having additional children. Double-digit inflation during the 1970s made two-earner, two-career families a virtual necessity for many."

Stephanie J. Ventura, chief of the reproductive statistics branch of the National Center for Health Statistics, said, "We've had these bumps and drops in the past, but 2009 will be critical."

Mr. Haub agreed. "If the economic crisis can be given a start date of early 2008," he said, "then evidence of a slump in the birth rate might become apparent as early as late 2008, but could not be really conclusive until well into 2009."

"It is certainly too soon to tell if this economic crisis will result in a sharp drop in the birth rate," he said, "but all the measures and indicators, along with the collapse of the mainstays of the economy, are much worse than in the 1970s."

In 2006 and 2007, the National Center for Health Statistics, part of the Centers for Disease Control and Prevention, recorded a birth rate of 14.3 per thousand people. That number declined to 13.9 in 2008 (most sharply near the end of the year).

The fertility rate among women 15-to-44 years old, which rose from 68.7 per 1,000 in 2006 to 69.2 in 2007, dipped to 68.4 in 2008.

The New York Times

Multimedia stories regarding how different people are coping during the recession, including a photo slideshow narrated by Scott Peterson of Selection 1.4, are available at: http://projects.nytimes.com/living-with-less

Selection 1.4

One barometer of economic health is how businesses are performing. We don't often hear about the small businesses. That's because most business writing focuses on the large, publicly traded companies. Here is an interesting story that gets inside how small, family businesses have been devastated by the recession by looking at how the Peterson family's business is fighting for survival.

Family Businesses Are Reeling in Recession
By DAMIEN CAVE

MIAMI—Using only strips of canvas and a little rope, Scott Peterson walked up a 50-foot flagpole here to remove a star-spangled banner with reds faded pink. His ancestors used the same method: the family business, originally Harold A. Peterson Steeplejack, opened in 1926.

And it will probably close in 2009. The Great Recession, especially its stranglehold on credit and new construction, appears to have mortally wounded what the Depression could not kill.

Published: July 13, 2009.

"It's not 'Oh, I don't have a job, I have to go find a new one,' " Mr. Peterson said. "We're losing a corporation that is 83 years old. We're losing our house. We're losing our credit. We're losing, other than our own physical bodies, everything."

Recessions, like bullies, always pick on the weak, but few victims feel more beaten down these days than the millions of Americans with family businesses. Most run small operations with just a few employees, and failure often means closing an office with a parent's name attached and deciding which relatives to fire.

They have been hit hard since the labor market began to weaken. Businesses with one to 19 employees, nearly all of them family run, lost 757,000 jobs from the second quarter of 2007 through the third quarter of 2008, according to figures from the Bureau of Labor Statistics, broken down by company size. That amounts to 53 percent of all private-sector losses for a group of companies with about 20 percent of all employees.

Recent surveys by the National Federation of Independent Business also show that small-business owners are reporting lower profits and fewer plans to add inventory or spend capital than at any time since the group began asking such questions in 1973.

Bill Dunkelberg, the federation's chief economist, says the market is being "cleansed" of unneeded goods and services, but other researchers emphasize that this ignores the broader civic and social role that companies like H.A. Peterson and Sons have played since Paul Revere took over his father's silversmith business in 1754.

"Outside looking in, people don't understand that business has often been an organizing point for the family," said Blaine McCormick, a professor at the Hankamer School of Business at Baylor University, who worked in his family's oil business growing up. "Everyone works in it; it's our livelihood and it's a meeting place where we form our identities and the stories that carry us through life."

The Petersons' company began in New Jersey with Harry Hagan, a German immigrant who learned rigging at sea and taught his stepson, Harold A. Peterson Sr., how to use ropes to lift objects or himself. They opened the business together when Mr. Peterson was just 16.

Flags were initially just a sideline. "Most of it was repairing steeples, smokestacks, water tanks, and painting them," said Harold Peterson Jr., 80, who said his father brought him into the business before he could shave, too. The elder Mr. Peterson made Junior, at age 14, scale a 125-foot wooden flagpole at a local school to fix a broken rope; later, the pair worked as a team, installing flags and building radio towers.

"We traveled not like father and son," Mr. Peterson said. "We were more like brothers."

The family moved to Florida in 1964. By the time Scott and his two older brothers reached high school a decade later, the steeplejack business had mostly petered out. Mr. Peterson went to work for Eastern Airlines—until at a family picnic, Scott and his brothers asked him to teach them how to climb.

Learning for the first time was tough. Walking up a vertical cylinder that narrows to a diameter of a few inches requires the balance of a dancer. The canvas slings are as narrow as toilet paper, lashed to the pole with rope, then placed under the left thigh and right foot. Stepping up is possible through leverage and friction, but a little wind or the slightest lean means spinning around, flipping or crashing to the ground.

"Climbing a flagpole and doing the work we do, being out in the middle of the air, over hundreds of feet off the ground, it's a rush," Scott Peterson said.

He and his older brother Mark persuaded their father to leave Eastern and revive the business. This time, they named it H.A. Peterson and Sons, and focused exclusively on flag installation and repair.

They did pretty well in the 1980s and '90s by piggybacking on the construction boom. Working together—at its peak, the company had six employees, all related—they installed flagpoles at the Miami Dolphins' new stadium, in countless new condominium developments and at the homes of Sylvester Stallone and the boxing promoter Don King. During its best years, the company brought in $500,000 in annual revenues.

Like many owners of family businesses, the Petersons also sewed themselves into their community. They signed on to maintain flags at local schools, worked with the Boy Scouts, teaching children the ceremony for burning used flags, and even now, they give some of their poorer, patriotic residential customers new flags for free.

Mr. Peterson Sr., who stopped climbing only a few months ago to take care of his ailing wife, said he would be heartbroken and ashamed if the company closed. He said he wanted to see the company's $120,000 in debt repaid.

"We've established ourselves as people of integrity," he said. "That integrity would be shot to hell if we said, 'O.K., it's bankruptcy. Goodbye.'"

Scott Peterson, 50, said that at this point he was just trying to make their monthly overhead of $15,000. He applied this spring for a loan backed by the Small Business Administration, but he said it was rejected because his credit score was too low—after several credit card issuers cut his credit limits despite on-time payments.

Flag maintenance, an anachronism even before the recession, has now become his main income source. On one recent workday, he drove his 1993 GMC van with 250,000 miles to jobs at three separate flagpoles, and each earned him around $160.

"It's not enough monthly to keep it even," he said, sweat pouring off his bald head after descending the last pole of the day. "We're just going down and down."

The stress has already taken a toll. His wife, Arelis, is now the company's only other employee, and when asked what she made of their predicament, she started crying. Their two daughters, 8 and 11, are struggling to understand why their mother can no longer afford lunch at McDonald's, and their father no longer sleeps through the night.

"The anxiety attack is instant," Mr. Peterson said.

Seeing businesses like his disappear all around his office in a small industrial park does not help. Of the six spaces here, two are now marked with red "for rent" signs. A third is on the way, and Mr. Peterson said he just hopes his company will not be the fourth.

"The reality is that you try and stay away from realizing that everything is about to go away," he said. "We're about to lose everything that we have."

Selection 1.5

During an economic downturn, movie ticket sales jump as people try to escape the misery of layoffs, pay cuts and foreclosures. Another sure winner is candy; there's nothing like a little sugar to soothe frayed nerves. Candy consumption is just one of many nontechnical indicators that reporters can use to show the severity of the economic times. This story is filled with enough names, details and descriptions to make readers hungry for more.

When Economy Sours, Tootsie Rolls Soothe Souls
By CHRISTINE HAUGHNEY

Raymond Schneider politely elbowed his way through crowds of customers as he made for the bulk candy bins at Dylan's Candy Bar across from Bloomingdale's in Manhattan. Since he was laid off in December, Mr. Schneider, a 33-year-old interior designer, says he has become a "gummy junkie," stocking up on sweets every time he shops for groceries.

"Sugar is comforting," he said as he scooped Red Licorice Scottie Dogs into a plastic bag. "There's nothing more stressful than growing financial insecurity everywhere."

Published: March 23, 2009.

The recession seems to have a sweet tooth. As unemployment has risen and 401(k)'s have shrunk, Americans, particularly adults, have been consuming growing volumes of candy, from Mary Janes and Tootsie Rolls to Gummy Bears and cheap chocolates, say candy makers, store owners and industry experts.

Theories vary on exactly why. For many, sugar lifts spirits dragged low by the languishing economy. For others, candy also provides a nostalgic reminder of better times. And not insignificantly, it is relatively cheap.

"People may indulge themselves a little bit more when times are tough," said Jack P. Russo, an analyst with the Edward Jones retail brokerage in St. Louis. "These are low-cost items that people can afford pretty easily."

At Candyality, a store in the Lakeview neighborhood of Chicago, business has jumped by nearly 80 percent compared with this time last year, and the owner, Terese McDonald, said she was struggling to keep up with the demand for Bit-O-Honeys, Swedish Fish and Sour Balls.

At the Candy Store in San Francisco, the owner, Diane Campbell, has tripled her orders for nostalgic candies like Necco Wafers and Mallo Cups in recent months. Many of her customers tell her that even though they are living on less, they're setting aside cash for candy.

"They put candy in their actual budget," she said.

Many big candy makers are reporting rising sales and surprising profits even as manufacturers of other products are struggling to stay afloat. Cadbury reported a 30 percent rise in profits for 2008 while Nestlé's profits grew by 10.9 percent, according to public filings. Hershey, which struggled for much of 2008, saw profits jump by 8.5 percent in the fourth quarter.

Lindt & Sprüngli, which specializes in more expensive products like Lindt and Ghirardelli chocolate, announced that even though it expects to close some of its luxury retail stores this year, it also expects chocolate sales to remain strong through mainstream retailers like Wal-Mart and Target.

"All is well in candy land," said Jamie Hallman, owner of the Sweetdish candy store in the Marina district of San Francisco.

In Manhattan, at the sweet-smelling confines of Economy Candy on the Lower East Side, the owner, Jerry Cohen, said he increased his orders by 10 percent in January and February to keep up with demand for candies like Sugar Daddies and Sour Razzles. On a recent Sunday, Mr. Cohen had about a dozen workers in the narrow store trying to keep the candy tables and penny candy bins restocked as shoppers—the vast majority of them adults—grabbed candy bars and dug their hands into bins of Tootsie Rolls and Bit-O-Honeys.

"We have been wiping out of inventory," he said.

Mr. Cohen's son, Mitchell, 23, who works long hours as a Wall Street investment banker, helps out at the store on some Sundays because, he said, he finds the mood uplifting. He noted that his Wall Street co-workers have also been eating more candy: The 10-pound candy bags he puts on his desk are being devoured in one week instead of the usual two.

"That's why I like going to the store on Sundays," Mitchell Cohen said. "Everyone is happy."

There may be historic precedent to the recessionary strength of the candy business. During the 1930s, candy companies thrived, introducing an array of confections that remain popular today. Snickers started in 1930. Tootsie Pops appeared in 1931. Mars bars with almonds and Three Musketeers bars followed in 1932.

Hershey, the dominant candy brand during the Depression, remained profitable enough through the 1930s for the company to finance its own work program for the unemployed, said Pamela Whitenack, Hershey's community archives director.

"Candy companies are relatively recession-proof," said Peter Liebhold, chairman of the Smithsonian Institution's work and industry division. "During the Great Depression, candy companies stayed in business."

Candy seems to conjure memories of times before bank collapses and government bailouts. Jackie Hague, vice president of marketing for the New England Confectionery Company in Revere, Mass., which makes Necco wafers and other candies, said the company has received an unusual number of letters, e-mail messages and telephone calls from customers saying their candies had helped them "flash back to childhood."

Indeed, store owners and manufacturers find that the hottest-selling candies these days are cheaper, old-fashioned ones. In addition to strong sales of Necco Wafers and Mary Janes, the New England Confectionery Company said sales of Sweetheart candies jumped 20 percent at Valentine's Day. Eastern Sales and Marketing, a major candy representative for manufacturers, has noticed "double digit growth" for Gummy Bears, Violet Gum and Jelly Bellies, according to John Anastasi, the company's senior vice president of the confectionery business unit.

Not everyone in the industry is benefiting from tighter wallets. Edgar Roesch, a food analyst with Soleil Securities, an investment research firm in New York, predicts that the recession may present more opportunities for more economical, mass-market brands like Hershey than for, say, gourmet truffles.

Until the fourth quarter of last year, he said, "Things like Hershey Kisses were losing out to higher-end brands." But this year, that trend has reversed.

Increased candy consumption may have already taken a toll on the waistlines of many New Yorkers.

Liz Josefsberg, who runs four Weight Watchers meetings a week in Manhattan, said talk of stress eating involving candy was taking up an increasing percentage of her meetings. "I'm hearing a lot about Skittles and Mary Janes," she said.

Since Piper Gray, 23, arrived in Manhattan from Memphis in September, she has lived on a tiny salary from a journalism internship and tries to remain optimistic about eventually landing permanent work, even though prospects look discouraging.

Beside two friends at Economy Candy on a recent Sunday afternoon, she sounded cheerful as she munched on mini Smooth 'N Melty nonpareils, joked about her addiction to Creme Eggs and scoffed at the merits of Swedish Fish. Candy has become her affordable escape.

"Apples and oatmeal only go so far," she wrote later in an e-mail message. "It's so tempting to pick up an 88-cent pack of Skittles as a little pick-me-up. So I won't feel so deprived."

Selection 1.6

David Leonhardt does a remarkable job of clearly explaining the challenges facing the U.S. economy. The 7,000-word story blends economics, history, politics and analysis without tangling up the reader. You get the feeling Leonhardt is having a conversation with you, explaining what he has learned over a glass of iced tea. He cleverly employs a number of devices—active verbs, questions, subheads and time elements—to move you through the story. Major paragraphs have topic sentences cluing you to what is coming next. This is great business writing.

The Big Fix

By DAVID LEONHARDT

I. Whither Growth?

The economy will recover. It won't recover anytime soon. It is likely to get significantly worse over the course of 2009, no matter what President Obama and Congress do. And resolving the financial crisis will require both aggressiveness and creativity. In fact, the main lesson from other crises of the past century is that governments tend to err on the side of too much caution—of taking the punch bowl away before the party has truly started up again. "The mistake the United States made during the Depression and the Japanese made during the

Published: February 1, 2009.

'90s was too much start-stop in their policies," said Timothy Geithner, Obama's choice for Treasury secretary, when I went to visit him in his transition office a few weeks ago. Japan announced stimulus measures even as it was cutting other government spending. Franklin Roosevelt flirted with fiscal discipline midway through the New Deal, and the country slipped back into decline.

Geithner arguably made a similar miscalculation himself last year as a top Federal Reserve official who was part of a team that allowed Lehman Brothers to fail. But he insisted that the Obama administration had learned history's lesson. "We're just not going to make that mistake," Geithner said. "We're not going to do that. We'll keep at it until it's done, whatever it takes."

Once governments finally decide to use the enormous resources at their disposal, they have typically been able to shock an economy back to life. They can put to work the people, money and equipment sitting idle, until the private sector is willing to begin using them again. The prescription developed almost a century ago by John Maynard Keynes does appear to work.

But while Washington has been preoccupied with stimulus and bailouts, another, equally important issue has received far less attention—and the resolution of it is far more uncertain. What will happen once the paddles have been applied and the economy's heart starts beating again? How should the new American economy be remade? Above all, how fast will it grow?

That last question may sound abstract, even technical, compared with the current crisis. Yet the consequences of a country's growth rate are not abstract at all. Slow growth makes almost all problems worse. Fast growth helps solve them. As Paul Romer, an economist at Stanford University, has said, the choices that determine a country's growth rate "dwarf all other economic-policy concerns."

Growth is the only way for a government to pay off its debts in a relatively quick and painless fashion, allowing tax revenues to increase without tax rates having to rise. That is essentially what happened in the years after World War II. When the war ended, the federal government's debt equaled 120 percent of the gross domestic product (more than twice as high as its likely level by the end of next year). The rapid economic growth of the 1950s and '60s—more than 4 percent a year, compared with 2.5 percent in this decade—quickly whittled that debt away. Over the coming 25 years, if growth could be lifted by just one-tenth of a percentage point a year, the extra tax revenue would completely pay for an $800 billion stimulus package.

Yet there are real concerns that the United States' economy won't grow enough to pay off its debts easily and ensure rising living standards, as happened in the postwar decades. The fraternity of growth experts in the economics profession predicts that the economy, on its current path, will grow more slowly in the next couple of decades than over the past couple. They are concerned in part because two of the economy's most powerful recent engines have been exposed as a mirage: the explosion in consumer debt and spending, which lifted short-term growth at the expense of future growth, and the great Wall Street boom, which depended partly on activities that had very little real value.

Richard Freeman, a Harvard economist, argues that our bubble economy had something in common with the old Soviet economy. The Soviet Union's growth was artificially raised by massive industrial output that ended up having little use. Ours was artificially raised by mortgage-backed securities, collateralized debt obligations and even the occasional Ponzi scheme.

Where will new, real sources of growth come from? Wall Street is not likely to cure the nation's economic problems. Neither, obviously, is Detroit. Nor is Silicon Valley, at least not by itself. Well before the housing bubble burst, the big productivity gains brought about by the 1990s technology boom seemed to be petering out, which suggests that the Internet may not be able to fuel decades of economic growth in the way that the industrial inventions of the early 20th century did. Annual economic growth in the current decade, even excluding the dismal contributions that 2008 and 2009 will make to the average, has been the slowest of any decade since the 1930s.

So for the first time in more than 70 years, the epicenter of the American economy can be placed outside of California or New York or the industrial Midwest. It can be placed in Washington. Washington won't merely be given the task of pulling the economy out of the immediate crisis. It will also have to figure out how to put the American economy on a more sustainable path—to help it achieve fast, broadly shared growth and do so without the benefit of a bubble. Obama said as much in his inauguration speech when he pledged to overhaul Washington's approach to education, health care, science and infrastructure, all in an effort to "lay a new foundation for growth."

For centuries, people have worried that economic growth had limits—that the only way for one group to prosper was at the expense of another. The pessimists, from Malthus and the Luddites and on, have been proved wrong again and again. Growth is not finite. But it is also not inevitable. It requires a strategy.

II. The Upside of a Downturn

Two weeks after the election, Rahm Emanuel, Obama's chief of staff, appeared before an audience of business executives and laid out an idea that Lawrence H. Summers, Obama's top economic adviser, later described to me as Rahm's Doctrine. "You never want a serious crisis to go to waste," Emanuel said. "What I mean by that is that it's an opportunity to do things you could not do before."

In part, the idea is standard political maneuvering. Obama had an ambitious agenda—on health care, energy and taxes—before the economy took a turn for the worse in the fall, and he has an interest in connecting the financial crisis to his pre-existing plans. "Things we had postponed for too long, that were long term, are now immediate and must be dealt with," Emanuel said in November. Of course, the existence of the crisis doesn't force the Obama administration to deal with education or health care. But the fact that the economy appears to be mired in its worst recession in a generation may well allow the administration to confront problems that have festered for years. That's the crux of the doctrine.

The counterargument is hardly trivial—namely, that the financial crisis is so serious that the administration shouldn't distract itself with other matters. That is a risk, as is the additional piling on of debt for investments that might not bear fruit for a long while. But Obama may not have the luxury of trying to deal with the problems separately. This crisis may be his one chance to begin transforming the economy and avoid future crises.

In the early 1980s, an economist named Mancur Olson developed a theory that could fairly be called the academic version of Rahm's Doctrine. Olson, a University of Maryland professor who died in 1998, is one of those academics little known to the public but famous among his peers. His seminal work, "The Rise and Decline of Nations," published in 1982, helped explain how stable, affluent societies tend to get in trouble. The book turns out to be a surprisingly useful guide to the current crisis.

In Olson's telling, successful countries give rise to interest groups that accumulate more and more influence over time. Eventually, the groups become powerful enough to win government favors, in the form of new laws or friendly regulators. These favors allow the groups to benefit at the expense of everyone else; not only do they end up with a larger piece of the economy's pie, but they do so in a way that keeps the pie from growing as much as it otherwise would. Trade barriers and tariffs are the classic example. They help the domestic manufacturer of a product at the expense of millions of consumers, who must pay high prices and choose from a limited selection of goods.

Olson's book was short but sprawling, touching on everything from the Great Depression to the caste system in India. His primary case study was Great Britain in the decades after World War II. As an economic and military giant for more than two centuries, it had accumulated one of history's great collections of interest groups—miners, financial traders and farmers, among others. These interest groups had so shackled Great Britain's economy by the 1970s that its high unemployment and slow growth came to be known as "British disease."

Germany and Japan, on the other hand, were forced to rebuild their economies and political systems after the war. Their interest groups were wiped away by the defeat. "In a crisis, there is an opportunity to rearrange things, because the status quo is blown up," Frank Levy, an M.I.T. economist and an Olson admirer, told me recently. If a country slowly glides down toward irrelevance, he said, the constituency for reform won't take shape. Olson's insight was that the defeated countries of World War II didn't rise in spite of crisis. They rose because of it.

The parallels to the modern-day United States, though not exact, are plain enough. This country's long period of economic preeminence has produced a set of interest groups that, in Olson's words, "reduce efficiency and aggregate income." Home builders and real estate agents pushed for housing subsidies, which made many of them rich but made the real estate bubble possible. Doctors, drug makers and other medical companies persuaded the federal government to pay for expensive treatments that have scant evidence of being effective. Those treatments are the primary reason this country spends so much more than any other on medicine. In these cases, and in others, interest groups successfully lobbied for actions that benefited them and hurt the larger economy.

Surely no interest group fits Olson's thesis as well as Wall Street. It used an enormous amount of leverage—debt—to grow to unprecedented size. At times Wall Street seemed ubiquitous. Eight Major League ballparks are named for financial-services companies, as are the theater for the Alvin Ailey dance company, a top children's hospital in New York and even a planned entrance of the St. Louis Zoo. At Princeton, the financial-engineering program, meant to educate future titans of finance, enrolled more undergraduates than any of the traditional engineering programs. Before the stock market crashed last year, finance companies earned 27 percent of the nation's corporate profits, up from about 15 percent in the 1970s and '80s. These profits bought political influence. Congress taxed the income of hedge-fund managers at a lower rate than most everyone else's. Regulators didn't ask too many hard questions and then often moved on to a Wall Street job of their own.

In good times—or good-enough times—the political will to beat back such policies simply doesn't exist. Their costs are too diffuse, and their benefits too concentrated. A crisis changes the dynamic. *It's an opportunity to do things you could not do before.*

England's crisis was the Winter of Discontent, in 1978–79, when strikes paralyzed the country and many public services shut down. The resulting furor helped elect Margaret Thatcher as prime minister and allowed her to sweep away some of the old economic order. Her laissez-faire reforms were flawed in some important ways—taken to an extreme, they helped create the current financial crisis—and they weren't the only reason for England's turnaround. But they made a difference. In the 30 years since her election, England has grown faster than Germany or Japan.

III. The Investment Gap

One good way to understand the current growth slowdown is to think of the debt-fueled consumer-spending spree of the past 20 years as a symbol of an even larger problem. As a country we have been spending too much on the present and not enough on the future. We have been consuming rather than investing. We're suffering from investment-deficit disorder.

You can find examples of this disorder in just about any realm of American life. Walk into a doctor's office and you will be asked to fill out a long form with the most basic kinds of information that you have provided dozens of times before. Walk into a doctor's office in many other rich countries and that information—as well as your medical history—will be stored in computers. These electronic records not only reduce hassle; they also reduce medical errors. Americans cannot avail themselves of this innovation despite the fact that the United States spends far more on health care, per person, than any other country. We are spending our money to consume medical treatments, many of which have only marginal health benefits, rather than to invest it in ways that would eventually have far broader benefits.

Along similar lines, Americans are indefatigable buyers of consumer electronics, yet a smaller share of households in the United States has broadband Internet service than in Canada, Japan, Britain, South Korea and about a dozen other countries. Then there's education: this country once led the world in educational attainment by a wide margin. It no longer does. And transportation: a trip from Boston to Washington, on the fastest train in this country, takes six-and-a-half hours. A trip from Paris to Marseilles, roughly the same distance, takes three hours—a result of the French government's commitment to infrastructure.

These are only a few examples. Tucked away in the many statistical tables at the Commerce Department are numbers on how much the government and the private sector spend on investment and research—on highways, software, medical research and other things likely to yield future benefits. Spending by the private sector hasn't changed much over time. It was equal to 17 percent of G.D.P. 50 years ago, and it is about 17 percent now. But spending by the government—federal, state and local—has changed. It has dropped from about 7 percent of G.D.P. in the 1950s to about 4 percent now.

Governments have a unique role to play in making investments for two main reasons. Some activities, like mass transportation and pollution reduction, have societal benefits but not necessarily financial ones, and the private sector simply won't undertake them. And while many other kinds of investments do bring big financial returns, only a fraction of those returns go to the original investor. This makes the private sector reluctant to jump in. As a result, economists say that the private sector tends to spend less on research and investment than is economically ideal.

Historically, the government has stepped into the void. It helped create new industries with its investments. Economic growth has many causes, including demographics and some forces that economists admit they don't understand. But government investment seems to have one of the best track records of lifting growth. In the 1950s and '60s, the G.I. Bill created a generation of college graduates, while the Interstate System of highways made the entire economy more productive. Later, the Defense Department developed the Internet, which spawned AOL, Google and the rest. The late '90s Internet boom was the only sustained period in the last 35 years when the economy grew at 4 percent a year. It was also the only time in the past 35 years when the incomes of the poor and the middle class rose at a healthy pace. Growth doesn't ensure rising living standards for everyone, but it sure helps.

Even so, the idea that the government would be playing a much larger role in promoting economic growth would have sounded radical, even among Democrats, until just a few months ago. After all, the European countries that have tried guiding huge swaths of their economies—that have kept their arms around the "commanding heights," in Lenin's enduring phrase—have grown even more slowly than this country in recent years. But the credit crunch and the deepening recession have changed the discussion here. The federal government seems as if it was doing too little to take advantage of the American economy's enormous assets: its size, its openness and its mobile, risk-taking work force. The government is also one of the few large entities today able to borrow at a low interest rate. It alone can raise the capital that could transform the economy in the kind of fundamental ways that Olson described.

"This recession is a critical economic problem—it is a crisis," Summers told me recently. "But a moment when there are millions of people who are unemployed, when the federal government can borrow money over the long term at under 3 percent and when we face long-run fiscal problems is also a moment of great opportunity to make investments in the future of the country that have lagged for a long time."

He then told a story that John F. Kennedy liked to tell, about an early-20th-century French marshal named Hubert Lyautey. "The guy says to his gardener, 'Could you plant a tree?' " Summers said. "The gardener says, 'Come on, it's going to take 50 years before you see anything out of that tree.' The guy says, 'It's going to take 50 years? Really? Then plant it this morning.' "

IV. Stimulus vs. Transformation

The Obama administration's first chance to build a new economy—
an investment economy—is the stimulus package that has been
dominating policy discussions in Washington. Obama has repeatedly
said he wants it to be a down payment on solving bigger problems.
The twin goals, he said recently, are to "immediately jump-start job
creation and long-term growth." But it is not easy to balance those
goals.

For the bill to provide effective stimulus, it simply has to spend
money—quickly. Employing people to dig ditches and fill them up
again would qualify. So would any of the "shovel ready" projects that
have made it onto the list of stimulus possibilities. Even the construction of a mob museum in Las Vegas, a project that was crossed off the
list after Republicans mocked it, would work to stimulate the economy, so long as ground was broken soon. Pork and stimulus aren't
mutually exclusive. But pork won't transform an economy. Neither
will the tax cuts that are likely to be in the plan.

Sometimes a project can give an economy a lift and also lead
to transformation, but sometimes the goals are at odds, at least in
the short term. Nothing demonstrates this quandary quite so well as
green jobs, which are often cited as the single best hope for driving
the post-bubble economy. Obama himself makes this case. Consumer
spending has been the economic engine of the past two decades, he has
said. Alternative energy will supposedly be the engine of the future—a
way to save the planet, reduce the amount of money flowing to hostile
oil-producing countries and revive the American economy, all at once.
Put in these terms, green jobs sounds like a free lunch.

Green jobs can certainly provide stimulus. Obama's proposal
includes subsidies for companies that make wind turbines, solar power
and other alternative energy sources, and these subsidies will create
some jobs. But the subsidies will not be nearly enough to eliminate the
gap between the cost of dirty, carbon-based energy and clean energy.
Dirty-energy sources—oil, gas and coal—are cheap. That's why we
have become so dependent on them.

The only way to create huge numbers of clean-energy jobs
would be to raise the cost of dirty-energy sources, as Obama's proposed cap-and-trade carbon-reduction program would do, to make
them more expensive than clean energy. This is where the green-jobs
dream gets complicated.

For starters, of the $700 billion we spend each year on energy,
more than half stays inside this country. It goes to coal companies or
utilities here, not to Iran or Russia. If we begin to use less electricity, those utilities will cut jobs. Just as important, the current, relatively low price of energy allows other companies—manufacturers,
retailers, even white-collar enterprises—to sell all sorts of things at
a profit. Raising that cost would raise the cost of almost everything

that businesses do. Some projects that would have been profitable to Boeing, Kroger or Microsoft in the current economy no longer will be. Jobs that would otherwise have been created won't be. As Rob Stavins, a leading environmental economist, says, "Green jobs will, to some degree, displace other jobs." Just think about what happened when gas prices began soaring last spring: sales of some hybrids increased, but vehicle sales fell overall.

None of this means that Obama's climate policy is a mistake. Raising the price of carbon makes urgent sense, for the well-being of the planet and of the human race. And the economic costs of a serious climate policy are unlikely to be nearly as big as the alarmists— lobbyists and members of Congress trying to protect old-line energy industries—suggest. Various analyses of Obama's cap-and-trade plan, including one by Stavins, suggest that after it is fully implemented, it would cost less than 1 percent of gross domestic product a year, or about $100 billion in today's terms. That cost is entirely manageable. But it's still a cost.

Or perhaps we should think of it as an investment. Like so much in the economy, our energy policy has been geared toward the short term. Inexpensive energy made daily life easier and less expensive for all of us. Building a green economy, on the other hand, will require some sacrifice. In the end, that sacrifice should pay a handsome return in the form of icecaps that don't melt and droughts that don't happen—events with costs of their own. Over time, the direct economic costs of a new energy policy may also fall. A cap-and-trade program will create incentives for the private sector to invest in alternative energy, which will lead to innovations and lower prices. Some of the new clean-energy spending, meanwhile, really will replace money now flowing overseas and create jobs here.

But all those benefits will come later. The costs will come sooner, which is a big reason we do not already have a green economy—or an investment economy.

V. Curing Inefficiencies

Washington's challenge on energy policy is to rewrite the rules so that the private sector can start building one of tomorrow's big industries. On health care, the challenge is keeping one of tomorrow's industries from growing too large.

For almost two decades, spending on health care grew rapidly, no matter what the rest of the economy was doing. Some of this is only natural. As a society gets richer and the basic comforts of life become commonplace, people will choose to spend more of their money on health and longevity instead of a third car or a fourth television.

Much of the increases in health care spending, however, are a result of government rules that have made the sector a fabulously—some say uniquely—inefficient sector. These inefficiencies have left the United States spending far more than other countries on medicine and, by many measures, getting worse results. The costs of health care are now so large that it has become one problem that cannot be solved by growth alone. It's qualitatively different from the other budget problems facing the government, like the Wall Street bailout, the stimulus, the war in Iraq or Social Security.

You can see that by looking at various costs as a share of one year of economic output—that is, gross domestic product. Surprisingly, the debt that the federal government has already accumulated doesn't present much of a problem. It is equal to about $6 trillion, or 40 percent of G.D.P., a level that is slightly lower than the average of the past six decades. The bailout, the stimulus and the rest of the deficits over the next two years will probably add about 15 percent of G.D.P. to the debt. That will take debt to almost 60 percent, which is above its long-term average but well below the levels of the 1950s. But the unfinanced parts of Medicare, the spending that the government has promised over and above the taxes it will collect in the coming decades requires another decimal place. They are equal to more than 200 percent of current G.D.P.

During the campaign, Obama talked about the need to control medical costs and mentioned a few ideas for doing so, but he rarely lingered on the topic. He spent more time talking about expanding health-insurance coverage, which would raise the government's bill. After the election, however, when time came to name a budget director, Obama sent a different message. He appointed Peter Orszag, who over the last two years has become one of the country's leading experts on the looming budget mess that is health care.

Orszag is a tall, 40-year-old Massachusetts native, made taller by his preference for cowboy boots, who has risen through the Democratic policy ranks over the last 15 years. He received a Ph.D. from the London School of Economics, later joined the Clinton White House and, from 2007, was the director of the Congressional Budget Office. While there, he devoted himself to studying health care, believing that it was far more important to the future of the budget than any other issue in front of Congress. He nearly doubled the number of health care analysts in the office, to 50. Obama highlighted this work when he announced Orszag's appointment in November.

In Orszag's final months on Capitol Hill, he specifically argued that health care reform should not wait until the financial system has been fixed. "One of the blessings in the current environment is that we have significant capacity to expand and sell Treasury debt," he told me recently. "If we didn't have that, and if the financial markets didn't have confidence that we would repay that debt, we would be in even more dire straits than we are." Absent a health care overhaul, the federal government's lenders around the world may eventually grow nervous about its ability to repay its debts. That, in turn, will cause them to demand higher interest rates to cover their risk when lending to the United States. Facing higher interest rates, the government won't be able to afford the kind of loans needed to respond to a future crisis, be it financial or military. The higher rates will also depress economic growth, aggravating every other problem.

So what should be done? Orszag was technically prohibited from advocating policies in his old job. But it wasn't very hard to read between the lines. In a series of speeches around the country, in testimony to Congress and in a blog that he started ("Director's Blog"), he laid out a fairly clear agenda.

Orszag would begin his talks by explaining that the problem is not one of demographics but one of medicine. "It's not primarily that we're going to have more 85-year-olds," he said during a September speech in California. "It's primarily that each 85-year-old in the future will cost us a lot more than they cost us today." The medical system will keep coming up with expensive new treatments, and Medicare will keep reimbursing them, even if they bring little benefit.

After this introduction, Orszag would typically pause and advise his audience not to get too depressed. He would put a map of the United States on the screen behind him, showing Medicare spending by region. The higher-spending regions were shaded darker than the lower-spending regions. Orszag would then explain that the variation cannot be explained by the health of the local population or the quality of care it receives. Darker areas didn't necessarily have sicker residents than lighter areas, nor did those residents necessarily receive better care. So, Orszag suggested, the goal of reform doesn't need to be remaking the American health care system in the image of, say, the Dutch system. The goal seems more attainable than that. It is remaking the system of a high-spending place, like southern New Jersey or Texas, in the image of a low-spending place, like Minnesota, New Mexico or Virginia.

To that end, Orszag has become intrigued by the work of Mitchell Seltzer, a hospital consultant in central New Jersey. Seltzer has collected large amounts of data from his clients on how various doctors treat patients, and his numbers present a very similar picture to the regional data. Seltzer told me that big-spending doctors typically explain their treatment by insisting they have sicker patients than their colleagues. In response he has made charts breaking down the costs of care into thin diagnostic categories, like "respiratory-system diagnosis with ventilator support, severity: 4," in order to compare doctors who were treating the same ailment. The charts make the point clearly. Doctors who spent more—on extra tests or high-tech treatments, for instance—didn't get better results than their more conservative colleagues. In many cases, patients of the aggressive doctors stay sicker longer and die sooner because of the risks that come with invasive care.

The first step toward turning "less efficient" doctors, in Seltzer's euphemism, into "efficient" doctors would be relatively uncontroversial. The government would have to create a national version of his database and, to do so, would need doctors and hospitals to have electronic medical records. The Obama administration plans to use the stimulus bill to help pay for the installation of such systems. It is then likely to mandate that, within five years, any doctor or hospital receiving Medicare payment must be using electronic records.

The next steps will be harder. Based on what the data show, Medicare will have to stop reimbursing some expensive treatments that don't do much good. Private insurers would likely follow Medicare's lead, as they have on other issues in the past. Doctors, many of whom make good money from extra treatments, are sure to object, just as Mancur Olson would have predicted. They will claim that, whatever the data show, the treatments are benefiting their patients. In a few cases—though, by definition, not most—they may be right. Even when they are not, their patients, desperate for hope, may fight for the treatment.

The most pessimistic point that Orszag routinely made during his time on Capitol Hill was that the political system didn't deal well with simmering, long-term problems. It often waited until those problems became a crisis, he would say. That may be a kind of corollary to Rahm's Doctrine, but it does highlight the task before the Obama administration. It will need to figure out how it can use one crisis as an excuse to prevent several more.

VI. Graduates Equal Growth

A great appeal of green jobs—or, for that matter, of a growing and efficient health care sector—is that they make it possible to imagine what tomorrow's economy might look like. They are concrete. When somebody wonders, What will replace Wall Street? What will replace housing? they can be given an answer.

As answers go, green jobs and health care are fine. But they probably aren't the best answers. The best one is less concrete. It also has a lot more historical evidence on its side.

Last year, two labor economists, Claudia Goldin and Lawrence Katz, published a book called "The Race Between Education and Technology." It is as much a work of history—the history of education—as it is a work of economics. Goldin and Katz set out to answer the question of how much an education really matters. They are themselves products of public schools, she of New York and he of Los Angeles, and they have been a couple for two decades. They are liberals (Katz served as the chief economist under Robert Reich in Bill Clinton's Labor Department), but their book has been praised by both the right and the left. "I read the Katz and Goldin book," Matthew Slaughter, an associate dean of Dartmouth's business school who was an economic adviser to George W. Bush, recently told me, "and there's part of me that can't fathom that half the presidential debates weren't about a couple of facts in that book." Summers wrote a blurb for the book, calling it "the definitive treatment" of income inequality.

The book's central fact is that the United States has lost its once-wide lead in educational attainment. South Korea and Denmark graduate a larger share of their population from college—and Australia, Japan and the United Kingdom are close on our heels.

Goldin and Katz explain that the original purpose of American education was political, to educate the citizens of a democracy. By the start of the 20th century, though, the purpose had become blatantly economic. As parents saw that high-school graduates were getting most of the good jobs, they started a grass-roots movement, known as the high-school movement, to demand free, public high schools in their communities. "Middletown," the classic 1929 sociological study of life in Indiana, reported that education "evokes the fervor of a religion, a means of salvation, among a large section of the population."

At the time, some European intellectuals dismissed the new American high schools as wasteful. Instead of offering narrowly tailored apprentice programs, the United States was accused of overeducating its masses (or at least its white masses). But Goldin and Katz, digging into old population surveys, show that the American system paid huge dividends. High-school graduates filled the ranks of companies like General Electric and John Deere and used their broad base of skills to help their employers become global powers. And these new white-collar workers weren't the only ones to benefit. A high-school education also paid off for blue-collar workers. Those with a diploma were far more likely to enter newer, better-paying, more technologically advanced industries. They became plumbers, jewelers, electricians, auto mechanics and railroad engineers.

Not only did mass education increase the size of the nation's economic pie; it also evened out the distribution. The spread of high schools—by 1940, half of teenagers were getting a diploma—meant that graduates were no longer an elite group. In economic terms, their supply had increased, which meant that the wage premium that came with a diploma was now spread among a larger group of workers. Sure enough, inequality fell rapidly in the middle decades of the 20th century.

But then the great education boom petered out, starting in the late 1960s. The country's worst high schools never got their graduation rates close to 100 percent, while many of the fast-growing community colleges and public colleges, which were educating middle-class and poorer students, had low graduation rates. Between the early 1950s and early '80s, the share of young adults receiving a bachelor's degree jumped to 24 percent, from 7 percent. In the 30 years since, the share has only risen to 32 percent. Nearly all of the recent gains have come among women. For the first time on record, young men in the last couple of decades haven't been much more educated than their fathers were.

Goldin and Katz are careful to say that economic growth is not simply a matter of investing in education. And we can all name exceptions to the general rule. Bill Gates dropped out of college (though, as Malcolm Gladwell explains in his recent book, "Outliers," Gates received a fabulously intense computer-programming education while in high school). Some college graduates struggle to make a good living, and many will lose their jobs in this recession. But these are exceptions. Goldin's and Katz's thesis is that the 20th century was the American century in large part because this country led the world in education. The last 30 years, when educational gains slowed markedly, have been years of slower growth and rising inequality.

Their argument happens to be supported by a rich body of economic literature that didn't even make it into the book. More-educated people are healthier, live longer and, of course, make more money. Countries that educate more of their citizens tend to grow faster than similar countries that do not. The same is true of states and regions within this country. Crucially, the income gains tend to come after the education gains. What distinguishes thriving Boston from the other struggling cities of New England? Part of the answer is the relative share of children who graduate from college. The two most affluent immigrant groups in modern America—Asian-Americans and Jews—are also the most educated. In recent decades, as the educational attainment of men has stagnated, so have their wages. The median male worker is roughly as educated as he was 30 years ago and makes roughly the same in hourly pay. The median female worker is far more educated than she was 30 years ago and makes 30 percent more than she did then.

There really is no mystery about why education would be the lifeblood of economic growth. On the most basic level, education helps people figure out how to make objects and accomplish tasks more efficiently. It allows companies to make complex products that the rest of the world wants to buy and thus creates high-wage jobs. Education may not be as tangible as green jobs. But it helps a society leverage every other investment it makes, be it in medicine, transportation or alternative energy. Education—educating more people and educating them better—appears to be the best single bet that a society can make.

Fortunately, we know much more than we did even a decade ago about how education works and doesn't work. In his book, "Whatever It Takes" (and in this magazine, where he is an editor), Paul Tough has described some of the most successful schools for poor and minority students. These schools tend to set rigorous standards, keep the students in school longer and create a disciplined, can-do culture.

Many of the schools, like several middle schools run by an organization called KIPP, have had terrific results. Students enter with test scores below the national average. They leave on a path to college.

The lessons of KIPP—some of the lessons, at least—also apply to schools that are not so poor. Last year, the Gates Foundation hired an economist named Thomas Kane to oversee a big new push to prepare students for college. Kane is one of the researchers whose work shows that teachers may matter more than anything else. Good teachers tend to receive high marks from parents, colleagues and principals, and they tend to teach their students much more than average teachers. Bad teachers tend to do poorly on all these metrics. The differences are usually apparent after just a couple of years on the job. Yet in a typical school system, both groups receive tenure.

The Obama administration has suggested that education reform is an important goal. The education secretary is Arne Duncan, the former school superintendent in Chicago, who pushed for education changes there based on empirical data. Obama advisers say that the administration plans to use the education money in the stimulus package as leverage. States that reward good teaching and use uniform testing standards—rather than the choose-your-own-yardstick approach of the No Child Left Behind law—may get more money.

But it is still unclear just how much of a push the administration will make. With the financial crisis looming so large, something as sprawling and perennially plagued as education can seem like a sideshow. Given everything else on its agenda, the Obama administration could end up financing a few promising pilot programs without actually changing much. States, for their part, will be cutting education spending to balance their budgets.

A few weeks ago, I drove to Shepherd University in West Virginia to get a glimpse of both the good and bad news for education. Shepherd is the kind of public college that will need to be at the center of any effort to improve higher education. Located in a small town in the Shenandoah Valley, it attracts mostly middle-class students—from the actual middle class, not the upper middle class—and it has a graduation rate of about 35 percent.

Several years ago, the state of West Virginia started a scholarship program, called Promise, in part to lift the graduation rate at places like Shepherd. The program is modeled after those in several Southern states, in which any high-school student with a certain minimum grade-point average (often 3.0) and certain SAT scores gets a hefty scholarship to any state school. When West Virginia officials were designing their program, though, they noticed a flaw with the other programs. The students weren't required to take a course load that was big enough to let them graduate in four years. In some cases they were required to keep a minimum grade-point average, which encouraged them, perversely, to take fewer courses. Many students drifted along for a few years and then dropped out.

So West Virginia changed the rules. It offered a bigger carrot— free tuition at any public college—but also a stick. Students had to take enough courses each semester so that they could graduate in four years. Judith Scott-Clayton, a young economist who analyzed the program, concluded that it had raised the on-time graduation rate by almost 7 percentage points in a state where many colleges have a graduation rate below 50 percent.

Given those results, the Promise scholarship might seem like an ideal public policy in a deep recession. It pays for school at a time when many families are struggling. It keeps students busy when jobs are hard to come by. It also has the potential to do some long-term good. But nearly everyone I interviewed in West Virginia—the students, the president of Shepherd and other education officials—worried that financing would be reduced soon. The program is expensive, and state revenue is declining. Something has to give.

VII. A Matter of Norms

What struck me about the Shepherd students I met was that they didn't seem to spend much time thinking about the credit requirement. It had become part of their reality. Many college students today assume they will not graduate in four years. Some even refer to themselves as second- or third-years, instead of sophomores or juniors. "It's just normal all around not to be done in four years," Chelsea Carter, a Shepherd student, told me. "People don't push you." Carter, in fact, introduced herself to me as a third-year. But she is also a Promise scholar, and she said she expected to graduate in four years. Her younger sister, now in her first year in the program at Shepherd, also plans to graduate in four years. For many Promise scholars, graduating on time has become the norm.

Economists don't talk much about cultural norms. They prefer to emphasize prices, taxes and other incentives. And the transformation of the American economy will depend very much on such incentives: financial aid, Medicare reimbursements, energy prices and marginal tax rates. But it will also depend on forces that aren't quite so easy to quantify.

Orszag, on his barnstorming tour to talk about the health care system, argued that his fellow economists were making a mistake by paying so little attention to norms. After all, doctors in Minnesota don't work under a different Medicare system than doctors in New Jersey. But they do act differently.

The norms of the last two decades or so—consume before invest; worry about the short term, not the long term—have been more than just a reflection of the economy. They have also affected the economy. Chief executives have fought for paychecks that their predecessors would have considered obscenely large. Technocrats inside Washington's regulatory agencies, after listening to their bosses talk endlessly about the dangers of overregulation, made quite sure that they weren't regulating too much. Financial engineering became a more appealing career track than actual engineering or science. In one of the small gems in their book, Goldin and Katz write that towns and cities with a large elderly population once devoted a higher-than-average share of their taxes to schools. Apparently, age made them see the benefits of education. In recent decades, though, the relationship switched. Older towns spent less than average on schools. You can imagine voters in these places asking themselves, "What's in it for me?"

By any standard, the Obama administration faces an imposing economic to-do list. It will try to end the financial crisis and recession as quickly as possible, even as it starts work on an agenda that will inspire opposition from a murderers' row of interest groups: Wall Street, Big Oil, Big Coal, the American Medical Association and teachers' unions. Some items on the agenda will fail.

But the same was true of the New Deal and the decades after World War II, the period that is obviously the model for the Obama years. Roosevelt and Truman both failed to pass universal health insurance or even a program like Medicare. Yet the successes of those years—Social Security, the highway system, the G.I. Bill, the National Science Foundation, the National Labor Relations Board—had a huge effect on the culture.

The American economy didn't simply grow rapidly in the late 1940s, 1950s and 1960s. It grew rapidly and gave an increasing share of its bounty to the vast middle class. Middle-class incomes soared during those years, while income growth at the very top of the ladder, which had been so great in the 1920s, slowed down. The effects were too great to be explained by a neat package of policies, just as the last few decades can't be explained only by education, investment and the like.

When Washington sets out to rewrite the rules for the economy, it can pass new laws and shift money from one program to another. But the effects of those changes are not likely to be merely the obvious ones. The changes can also send signals. They can influence millions of individual decisions—about the schools people attend, the jobs they choose, the medical care they request—and, in the process, reshape the economy.

A Conversation with ... **David Leonhardt**

ECONOMIC SCENE COLUMNIST; STAFF WRITER,
THE NEW YORK TIMES MAGAZINE

© The New York Times

David Leonhardt has been writing about economics for The New York Times since 2000 and has been a columnist since 2006. He is a 2009 winner of a Gerald Loeb Award for his New York Times Magazine story "Obamanomics." A New York native, he studied applied mathematics at Yale. Before coming to The Times, he worked for Business Week magazine in Chicago and New York and for the metro desk of The Washington Post. The following is an edited transcript of a telephone interview.

How long had you been at The New York Times?
Just about 10 years.

Did you study or receive training before becoming an economics writer?
Certainly, no formal training. I learned on the job. I had some training at Business Week, where people taught me how to read company reports and how to use the Bloomberg terminal. I did study math, so I'm comfortable with the mathematical part of it, but I took only a couple of economics classes in college.

If you were a math major, why did you go into journalism?
I spent time working in college for my college paper. It was sort of strange that I decided to be a math major rather than a journalism major. I didn't take any formal journalism education, but I spent so much time working on the college paper [Yale Daily News]—five days a week—that I got fabulous training. I also spent two summers at Business Week while in college, a summer at The New Haven Register and one at The Boston Globe.

Do you like talking to economists?
I find it hard to talk to a lot of economists—they talk in code, they miss the forest for the trees. The key is finding the ones who don't do that and who figure out how to explain the world to the rest of us. Fortunately, there are a lot of these economists, too, and they're a pleasure to talk to.

What is your role as an economics writer?

I want to cut through a lot of parts of the economy that don't make sense to people. These are comprehensible things. It is just they are often explained poorly.

Do you feel pressure to forecast the direction of the economy?

There are always certain pressures to do forecasting. I don't love that because no one knows what the future holds. What is more important is to talk about the patterns we know from the past which in all likelihood will be relevant for the future.

One example is education. Do people who go to college find they have overeducated themselves? The results are really clear on that point: Evidence shows it [education] is absolutely the best investment people can make. Another is taxes. Cutting taxes does not get rid of the deficit. There are all sorts of things we can learn about these issues from the past. I think it is very important we just don't say, "Well, we don't really know if education pays off," or "We don't know if you can cut taxes and eliminate the deficit." Since we know the broad-brush answers to those questions, we shouldn't pretend that two equally plausible views exist and then give these views equal weight.

What is the biggest challenge?

The biggest challenge is figuring out how to explain things in a way that makes sense and that isn't dumb-downed. Far too often in journalism we say: "Event A happened and then event B happened." A normal, intelligent person is left asking, "Well, why? How did A cause B to happen? I don't get this." That is a very common journalistic device. My favorite is when we say the market fell today because of some event. My response is, "Oh, really—how do you know? Or is that the explanation we came up with after the fact?" Too often, we don't do a good enough job being clear.

Why isn't economics writing better?

I think because it is hard to do. You can't just assert—you have to explain. You have to think through the arguments you are making and the patterns you are explaining and ask yourself, "Would this make sense to a smart person who has no expertise in this issue?" You have to have this approach in mind. I think too often people are worrying about other things—things that are important to be worrying about, but not the only things that are important. They are worried about sounding sophisticated to their sources, or they are worrying about getting the story right. They are not asking themselves: Am I being clear?

What advice do you have for aspiring business writers?

People need to get comfortable with numbers and get comfortable with Excel. That allows you to figure out these issues for yourself rather than having to rely on other people telling you things.

It took me awhile, but I really noticed a huge difference when I got comfortable looking at the numbers in the monthly jobs report myself, as opposed to just calling economists and then asking them, "What do you make of these numbers?" When I got to the point of taking the numbers and then putting them in an Excel spreadsheet, playing around with them a bit to form my own impressions and then talking to economists, it made a huge difference. You don't have to just say, "Tell me, what are your views?" You can ask, "Hey I noticed this; is it important?" This kind of thing should be done by anyone analyzing a government budget. If you just rely on city council members to give you their impressions of the budget, you are not going to have nearly as granular an understanding as if you can actually get into the numbers yourself and say, "Wait a minute—it looks like this."

Are people born as analytical thinkers, or do you have to learn it?
I am still learning. If I got to play journalism dean, I wouldn't let anyone graduate from my school without a statistics class and without being able to use Excel. It is not just about numbers. I would put a real, real emphasis on this explanatory stuff. I would make people read the masters of this kind of explanatory form—people like Atul Gawande at The New Yorker and Joe Nocera here at The Times. There are lots of writers like this. The New Yorker is really, really good at this. I think these skills are absolutely learnable, and I don't think there is enough time spent teaching them, although I am sure some places do a fine job of teaching these skills.

MAKING**CONNECTIONS**

1

What is a leading indicator? Brainstorm some indicators you might track to measure the health of the economy. From this list, generate three story angles you could use to explore the health of the economy.

2

Tax cuts and public works projects are examples of government stimulus. What are the pros and cons of the government getting involved in managing the economy?

3

In tough economic times, consumers look for an escape. Besides candy, what are several areas that will benefit from increased consumer spending during a recession? How could you use these ideas to write stories about the economy?

BUSINESS CONCEPTS REVIEW

Depression   A severe version of a recession, a prolonged economic downturn marked by high unemployment, falling prices, falling productivity and falling personal income.

Economic indicator   Any statistic used to predict or measure performance of the economy. Some indicators are predictive while others are lagging statistics used to measure past performance.

Economic stimulus   Changes in government fiscal policy aimed at boosting economic activity during a recession such as cutting taxes or increasing government spending.

Free market   A market where buyers and sellers are allowed to enter into transactions without government regulation or interference. Prices are allowed to rise and fall in line with the laws of supply and demand.

Great Depression   A deep global recession that began with the stock market crash on Wall Street in October 1929 and continued throughout the 1930s. One in four U.S. workers lost their jobs. Manufacturing output fell to half its 1929 level.

Gross domestic product   The market value of all final goods and services produced within a country in a given time period. GDP is comprised of consumer and government purchases, private domestic investment and net exports of goods and services.

Lagging indicator   Economic statistic that follows or trails performance in the economy. One example is the unemployment rate. Businesses lay off workers after conditions worsen, so this is considered a lagging indicator.

Leading indicator   Economic statistic that tends to move with or ahead of general economic activity. Stock prices generally rise in anticipation of future economic activity.

Recession   A downturn in economic activity defined as two consecutive quarters of decline in gross domestic product.

inflation

FEW THINGS AFFECT A CONSUMER'S BEHAVIOR more than price. "How much does it cost?" is one of the first questions you consider when evaluating a purchase. If it's on sale, you might be more likely to buy. Or if it's the latest and greatest in gadgets, say a new iPod, you might be willing to pay full price. Perhaps you'd even drive across town if you can find a better deal somewhere else.

Price is how consumers keep score. So what factors influence the number on the sales tag? And, your personal pocketbook concerns aside, why should you or your readers care if prices are rising or falling? Because prices matter. As prices rise, your money buys less. This is called inflation. No one likes to pay more for the same goods they bought a week or a month ago. Left unchecked, inflation erodes value.

Economists teach us that higher prices are caused by shortages. The reverse is also true. An excess supply of anything—T-shirts, running shoes, gasoline—pushes the price of that item downward. Even valuable commodities such as gold, silver, diamonds and oil don't hold value if there is a glut.

But understanding prices is only half the battle. Experienced business journalists know that a price becomes meaningful only when it's expressed in relative terms. You need a benchmark of comparison. It could be as simple as comparing the cost of an ice cream cone to that of a similar-sized frozen yogurt bar. Or you might use time as your yardstick, measuring how much gasoline costs now vs. during the 1970s.

Drawing conclusions based on what you've found can be tricky. Let's say the price of a gallon of gas has more than doubled in the past decade. That might seem like awfully big news. But what if upon further examination you find that consumers are spending relatively the same percentage of their income, or less, on gas than they were 25 years ago? Context is everything when you write about prices.

On the other end of the spectrum, lower prices might seem like a good deal—that is, until you realize that lower prices also mean smaller paychecks. In deflationary times, employers cut wages and jobs. A general decline in prices is called deflation. Deflation accompanied the Great Depression in the 1930s. Persistently falling prices also were at the heart of Japan's so-called lost decade after the catastrophic collapse of its real estate bubble at the end of the 1980s—a period that some experts draw parallels to the Great Recession of 2007–2009.

What's the best way to measure whether prices are rising or falling? The granddaddy of price gauges is the Consumer Price Index produced by the federal government. It looks at a market basket of commonly purchased goods and compares the price from one period to the next. There are other price gauges—one being interest rates. An interest rate is the price a bank charges borrowers for the use of money the bank lends out. There are many different interest rates, but if rates rise, borrowing gets more expensive.

The stories in this chapter tackle the issue of inflation from many vantage points—the gas pump, the retail store, the consumer pocketbook and, of course, the Federal Reserve. If after reading these stories you feel you have only scratched the surface it's because you have. The issues surrounding prices are complicated. Even the folks at the Fed sometimes have trouble deciding what's going on. As Edmund L. Andrews writes at the end of this chapter in a revealing profile of Alan Greenspan, the Fed chairman once became exasperated and said, "We really do not know how this system works."

Selection 2.1

Daniel Gross does an excellent job of keeping the story clear and simple as he writes about why consumers and economists have two very different views of the Consumer Price Index, or CPI. Short sentences, active verbs, conversational quotes and topic sentences at the beginning of key paragraphs make the story easy to follow.

Economic View
If You Don't Eat or Drive, Inflation's No Problem
By DANIEL GROSS

Aside from the stuff that's becoming more expensive, like food and energy, there is no problem with inflation in the economy. That's the message economists want us to take from recent inflation reports.

On Oct. 14, the Bureau of Labor Statistics said the Consumer Price Index, the main inflation gauge, rose by a whopping 1.2 percent in September and by 4.7 percent in the last 12 months. The bureau also said the Producer Price Index, which measures inflation experienced by businesses, rose 1.9 percent in September alone.

Amid these alarming reports, many economists urged Americans to remain calm and to focus on the so-called core C.P.I.—the inflation measure that excludes the volatile costs of energy and food. The core rate rose just 0.1 percent in September, and is up only 2 percent in the last 12 months.

Published: October 23, 2005.

The dueling numbers seem to offer a classic case of how economists and consumers view the world differently. If only we lived in some futuristic biosphere where we didn't need energy or food, inflation wouldn't matter.

Government economists have been stripping out energy and food costs from the price gauge for more than three decades. After the Arab oil embargo of 1973, Arthur Burns, who was then the chairman of the Federal Reserve, correctly reasoned that temporary shifts in the price of oil shouldn't influence monetary policy unduly. So he asked Fed economists to show him a measure of price changes that excluded energy costs. Later, he asked for one that also excluded food costs.

Steven Roach, chief economist at Morgan Stanley, was an economist at the Fed at the time. "When we were asked to strip out some of the most important things that people buy, my reaction was, 'You've got to be nuts,'" he said. "These are the vital necessities of life."

But Mr. Roach, like most other economists, has come to see the virtues of distinguishing between the so-called headline C.P.I. and the core C.P.I.

Prices of food and energy are notoriously volatile, and susceptible to supply shocks and acts of nature. Inflation in these vital sectors doesn't necessarily indicate inflation across the economy. Mr. Roach notes that in the last year, consumer energy prices have risen 35 percent, while prices of other goods and services are up just 2 percent.

Economists also say the utility of the inflation measure depends on the question you are trying to answer. "If you want to know how much more it costs you to live this year than last year, look at the headline C.P.I.," said Ann L. Owen, associate professor of economics at Hamilton College in Clinton, N.Y., and a former economist at the Federal Reserve. "And from a consumer's perspective, there's nothing good about a 4.7 percent increase in headline inflation in 12 months."

Economists at the Fed aren't obsessed with short-term pocketbook issues like high oil prices—and not just because many of them commute to work in Washington on the Metro. Rather, they focus on long-term economy-wide issues.

"You want to make sure that short-term monetary policy isn't responding to a phenomenon that is just going to go away in a few months, or even a year," said Stephen G. Cecchetti, economics professor at Brandeis University. "A change in an interest rate today will have an effect on inflation one to two years from today." We would not have wanted the Fed to act as if the post-Katrina spike in gasoline prices were permanent, he noted.

What's more, the Fed tends to focus on things that it can control. Not even a Fed chairman as powerful as Alan Greenspan can affect the price of oil by manipulating interest rates. "There's nothing the central bank can do about that, unless it figures out how to produce more oil," said Michael F. Bryan, vice president and economist at the Federal Reserve Bank of Cleveland.

But the Fed can control the amount of money circulating in the economy relative to the quantity of goods available. "So it tries to find the inflation signal common to all prices throughout the economy," Mr. Bryan said.

Thus considered, the core C.P.I. may be the best tool the Fed has to monitor long-term changes in prices.

Still, economists see two good reasons not to ignore the headline number today. First, inflation in a crucial category like energy can worm its way into the entire system. "If high energy costs persist, and if they continue to rise, they may ultimately seep into the core," Professor Owen said. The second reason has less to do with hard economic realities than with softer perceptions. The cost of gasoline is the economy's most visible price. People see it every day even if they don't buy gas every day, said Matthew Martin, senior economist at Economy.com. And most people buy food every week.

"If prices for those two things go up quickly, consumers will form the impression that inflation is high," he said. "And if consumers begin to expect more inflation, they might be more tolerant of price increases."

If that happens, the headline C.P.I. number could dominate the headlines.

Two Ways to Measure Prices

When food and energy prices are included, the 12-month inflation rate has surged to almost 5 percent. But the "core" rate, which excludes those two categories, has followed a much calmer path.

Inflation
12-month change in consumer prices

All items ▶

Excluding food and energy

'95   '97   '99   '01   '03   '05

Source: Bureau of Labor Statistics

Selection 2.2

Matt Richtel finds plenty of cheapskates who are worried about money. The object here is to dig up individual stories that tantalize with specifics—so readers keep reading to find out what bizarre things the next person has to say. The more bizarre, the better—like the Missouri woman who plans to start burying her used cleaning rags and her dogs' feces, or the nurse who collects used clothes and furniture people leave on the street.

Austere Times? Perfect

By MATT RICHTEL

SAN FRANCISCO—Millions of Americans have trimmed expenses because they have had their jobs or hours cut, or fear they will. But a subset of savers are reducing costs not just with purpose, but with relish. These are the gleefully frugal.

"I'm enjoying this," said Becky Martin, 52, who has cut up her 10 credit cards, borrows movies from the library instead of renting them, and grows her own fruits and vegetables—even though her family is comfortable.

Ms. Martin is a real estate investor, her husband is a plastic surgeon, and their home sits on the 12th hole of a Cincinnati country club.

"It's a chance to pass along the frugal lifestyle that my mother gave to me," she says, noting that her sensibilities seem to be rubbing off not just on her sons, but also on her husband. "We're on the same page financially for the first time in years, and it's fabulous."

Americans' spending is down and their personal savings are up—sharply. The savings rate in the United States, which had fallen steadily since the early 1980s, dropped to less than 1 percent in August of 2008. It has since spiked to 5 percent.

"It's huge," said Martha Olney, an economics professor at the University of California, Berkeley, who specializes in the Great Depression, consumerism and indebtedness. The rapid reversal is even more remarkable, she said, because in recessions consumers usually save less money. Not this time. "It implies a re-emergence of thrift as a value," she said.

The gleefully frugal happily seek new ways to economize and take pride in outsaving the Joneses. The mantra is cut, cut, cut— magazine and cable subscriptions, credit cards, fancy coffee drinks and your own hair.

In San Francisco, Cooper Marcus, 36, has started choosing recipes based on the ingredients on sale at the market. Mr. Marcus canceled the family's subscription to Netflix, his premium cable package and a wine club membership. He uses a program on his iPhone to find the cheapest gas and drives out of his way to save 50 cents per gallon.

"It seems a little crazy," he laughs, then adds: "I'm frugal and loving it."

Kellee Sikes, 37, a consultant in Kirkwood, Mo., no longer uses paper napkins. Ms. Sikes uses organic cloth ones until they get threadbare and then uses them as cleaning rags. When they are no longer useful, she puts them in the in-ground waste composter in the backyard. She plans to start burying her dogs' feces there, which saves on the cost of sending refuse to a landfill.

"I recently heard a phrase: 'Never waste a crisis,'" Ms. Sikes said. "I love it. This is a chance for us to re-examine what's important."

Indeed, the recession has given penny pinchers—once closeted in a society that valued what one had, not what one saved—license to speak up.

"There is no joy in other people suffering, but this validates the choices I've made," said Vicki Robin, author of "Your Money or Your Life," a guide to saving money that was a best seller in the 1990s and was re-released last year.

Currently, there are dozens of Web sites and blogs devoted to celebrating conspicuous cutting, like Dollar Stretcher (www.stretcher .com), All Things Frugal (allthingsfrugal.com), Frugal Mom (www .frugalmom.net), and on and on. The Web site meetup.com, which helps people of like interests gather offline, lists 57 "frugal living" groups around the country, including eight formed in February and nine in March.

One part of the gleefully frugal movement, frugalistas—frugal fashionistas who refuse to sacrifice style—may have been popularized in Britain before crossing the Atlantic. But Americans have taken it on as their own.

A Virginia group, the Frugal and Fabulous Moms, tells prospective members: "If you are a coupon-clipping, deal-seeking, stylish and fabulous mom that loves a great deal, then this group is for you!"

A San Francisco group met one Sunday last month for an exercise in fashion frugality: a clothing swap. About 80 women exchanged clothing, shoes and accessories and they are planning another event for April 20 where they hope to have 400 participants.

"When a woman gets a compliment on a dress she got at a swap or the Salvation Army, she feels almost proud," said Suzanne Agasi, organizer of the event and operator of the Web site clothingswaps .com. People at the event "feel like they've scored," she said.

"My behavior has become less strange and more of a resource," said Katy Wolk-Stanley, 41, a nurse in Portland, Ore. A practicing penny-pincher for the last decade, she is now spreading her gospel. Last May, she started a blog with tips and tactics for cutting back called The Non-Consumer Advocate.

She knows whereof she blogs. She darns socks, dries clothes on a line she recently hung inside her house (even though it takes a few days for the clothes to dry inside), washes and reuses plastic bags and takes used clothes and furniture people leave on the street—like the slightly torn Garnet Hill duvet cover she found recently.

"It was wet, and covered with dog hair," she said. "I washed it really well a couple of times and mended it." Her quest for money-saving ideas "is very energizing," she says. "You see opportunities everywhere."

Ms. Wolk-Stanley says she is not cheap. She's sensible. Why spend on new things when there are viable alternatives? And she contends she does not judge others.

"If everyone followed this advice, it would be catastrophic to the economy," she said.

Indeed, economists call it the Paradox of Thrift. While saving is desirable, if everyone does it then consumption falls, businesses fail and the economy grinds to a halt. Professor Olney, from Berkeley, said that the increased rate of savings would most likely slow down the pace of recovery but she also said that a higher savings rate was not inconsistent with a strong economy; from the 1950s to the early 1980s, the savings rate hovered around 9 percent, according to the Bureau of Economic Analysis.

Although the children of the Great Depression raised the spend-thrift baby boom generation, Ms. Martin, from Ohio, echoes other penny pinchers in hoping that the recession spawns a new generation of frugality. Already, her 14-year-old son has picked up her lead. "He is not beyond stopping and pulling things out from someone's trash," she said. He found one sectional sofa left on the sidewalk that he resold on the Internet for $200.

"I'm very proud of him."

Selection 2.3

Taking people to a new venue outside their usual field of vision is a great way to add perspective and capture readers' attention about a subject they have already read about—falling housing prices. Mark Landler offers a new spin on an old story by transporting readers to Europe, where they find out things are even worse than in the United States. Notice Landler's choice of verbs here—prices are "swooning," "soaring," "falling" and "surging." The economy is "tightening," and people are "suffering," amid a market that has been "amplified" and "aggravated" by boom and a subsequent bust.

Housing Woes in U.S. Spread Around Globe

By MARK LANDLER

DUBLIN—The collapse of the housing bubble in the United States is mutating into a global phenomenon, with real estate prices swooning from the Irish countryside and the Spanish coast to Baltic seaports and even parts of northern India.

This synchronized global slowdown, which has become increasingly stark in recent months, is hobbling economic growth worldwide, affecting not just homes but jobs as well.

In Ireland, Spain, Britain and elsewhere, housing markets that soared over the last decade are falling back to earth. Property analysts predict that some countries, like this one, will face an even more wrenching adjustment than that of the United States, including the possibility that the downturn could become a wholesale collapse.

To some extent, the world's problems are a result of American contagion. As home financing and credit tightens in response to the crisis that began in the subprime mortgage market, analysts worry that other countries could suffer the mortgage defaults and foreclosures that have afflicted California, Florida and other states.

Citing the reverberations of the American housing bust and credit squeeze, the International Monetary Fund last Wednesday cut its forecast for global economic growth this year and warned that the malaise could extend into 2009.

"The problems in the U.S. are being transmitted to Europe," said Michael Ball, professor of urban and property economics at the University of Reading in Britain, who studies housing prices. "What's happening now is an awful lot more grief than we expected."

For countries like Ireland, where prices were even more inflated than in the United States, it has been a painful education, as homeowners learn the American vocabulary of misery.

"We know we're already in negative equity," said Emma Linnane, a 31-year-old university administrator.

She bought a cozy, one-bedroom apartment in the Dublin suburbs with her fiancé, Paul Colgan, in May 2006, at the peak of the market. They paid $575,000—at least $100,000 more than it would fetch today. "I sometimes get shivers thinking about it," Ms. Linnane said, "but I'll let the reality hit me when I go to sell it."

That reality is spreading. Once-sizzling housing markets in Eastern Europe and the Baltic states are cooling rapidly, as nervous Western Europeans stop buying investment properties in Warsaw, Tallinn, Estonia and other real estate Klondikes.

Published: April 14, 2008.

Further east, in India and southern China, prices are no longer surging. With stock markets down sharply after reaching heady levels, people do not have as much cash to buy property. Sales of apartments in Hong Kong, a normally hyperactive market, have slowed recently, with prices for mass-market flats starting to drop.

In New Delhi and other parts of northern India, prices have fallen 20 percent over the last year. Sanjay Dutt, an executive director in the Mumbai office of Cushman & Wakefield, the real estate firm, describes it as an erosion of confidence.

Much of the retrenchment seems to be following the basic law of gravity: what goes up must come down. With low interest rates helping to inflate housing bubbles in many countries, economists said the confluence of falling prices was predictable, if unsettling.

This is not the first housing downturn to cross borders, but its reverberations have been amplified by the integration of financial markets. When faulty American mortgages end up on the books of European banks, the problems of the United States aggravate the world's problems.

Consider Britain, which had one of Europe's most robust housing markets, with less of an oversupply than in Ireland or Spain. Then last summer came the subprime crisis across the Atlantic.

Within two months, mortgage approvals dropped 31 percent, compared with the previous year. And by March, average housing prices had fallen 2.5 percent, the largest monthly decline since 1992.

"The boom in house prices was actually much bigger here than in the U.S.," said Kelvin Davidson, an economist at Capital Economics in London. "If anything, people should be more worried than in the U.S."

Britain has one of the most developed home-financing industries, not far behind that of the United States. The amount of outstanding mortgage debt, as a share of total economic output, is higher there than in the United States, according to a study by the International Monetary Fund.

"The U.K. followed the U.S. into never-never land, pushing mortgages out the door, believing that prices would go up forever," said Allan Saunderson, the managing editor of Property Finance Europe, a newsletter for investors.

Still, the problems in Britain pale next to those of Spain and Ireland. Residential investment accounts for 12 percent of the Irish economy and 9 percent of the Spanish economy, compared with 5 percent in Britain and 4 percent in the United States, according to the I.M.F.

The glut of housing has brought new construction to a standstill, driving up unemployment and dimming the prospects for two of Europe's stellar performers over the last decade.

"We're waking up from the property dream and finding ourselves in a situation where prices are falling in Spain for the first time," said Fernando Encinar, a founder of Idealista.com, a real estate Web site.

In Spain, more than four million homes were built in the last decade, more than in Germany, Britain and France combined. Average house prices tripled in parts of the country, as Spain's torrid economy attracted immigrants and Northern Europeans snapped up holiday homes along the Costa del Sol.

Now, though, thousands of those houses stand empty. The I.M.F. estimates that property is overvalued by more than 15 percent. With mortgages drying up and prices swooning, speculators who once viewed Spanish property as a no-lose proposition are confronting hard reality.

In 2005, Julian Felipe Fernandez bought three small apartments, as an investment, in a huge development being built outside Madrid. He paid 100,000 euros as a deposit for the units, and now he is eager to sell them to avoid having to take on a costly mortgage. But with the market stalled, Mr. Fernandez's asking price is what he paid for them.

"Three years ago, it looked like I would be able to flip them for a nice profit before they were finished," he said. "I just want to get them off my hands, to get rid of this headache."

If he unloads them, he will be lucky. Enric Bueno, head of marketing for Ibusa, a real estate company in Barcelona, said his firm was closing six or seven sales a month, compared with 40 a month a year ago.

"Things are really bad," Mr. Bueno said. "If this goes on for five years, we won't make it."

Economists have been busy cutting their growth forecasts for Spain, with a few saying that it may stagnate this summer. BBVA, a leading Spanish bank, forecasts that unemployment will rise to an average of 11 percent this year, from 8.6 percent in 2007.

Such cutbacks are well under way in Ireland, where the taxi drivers complain that their ranks are being swollen by laid-off home builders. The housing collapse has brought an abrupt end to more than a decade of pell-mell growth that earned Ireland the nickname "the Celtic tiger."

Today, the mood in this country feels like a wake, and not an Irish one. Average house prices fell 7 percent last year, the most in Europe, according to the Royal Institution of Chartered Surveyors, a British real estate group. They are likely to fall by a similar amount this year.

After a 16-year boom that was interrupted only briefly after the Sept. 11 terrorist attacks, Ireland has the most overvalued housing market among developed countries, according to the I.M.F. In its recent economic outlook, the fund calculated that prices are 30 percent higher than they should be, given Ireland's economic fundamentals.

For many Irish, accepting that reality is like passing through the seven stages of grief. Some homeowners are still in denial, brokers said, asking $5 million for houses worth no more than $4 million. But developers have begun cutting prices for smaller apartments like the one owned by Emma Linnane.

"Last year was our 'wake up in the middle of the night with sweat pouring down your face' period," said David Bewley, a director at the Lisney real estate agency. "Now we've grown up."

Not all the omens are negative. Mr. Bewley said houses were selling again, albeit for 25 percent less. Ireland has not yet suffered widespread incidences of defaulting mortgages or foreclosures in this downturn, in part because lenders have not been as aggressive as those in the United States.

But some worry that the housing meltdown could spoil Ireland's recipe for success. Like Spain, it attracted lots of foreign workers, many of whom came for well-paying jobs in the construction industry. That fueled the Irish rental market, which has remained buoyant and been a source of income for Ireland's many real estate speculators.

"If the immigrants go back home, will this hurt the rental market?" asked Ronan O'Driscoll, a director in the Dublin office of Savills, a real estate firm. "If that happens, it would definitely cause foreclosures."

Reporting was contributed by
Victoria Burnett in Madrid, Eamon Quinn in Dublin,
Heather Timmons in New Delhi and Julia Werdigier in London.

Selection 2.4

Good business journalism takes readers beyond the facts and numbers and helps them understand the bigger picture. In this case, Louis Uchitelle looks at what impact, beyond the obvious, higher oil prices will have on the economy. The result is an interesting story about how oil is used to produce items like plastics, tires, toiletries, light bulbs, cushions and computer screens. Businesses try to pass these costs on, but economic conditions and competitive factors don't always allow them to do so.

Oil Prices Raise Cost of Making Range of Goods

By LOUIS UCHITELLE

Surging oil prices are beginning to cut into the profits of a wide range of American businesses, pushing many to raise prices and maneuver aggressively to offset the rising cost of merchandise made from petroleum.

Published: June 8, 2008.

Airlines, package shippers and car owners are no longer the only ones being squeezed by the ever-mounting price of oil, which shot up almost $11 a barrel on Friday alone, to $138.54, a record.

Companies that make hard goods using raw materials derived from oil, like tires, toiletries, plastic packaging and computer screens, are watching their costs skyrocket, and they find themselves forced into unpleasant choices: Should they raise prices, shift to less costly procedures, cut workers, or all three?

The Goodyear Tire and Rubber Company is trying to adapt. Its raw material of choice now is natural rubber rather than synthetic rubber, made from oil. To sustain profits, it is making more high-end tires for consumers willing to pay upwards of $100 to replace each tire on their cars.

These steps have not been enough, however, particularly now that the cost of natural rubber is also rising sharply, along with that of many other commodities. So Goodyear has raised the prices of its tires by 15 percent in just four months.

"Our strategy is to raise prices and improve the mix to offset the cost of raw materials," said Keith Price, a Goodyear spokesman. "No one has predicted how long we can continue to do that."

The sense that many companies may be hitting a wall is palpable. Corporate profits peaked last spring and have shrunk since then, Moody's Economy.com reports, drawing on Commerce Department data.

The housing crisis and the weakening economy are big reasons, but oil prices are adding greatly to the pressure on profits as retailers fail to pass along higher prices to consumers. That helps to explain why expensive oil has not yet pushed up the inflation rate.

So far this year, the nation's employers have been cutting jobs at an accelerating pace, particularly last month, when the unemployment rate jumped to 5.5 percent from 5 percent. But with the vise on corporate profits tightening and the price of oil continuing to climb, more dire action, including job cuts and higher prices, may be in store, economists say, although there is still room to avoid such steps.

"Companies came into this period with extraordinarily high profit margins," said Edward McKelvey, chief domestic economist at Goldman Sachs, "and some of the surge in raw material costs will be absorbed by lowering those profits."

Still, the prevailing attitude that the economy could just keep absorbing higher oil prices is being tested—for the first time in nearly 30 years. Adjusted for inflation, a barrel of crude is now more expensive than it was in 1980, the previous peak.

"The conventional wisdom a couple of years ago was that oil did not have that much leverage over the economy," said Daniel Yergin, chairman of Cambridge Energy Research Associates. "But now it plainly does. People are suddenly paying much more attention to their energy costs and trying to figure out how to manage them."

Goodyear has kept its head above water in part by passing along some of the higher prices to dealers. The dealers, however, have not been able to pass along all of those increases to consumers and are absorbing the difference in lower profits.

Since last spring, the average profits of the nation's corporations—from behemoths like Goodyear to small neighborhood retailers—have declined at an annual rate of nearly 6 percent, government data show.

Even companies that have been performing well in the economic downturn are sounding notes of caution. Take Costco, the discount retail chain, which offers a wide array of consumer goods, food, wine, furniture, appliances, beauty aids and much more.

Costco's profit was up in the first quarter, but James D. Sinegal, the chief executive, says he is "starting to be confronted with unprecedented price increases" for the merchandise that Costco buys to stock its stores. His first response has been to buy in extra large quantities so that he has stock on hand to carry him through subsequent price increases.

"We just made a big purchase of Tumi luggage," Mr. Sinegal said.

Procter & Gamble finds itself in a similar predicament. For its fiscal year beginning next month, it expects to spend an additional $2 billion on oil-based raw materials and commodities. That is double last year's increase, and it is carved from total revenue of just under $80 billion.

Price increases have helped to offset this cost. They have averaged nearly 5 percent for paper towels, bath tissues and diapers, all made with chemicals derived from oil, said Paul Fox, a company spokesman.

Natural oils have been substituted for ingredients made from petroleum; for example, palm oil now goes into a variety of laundry soaps. But like rubber, the cost of palm oil and other natural commodities is rising.

Trying to hold down raw material costs, Procter & Gamble has resorted to "compacting" a few laundry products, Mr. Fox said, so that the same amount of detergent fits into smaller and less costly containers made of plastic, which is derived from oil.

Still, the company's operating profit edged down to 20.1 percent of revenue in the first quarter, from 21.9 percent in each of the two previous quarters. "That 20.1 percent was down, but it was an improvement on the advance guidance we had given for that quarter," Mr. Fox said.

No business in America produces more of the oil-based ingredients that go into the nation's products than the Dow Chemical Company, based in Midland, Mich. From Dow's petrochemical operations come the basic ingredients of a wide variety of plastic bottles and packaging, including numerous containers once made of glass or tin.

Indeed, paint, computer and television screens, mobile phones, light bulbs, cushions, paper, mattresses, car seats, carpets, steering wheels and polyesters are all made with ingredients that Dow and other chemical companies refine from oil and natural gas.

Dow normally raises prices piecemeal. Last month, though, the surge in the cost of oil and natural gas, the company's principal raw materials, produced a rare across-the-board price increase of as much as 20 percent.

"We have taken out head count, automated, been very diligent on cost control," said Andrew Liveris, Dow's chairman and chief executive, "but these surges in energy prices are just one surge too many."

Dow's sweeping price increases will probably have a domino effect, resulting in higher prices or, more likely, shrinking profits, analysts say. Constrained by the weak economy and fewer wage earners among their customers, the nation's retailers have so far not been able to pass on to consumers much of the rising cost of products that depend on oil. The Consumer Price Index, minus food and energy, is barely rising.

"One of the surprises," said Patrick Jackman, a senior economist in the consumer price division of the Bureau of Labor Statistics, "is that the oil price surges of the 1970s passed through fairly quickly into consumer prices, and this time that is not happening."

Selection 2.5

Some of the best stories define a problem and then lay out a possible scenario for the reader. These are difficult stories to write because they can easily become overwhelming. One approach is to cast the characters in terms of winners and losers. Peter S. Goodman does a good job of setting this story up and then simply explaining what could happen globally should we see a period of falling prices. Uncertainty adds an element of drama to the story. Here's how Goodman handles this: "Not since the Great Depression have so many countries faced so much trouble at once. The financial crisis has gone global, like a virus mutating in the face of every experimental cure."

Fear of Deflation Lurks as Global Demand Drops
By PETER S. GOODMAN

As dozens of countries slip deeper into financial distress, a new threat may be gathering force within the American economy—the prospect that goods will pile up waiting for buyers and prices will fall, suffocating fresh investment and worsening joblessness for months or even years.

Published: October 31, 2008.

The word for this is deflation, or declining prices, a term that gives economists chills.

Deflation accompanied the Depression of the 1930s. Persistently falling prices also were at the heart of Japan's so-called lost decade after the catastrophic collapse of its real estate bubble at the end of the 1980s—a period in which some experts now find parallels to the American predicament.

"That certainly is the snapshot of the risk I see," said Robert J. Barbera, chief economist at the research and trading firm ITG. "It is the crisis we face."

With economies around the globe weakening, demand for oil, copper, grains and other commodities has diminished, bringing down prices of these raw materials. But prices have yet to decline noticeably for most goods and services, with one conspicuous exception—houses. Still, reduced demand is beginning to soften prices for a few products, like furniture and bedding, which are down slightly since the beginning of 2007, according to government data. Prices are also falling for some appliances, tools and hardware.

Only a few months ago, American policy makers were worried about the reverse problem—rising prices, or inflation—as then-soaring costs for oil and food filtered through the economy. In July, average prices were 5.6 percent higher than a year earlier—the fastest pace of inflation since 1991. But by the end of September, annual inflation had dipped to 4.9 percent and was widely expected to go lower.

The new worry is that in the worst case, the end of inflation may be the beginning of something malevolent: a long, slow retrenchment in which consumers and businesses worldwide lose the wherewithal to buy, sending prices down for many goods. Though still considered unlikely, that would prompt businesses to slow production and accelerate layoffs, taking more paychecks out of the economy and further weakening demand.

The danger of this is the difficulty of a cure. Policy makers can generally choke off inflation by raising interest rates, dampening economic activity and reducing demand for goods. But as Japan discovered, an economy may remain ensnared by deflation for many years, even when interest rates are dropped to zero: falling prices make companies reluctant to invest even when credit is free.

Through much of the 1990s, prices for property and many goods kept falling in Japan. As layoffs increased and purchasing power declined, prices fell lower still, in a downward spiral of diminishing fortunes. Some fear the American economy could be sinking toward a similar fate, if a recession is deep and prolonged, as consumers lose spending power just as much of Europe, Asia and Latin America succumb to a slowdown.

"That's a meaningful risk at this point," said Nouriel Roubini, an economist at New York University's Stern School of Business, who forecast the financial crisis well in advance and has been warning of deflation for months. "We could get into a vicious circle of deepening malaise."

Most economists—Mr. Roubini and Mr. Barbera included—say American policy makers have tools to avert the sort of deflationary black hole that captured Japan. Deflation fears last broke out in the United States in 2003, but the Federal Reserve defeated the menace with low interest rates that kept the economy growing. This time, the Fed is again being aggressive, dropping its target rate to 1 percent this week. And the government's various bailout plans have also pumped money into the economy.

"If you print enough money, you can create inflation," said Kenneth S. Rogoff, a former chief economist at the International Monetary Fund and now a professor at Harvard.

But even as American authorities unleash credit, the threat has intensified. Not since the Depression have so many countries faced so much trouble at once. The financial crisis has gone global, like a virus mutating in the face of every experimental cure. From South Korea to Iceland to Brazil, the pandemic has spread, bringing with it a tightening of credit that has starved even healthy companies of finance.

"We're entering a really fierce global recession," Mr. Rogoff said. "A significant financial crisis has been allowed to morph into a full-fledged global panic. It's a very dangerous situation. The danger is that instead of having a few bad years, we'll have another lost decade."

Global economic growth has flourished in recent years, much of it fertilized with borrowed investment. This raised kingdoms of houses in Florida and California, steel mills in Ukraine, slaughterhouses in Brazil and shopping malls in Turkey.

That tide is now moving in reverse. Banks and other financial institutions are reckoning with hundreds of billions of dollars worth of disastrous investments. As they struggle to rebuild their capital, they are halting loans to many customers, demanding swift repayment from others and dumping assets—homes sold out of foreclosure, investments linked to mortgages and corporate loans. Selling is pushing prices down further, making the assets left on balance sheets worth less, in some cases prompting another round of sales.

"You get this adverse feedback loop where assets keep falling in value," Mr. Barbera said. "You're essentially putting big downward pressure on the global economy."

In past crises, like those that devastated Mexico in 1994 and much of Asia in 1997 and 1998, weak economies managed to recover by exporting aggressively, not least to the United States. But American consumers are battered this time. After years of borrowing against homes and tapping credit cards, consumers are pulling back.

From Asia to Latin America, exports are slowing and should continue to do so as the global appetite shrinks. This is spawning fears that major producers like China and India—which vastly expanded production capacity in recent years—will have to dump products on world markets to keep factories running and stave off unemployment, pressing prices lower.

Earlier this year, some analysts suggested that American businesses might continue to prosper, even as consumers pulled back at home, by selling into foreign markets. Caterpillar, the construction equipment manufacturer, might suffer declining sales in the United States, the argument went, but huge projects from Russia to Dubai required front-end loaders. Australia and Brazil needed earth-movers to expand mining operations as they sent iron ore toward smelters in Northeast Asia.

But as much of the planet now struggles, Caterpillar is worried. "Next year, no doubt, will be a challenge," Caterpillar's chief executive, James W. Owens, recently warned.

China has long been at the center of claims that the world could keep growing regardless of American troubles. China has been importing cotton from India and the United States; electronics components from South Korea, Malaysia and Taiwan; timber from Russia and Africa; and oil from the Middle East.

But many of the finished goods China produces with these materials have ultimately landed in the United States, Europe and Japan. When consumers pull back in those countries, Chinese factories feel the impact, along with their suppliers around the globe.

Fewer laptop computers shipped from China spells less demand for chips. Last week, Toshiba—Japan's largest chip maker—said it lost $275 million from July to September, blaming its troubles on a world glut.

Lower demand for flat-screen televisions means less need for flat-panel glass displays. This month, Samsung, the Korean electronics giant, said a global oversupply in that item caused its biggest dip in quarterly profits in three years.

Now, a glut of products may be building in the United States. Orders for trucks used by business have plummeted. Investments in industrial equipment are declining. Yet inventories have grown.

"I worry about an economy that looks like Japan," said Barry P. Bosworth, a senior fellow at the Brookings Institution. "We're going to be struggling with how to put this back together again for several more years."

Selection 2.6

What is the best way to make sense of deflation? In this posting to The Times'
Economix blog, University of Chicago economist Casey B. Mulligan looks to
history and offers some insights. Mulligan examines falling prices during the
Great Depression years, 1929–1933, drawing parallels to the 2008 drop in
prices that occurred after the housing bubble burst. His conclusion: The 2008
price drop was ominously similar to that of 1929. Many who commented on
Mulligan's posting feared that what he had to say might be true, with prices
falling through 2012. As one person wrote on the blog: "It may be a great time
to be older and retiring with a fixed pension and savings in Treasuries."

ECONOMIX
Deflation: 1929 vs. Today
By CASEY B. MULLIGAN

The Great Depression years 1929–33 featured a large and prolonged deflation. January 2009 reversed a deflation pattern for 2008
that was ominously similar to 1929's.

During most of our lifetimes, the prices of things we buy have
generally increased over time. We can name some exceptions, like toys
over the last decade and computer equipment over the last couple of
decades, but otherwise most items (even houses) have prices that are
higher now than they were 10, 20 or 30 years ago.

This general increase in consumer prices—often called
inflation—has become familiar. Employees expect regular pay raises,
and employers can normally afford them because they are increasing
the prices of the products they sell.

Just as important, familiarity with inflation comforts lenders
who offer loans to consumers and businesses under the assumption
that those borrowers will tend to have incomes that rise together with
all other prices. That is, lenders typically arrange for repayment at
regular intervals in specific dollar amounts—like the regular monthly
payment on a home mortgage—and inflation helps borrowers "grow
into" their loan payments.

On rare occasions, consumer price trends suddenly change
directions.

Nineteen twenty-nine was one of those occasions. Consumer
prices were pretty constant during the 1920s. The chart below [see
page 58] picks up the story in January 1929 with the red line [1929–30].
That line measures the (seasonally unadjusted) consumer price index
in each month through July 1930, normalized so that October 1929 is

Published: February 25, 2009. Text and comments available at: http://economix.blogs.nytimes
.com/2009/02/25/deflation-1929-vs-today/

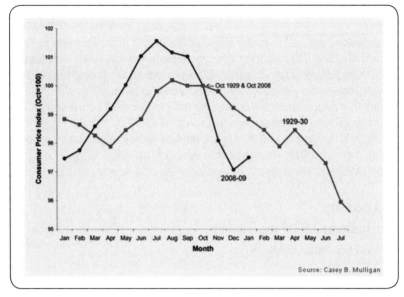

Source: Casey B. Mulligan

The New York Times

100 (for example, the value of 97.9 in April 1929 means that prices then were 2.1 percent lower than they would be in October).

Prices were heading up in the spring and summer of 1929, during which time lenders might have expected that the typical homeowner would obtain a pay raise and the typical farmer would someday fetch more for his crops—in both cases making it easy to pay back their respective mortgages.

In the fall of 1929, the inflation stopped (incidentally, the stock market crashed in late October of that year) and prices headed down, falling almost every month for almost four years. By the spring of 1933, this deflation brought prices down almost 50 percent from their 1929 peak. It was difficult for homeowners and farmers to make their mortgage payments when their paychecks had been cut in half.

The blue series [2008–09] in the chart shows the consumer price index for 2008 and 2009. Like the 1929 series, the 2008 series is normalized so that October is 100.

The chart shows how consumer prices also rose in the spring and early summer of 2008. Inflation had stopped by the fall (there was a stock market crash in October 2008, too), and consumer prices headed down. In fact, the deflation at the end of 2008 brought prices down more than 4 percent in a couple of months, as compared to the 1 percent drop at the end of 1929.

Price reductions since the summer of 2008 have been attributed to declines in prices of commodities, like fuel and food. That's not the whole story, because other prices (notably housing prices) were falling in 2008. Moreover, the role of commodity prices adds to the similarity between 1929 and 2008, because commodity prices were falling in 1929–33 too.

If the Great Depression consumer price parallel were to continue beyond 2008, we would be in for a sustained deflation until the year 2012. At that point, with most borrowers earning less than half what they were when they applied for the loan, today's mortgage problems would seem minor.

Thus, January's C.P.I. report released on Friday was a welcome return to something familiar: inflation.

Selection 2.7

The Federal Reserve is the nation's chief inflation fighter, which is why this chapter wouldn't be complete without a story about the Fed. This story offers insights into the Fed, how it is run and why it enjoys a certain mystique. Edmund L. Andrews does a remarkable job of pulling back the curtain on former Fed chairman Alan Greenspan. He captures the man in a two-sentence nut graf: "Mr. Greenspan abhorred rules, was skeptical about economic models and jettisoned practices that were enshrined by the likes of Paul A. Volcker, his predecessor, and Milton Friedman, a winner of the Nobel in economic science. If Mr. Greenspan stood for anything, it was flexibility and the freedom from dogma." Drafting a nut graf, a brief summary of your focus, is a great way to start writing when you're stuck. As you work on your story, go back and rewrite the nut graf several times. The result will be not just a stronger focus but a better story.

THE GREENSPAN EFFECT
The Doctrine Was Not to Have One
By EDMUND L. ANDREWS

JACKSON HOLE, Wyo., Aug. 25—Alan Greenspan was at the height of his success as chairman of the Federal Reserve in November 1999: the economy was booming, inflation was negligible and people at all levels were becoming wealthier.

But even as Mr. Greenspan was being celebrated as the economy's "maestro," he sounded far less omniscient behind closed doors.

"We really do not know how this system works," he told members of the Fed's policy-making committee in Washington, according to transcripts released earlier this year. "It's clearly new. The old models just are not working."

Now, as he nears the end of his 18-year tenure in the job, Mr. Greenspan is leaving a brilliant record but a murky legacy.

Published: August 26, 2005. The series "The Greenspan Effect" is available at: http://topics.nytimes .com/top/news/business/series/the-greenspan-effect/index.html

Despite numerous economic shocks and financial excesses, unemployment and inflation are both lower now than many economists considered possible when Mr. Greenspan took office in 1987. But whoever moves into his spacious office on Constitution Avenue early next year faces a near-impossible task in replicating Mr. Greenspan's success in managing monetary policy.

That is because Mr. Greenspan abhorred rules, was skeptical about economic models and jettisoned practices that were enshrined by the likes of Paul A. Volcker, his predecessor, and Milton Friedman, a winner of the Nobel in economic science. If Mr. Greenspan stood for anything, it was flexibility and the freedom from dogma.

"The Greenspan standard has for the most part meant what Greenspan wanted to do," said Alan S. Blinder, a professor of economics at Princeton and a former vice chairman of the Federal Reserve.

Mr. Blinder will be one of many economists at a Federal Reserve symposium beginning here Friday that will be devoted to discussions about the "post-Greenspan era." Before that, however, the gathering will open with what is expected to be Mr. Greenspan's swan song speech as chairman of the Fed.

Mr. Greenspan, whose term as a Fed governor expires in January and cannot be renewed, is thought likely to devote his speech to the lessons he learned running the central bank longer than all but one of his predecessors, William McChesney Martin Jr. Expected to be listening particularly closely at the conference are three of the leading candidates to succeed him: Ben S. Bernanke, President Bush's chief economic adviser; Martin S. Feldstein, an economist at Harvard; and R. Glenn Hubbard of Columbia University.

But for all his triumphs, Mr. Greenspan also presided over a stock market bubble that burst and, in helping minimize the damage from that fiasco, laid the groundwork for the housing boom—and potential bust—that followed.

Moreover, the United States has run up heavy foreign debt partly because the Federal Reserve drove interest rates so low that Americans borrowed more and saved less.

Mr. Greenspan's approach to such challenges was to roll with the punches, basing his management of the economy on a refusal to believe in firm rules, doctrines or models.

"A surprising problem is that a number of economists are not able to distinguish between the economic models we construct and the real world," he remarked back in 1984, when he was still head of a private consulting firm.

As Fed chairman, Mr. Greenspan has celebrated the hunt for "anomalies" or trends that seemed to defy what the models predict. He had little faith in widely accepted concepts like the "natural rate" of unemployment, which many economists long believed to be about 6 percent.

He jettisoned the practice of basing policy on growth in the money supply, a concept enshrined by Mr. Friedman as the best way to prevent inflation.

And though he has cultivated the reputation of a hard-liner on reducing inflation, Mr. Greenspan has often put more emphasis on driving up employment.

At 79, his hair is thinning and his gait is becoming stiffer. But he may be as famous as any pop star; he is certainly a larger-than-life figure for political leaders and economists. At a hearing in July before the House Financial Services Committee, lawmakers from both parties showered him with so much praise that they began running out of accolades.

"All the adjectives have been used up," complained Representative Steve Pearce, Republican of New Mexico, who then declared that Mr. Greenspan was a "handsome man."

By almost all accounts, Mr. Greenspan has been an exceptionally successful steward for the economy. In the last 18 years, the nation has endured only two recessions, one of them quite mild. There were four downturns in the previous 18 years.

The core rate of inflation has edged down to about 2 percent from 4 percent when he took office. Unemployment has averaged 5.5 percent over the last 18 years, compared with nearly 7 percent in the previous 18 years, and it is now down to about 5 percent.

Mr. Blinder, a Democrat who battled with Mr. Greenspan over the Fed's communication policy, said his former boss might well be the best central banker who ever lived.

Allen Sinai, chief global economist at Decision Economics, pointed to one reason Mr. Greenspan was so willing to rely on his gut instincts. "He didn't go to one of the top schools: Harvard or M.I.T. or Stanford or Northwestern," Mr. Sinai said. "I think that was an advantage. He didn't get brainwashed into one of the doctrines."

A devout believer in free markets and at one time a disciple of Ayn Rand, the libertarian philosopher, Mr. Greenspan—who studied at New York University—served as chairman of the Council of Economic Advisers under President Gerald R. Ford. As head of Townsend-Greenspan, the forecasting firm he ran both before and after his White House years, Mr. Greenspan made his reputation by poring through vast amounts of industry data to tease out economic trends.

Named by President Ronald Reagan to succeed Mr. Volcker as Fed chairman in 1987, Mr. Greenspan brought both his passion for detail and a cool head for crises.

The first crisis arrived barely two months after he arrived when the stock market crashed more than 500 points on Oct. 19, 1987.

Mr. Greenspan, initially mistrusted as a weak successor to the iron-willed Mr. Volcker, quickly soothed the economy by assuring banks that the Fed would provide enough money to keep financial markets functioning. With the Fed offering money to all takers, interest rates edged down, markets recovered and the crash turned out to be little more than a pause in the bull market.

Years later, Mr. Greenspan said one of his proudest achievements was the fact that he had been able to sleep the night after Black Monday.

But Mr. Greenspan gradually ushered in a host of more enduring changes at the Fed. With memories of the 1970's era of soaring prices still strong, he initiated "pre-emptive" changes in interest rates to head off inflation before it actually arrived, calling the practice "leaning against the wind."

By relentlessly raising interest rates in 1989, the Fed contributed to an unexpectedly sharp economic downturn that played a major role in the election defeat of the first President Bush in 1992. The second attempt, a sharp rise in rates in 1994 and 1995, went more smoothly: inflation remained low, the economy cooled briefly and then began its biggest growth spurt in decades.

Many economists say Mr. Greenspan's signal triumph was being among the first to recognize that starting in the mid-1990's, the United States had entered a sustained period of faster productivity growth. The increase had profound implications, because it meant that the economy could grow faster and unemployment could fall lower than had ever seemed possible without fueling inflation.

The productivity shift was not apparent in official government statistics, and Mr. Greenspan found himself bucking his own staff economists as well as Fed governors like Janet Yellen and Laurence H. Meyer.

At the time, most economists assumed inflation would heat up once unemployment dipped below 5.5 percent. But Mr. Greenspan, convinced that investments in computers and information technology were finally paying off in faster productivity, was content to let unemployment sink to less than 4 percent. "He was confident in his judgment and he was right," Mr. Blinder said. "The lesson is that sometimes you can't wait for the data to be definitive."

Some economists point to an even broader legacy for future Fed policy. Before Mr. Greenspan took over, they note, policy makers focused almost entirely on changes in demand as the determinant of inflation. The surge in productivity showed that changes on the economy's supply side could be equally, if not more, important.

Critics of Mr. Greenspan contend that he has relied too heavily on his own judgment and not enough on consistent principles.

"We've moved further away from a rules-based system," said Brian S. Wesbury, chief investment strategist at Claymore Advisers. "We have a Greenspan standard, but we don't have any kind of a Fed standard."

If the Fed had adopted an explicit numerical inflation target—something that many other central banks use but that Mr. Greenspan has rejected as too restrictive—Mr. Wesbury contended that the Fed might have avoided much of the volatility since 2000.

With little inflation in sight, the Fed might have raised interest rates less than it did in 1999, which might have softened the downturn that followed. That in turn might have made the Fed less eager to drive down rates when the stock market fell sharply in 2000, causing less of a potential bubble in housing prices today.

Other analysts contend that Mr. Greenspan's judgment has generally been correct, but that the Fed cannot afford to rely on the individual judgment of future chairmen.

"If you are Alan Greenspan, it's hard to make a rule that would do any better," said Allen H. Meltzer, professor of economics at Carnegie Mellon University and author of a history of the Fed. "On the other hand, we have had 12 chairmen at the Federal Reserve since 1913, and some of them have made massive blunders."

Mr. Greenspan remains convinced that the economy is simply too complex and fast moving to be subject to a single policy rule or predictable with any single economic model. If he has one consistent message, it is that nothing is permanent.

While many economists warn that the United States has become dangerously loaded up with foreign debt, Mr. Greenspan has argued that the globalization of finance and other changes may have created a global "savings glut" that allows the United States to borrow much more than would have been possible 20 years ago.

His alternative to firm rules is "risk management," a strategy of making policy based on a range of possible outcomes. The clearest example came in 2003, when the Fed worried about the slim possibility of a broad deflation, a downward spiral in consumer prices.

Though Fed officials viewed deflation as highly unlikely, they figured the damage would be heavy if it did occur. Mr. Greenspan cut short-term rates to 1 percent in 2003, then promised to keep them at that level for a "considerable period" that turned out to be a year.

The biggest risk for his successor could turn out to be a collapse in housing prices after the frenetic run-up that has resulted in part from the Fed's policy of keeping interest rates so low. But another key principle of the Greenspan Fed, which most experts have come to accept, is that the central bank should focus on economic fundamentals and not try to prematurely pop a market bubble in stock prices or real estate prices.

After the stock market bubble burst in 2000, Mr. Greenspan argued that the Fed would have made a mistake if it had tried to curb speculation by raising interest rates or making it harder for investors to buy stock with borrowed money.

It was better, he argued, to fix things afterward by cutting interest rates. With evidence of speculative excess in many housing markets, Mr. Greenspan is now warning that investors may be overconfident that interest rates will stay low and that housing prices will continue to soar.

But if housing prices do turn out to be a bubble that bursts, trapping homeowners who used exotic new mortgages to borrow far more than was once allowed, Mr. Greenspan will no longer be around to take the blame—or clean up the mess.

MAKING**CONNECTIONS**

1

The Consumer Price Index is one way the federal government tracks prices. The first story in this chapter lays the foundation for a larger discussion of how the CIP measures inflation. Write a lede for a straight news story using the most recent Consumer Price Index.

2

Discuss what impact the most recent recession has had on consumers who become "gleeful" about saving money. What are the longer-term implications for the economy if consumers save more and spend less? Can you draw any analogies to make these implications more clear?

3

Oil prices have a major impact on inflation that stretches beyond fuel and gasoline. Why is this true? Offer three examples of stories you could write about the impact of higher oil prices on the economy, beyond the obvious candidates such as gasoline and fuel oil.

BUSINESS CONCEPTS REVIEW

Consumer price index	A widely used quoted inflation statistic compiled monthly by the Bureau of Labor Statistics. The CPI measures the weighted average of a predetermined market basket that includes such items as food, transportation, shelter, utilities and clothing. The index is calculated by taking the changes in price of the market basket and then comparing that average with a benchmark year.
Consumer spending	The purchase of goods and services by individuals. Whether consumers are spending is a measure of the health of the economy.
Deflation	Decline in the price of goods and services due to changes in the economy—the reverse of inflation. Linked to recessions and the Great Depression. Not to be confused with disinflation—a slowdown in the inflation rate.
Federal Reserve System	The U.S. central bank and regulator of the nation's financial and monetary system, established by the Federal Reserve Act of 1913. The Fed's main functions are to regulate the money supply and set reserve requirements for member banks.
GDP deflator	Measures changes in price of all new domestically produced final goods and services in the economy. The deflator is calculated by dividing current dollar GDP by constant dollar GDP. The index is considered a broader measure of changes in price since it includes all goods and services and is not based on a fixed market basket of goods.
Inflation	An increase in the level of prices. Occurs when money in the economy increases faster than the supply of goods.
IMF	The International Monetary Fund (IMF) was established in 1944 to prevent currency devaluations and stabilize exchange rates worldwide.
Interest rate	The price of money, or amount charged by a lender, for the use of funds lent to borrowers. The interest rate is usually expressed as an annual rate.
Monetary policy	The regulation of the supply of money and interest rates by a central bank such as the Federal Reserve.
Money supply	Amount of money in the economy consisting of cash in circulation, deposits in savings and checking accounts. An increase in money supply tends to push interest rates down, but can also lead to an increase in prices. Tightening the money supply raises interest rates.
Mortgage	A debt where the borrower gives the lender a lien against property. The mortgage is repaid over time with a set schedule of payments.
Stagflation	Period marked by falling or slowing economic growth and rising prices.

CHAPTER 3

jobs and unemployment

● HARDLY A DAY GOES BY WHEN there isn't a major story in the news about jobs. Companies are always growing, expanding, merging, acquiring or shutting down. All of these actions have implications for their employees and the communities in which they live. Without jobs, an economy grinds to a halt. Stores close because there are no shoppers. Tax revenues dry up and government projects—such as new roads, schools or social programs—wither. Crime rises and social unrest foments.

Writing about jobs is one of the best beats around. Simply put, there are so many stories to report; many are low-hanging fruit just waiting to be picked. And while people may have trouble understanding finance, banking or law, everybody knows what it means to work a job or to lose one. Jobs provide people with a standard of living. Workers may hate their jobs, but they care a lot about having a paycheck.

Good journalists are always on the lookout for two things—stories that involve people and stories that involve conflict. Conflict gives stories tension and makes storytelling easier. The labor market has had plenty of conflict lately. It has been in a state of perpetual change for three decades, as virtually every sector of the U.S. economy has been ravaged by job cuts, mergers and corporate restructuring.

The trend started with high-wage manufacturing jobs exiting the United States in the late 1970s. It continues today with white-collar service jobs moving overseas. Desktop computers, cell phones and the Internet have eliminated the need for work to be tied to a specific location. Salesmen have virtual offices; X-rays and medical tests can be transmitted digitally for processing and then be sent back to the United States. Manufacturing has become a global enterprise, too. Seventy percent of the parts for Boeing's new monster jetliner, dubbed the 787 Dreamliner, are being constructed by subcontractors spanning from Italy to Japan.[1] The parts are then being shipped to the United States for final assembly.[2]

The result of all these changes is that American business has become far more efficient. Productivity has surged. These lower costs are being passed on to the consumer in the form of lower prices. Consumers are seeing better deals on flat screen TVs, electronics, furniture and clothing because of a well-developed global supply chain. The unfortunate trade-off is that jobs are far less secure now than they were a decade or two ago. People no longer work one job for most of their life, retiring with a gold watch and a company pension. Firms like General Motors and United Airlines, once stalwarts of American business, have filed for bankruptcy, laying off tens of thousands of workers.

As you'll see in this chapter, stories about jobs can be tackled from a number of different vantage points: sociology, economics, finance, demographics and race, to name just a few. Yes, knowing how the government calculates the unemployment rate is worthwhile, but in most newsrooms that only gets you to first base. Reading, research and lots of interviewing are key to rounding out the story, says New York Times economics writer Louis Uchitelle. "You keep reporting and you come up with a framework," he says. "There are plenty of stories that I start out to do and have to abandon because some idea I have or some conception I have isn't there."[3]

Beginning journalists covering labor and employment should think of themselves as behaviorists, chronicling the human events around them. What is happening is always important. But even more valuable is uncovering the *why* behind a particular trend or event. Why, for example, are Mexicans immigrating to the United States when U.S. companies are sending jobs to Mexico? Why did record numbers of women enter the work force only to start leaving in record numbers decades later? And what impact does a college education have on how much money you earn during your lifetime?

Labor is one exciting beat. The stories in this chapter should give you a cross-section of the road ahead. There is no one way to report on jobs and the labor force. So tackle it with enthusiasm and a dogged persistence, insisting on answers to questions that so often elude us. Happy hunting.

Selection 3.1

When it comes to jobs, who gets hurt the most when the economy turns downward? The less-educated and lower-income workers suffer the brunt of the job losses. College graduates tend to fare better. But there are some distinct patterns beyond income that are worth noting in the Great Recession of 2007–2009. For example, men have been hit harder than women, and homeowners and investors are hurting more than renters or retirees who rely on Social Security. In this column, part of the Wednesday "Economic Scene" feature, David Leonhardt discusses these patterns by examining one California desert town. The approach allows Leonhardt to put a face on the job numbers by offering examples of different groups affected by the recession. We quickly get a picture of the winners and the losers.

ECONOMIC SCENE
Job Losses Show Breadth of Recession
By DAVID LEONHARDT

What does the worst recession in a generation look like?

It is both deep and broad. Every state in the country, with the exception of a band stretching from the Dakotas down to Texas, is now shedding jobs at a rapid pace. And even that band has recently begun to suffer, because of the sharp fall in both oil and crop prices.

Unlike the last two recessions—earlier this decade and in the early 1990s—this one is causing much more job loss among the less educated than among college graduates. Those earlier recessions introduced the country to the concept of mass white-collar layoffs. The brunt of the layoffs in this recession is falling on construction workers, hotel workers, retail workers and others without a four-year degree.

The Great Recession of 2008 (and beyond) is hurting men more than women. It is hurting homeowners and investors more than renters or retirees who rely on Social Security checks. It is hurting Latinos more than any other ethnic group. A year ago, a greater share of Latinos held jobs than whites. Today, the two have switched places.

If the Great Recession, as some have called it, has a capital city, it is El Centro, Calif., due east of San Diego, in the desert of California's Inland Valley. El Centro has the highest unemployment rate in the nation, a depressionlike 22.6 percent.

It's an agricultural area—because of water pumped in from the Colorado River, which allows lettuce, broccoli and the like to grow—and unemployment is in double digits even in good times. But El Centro has lately been hit by the brutal combination of a drought, a housing bust and a falling peso, which cuts into the buying power of Mexicans who cross the border to shop.

Until recently, El Centro was one of those relatively cheap inland California areas where construction and home sales were booming. Today, it is pockmarked with "bank-owned" for sale signs. A wallboard factory in nearby Plaster City—its actual name—has laid off workers once kept busy by the housing boom. Even Wal-Mart has cut jobs, Sam Couchman, who runs the county's work force development office, told me.

Published: March 3, 2009.

You often hear that recessions exact the biggest price on the most vulnerable workers. And that's true about this recession, at least for the moment. But it isn't the whole story. Just look at Wall Street, where a generation-long bubble seems to lose a bit more air every day.

In the long run, this Great Recession may end up afflicting the comfortable more than the afflicted.

The main reason that recessions tend to increase inequality is that lower-income workers are concentrated in boom-and-bust industries. Agriculture is the classic example. In recent years, construction has become the most important one.

By the start of this decade, the construction sector employed more men without a college education than the manufacturing sector did, Lawrence Katz, the Harvard labor economist, points out. (As recently as 1980, three times as many such men worked in manufacturing as construction.) The housing boom was like a giant jobs program for many workers who otherwise would have struggled to find decent paying work.

The housing bust has forced many of them into precisely that struggle and helps explain the recession's outsize toll on Latinos and men. In the summer of 2005, just as the real estate market was peaking, I spent a day visiting home construction sites in Frederick, Md., something of a Washington exurb, interviewing the workers. They were almost exclusively Latino.

At the time, the national unemployment rate for Latino men was 3.6 percent. Today, when there aren't many homes being built in Frederick or anywhere else, that unemployment rate is 11 percent. And this number understates the damage, since it excludes a considerable number of immigrants who have returned home.

Frederick was typical of the boom in another way, too. It wasn't nearly as affluent as some closer suburbs. Now the bust is widening that gap.

If you look at the interactive map with this column, you will see the places that already had high unemployment before the recession have also had some of the largest increases. Some are victims of the housing bust, like inland California. Others are manufacturing centers, as in Michigan and North Carolina, whose long-term decline is accelerating. Rhode Island, home to both factories and Boston exurbs, has one of the highest jobless rates in the nation.

All of these trends will serve to increase inequality. Yet I still think the Great Recession will eventually end up compressing the rungs on the nation's economic ladder. Why? For the same three fundamental reasons that the Great Depression did.

The first is the stock market crash. Clearly, it has hurt wealthy and upper middle-class families, who own the bulk of stock, more than others. In addition, thousands of high-paying Wall Street jobs—jobs that have helped the share of income flowing to the top 1 percent of earners soar in recent decades—will disappear.

Hard as it may be to believe, the crash will also help a lot of young families. The stocks that they buy in coming years are likely to appreciate far more than they would have if the Dow were still above 14,000. The same is true of future house purchases for the one in three families still renting a home.

The second reason is government policy. The Obama administration plans to raise taxes on the affluent, cut them for everyone else (so long as the government can afford it, that is) and take other steps to reduce inequality. Franklin D. Roosevelt did something similar and it had a huge effect.

Of course, these two factors both boil down to redistribution. One group is benefiting at the expense of another. Yes, many of the people on the losing end of that shift have done quite well in recent years, far better than most Americans. Still, the shift isn't making the economic pie any bigger. It is simply being divided differently.

Which is why the third factor—education—is the most important of all. It can make the pie larger and divide it more evenly.

That was the legacy of the great surge in school enrollment during the Great Depression. Teenagers who once would have dropped out to do factory work instead stayed in high school, notes Claudia Goldin, an economist who recently wrote a history of education with Mr. Katz.

In the manufacturing-heavy mid-Atlantic states, the high school graduation rate was just above 20 percent in the late 1920s. By 1940, it was almost 60 percent. These graduates then became the skilled workers and teachers who helped build the great post-World War II American economy.

Nothing would benefit tomorrow's economy more than a similar surge. And there is some evidence that it's starting to happen. In El Centro, enrollment at Imperial Valley Community College jumped 11 percent this semester. Ed Gould, the college president, said he expected applications to keep rising next year.

Unfortunately, California—one of the states hit hardest by the Great Recession—is in the midst of a fiscal crisis. So Imperial Valley's budget is being capped. Next year, Mr. Gould expects he will have to tell some students that they can't take a full load of classes, just when they most need help.

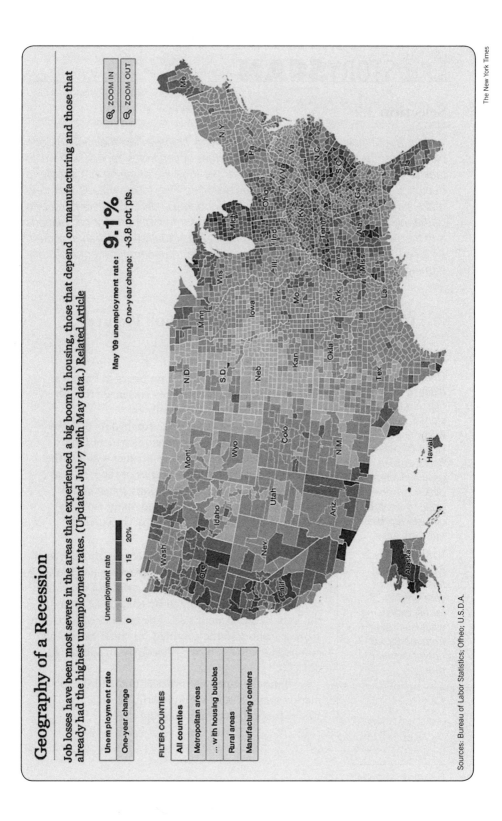

Geography of a Recession

Job losses have been most severe in the areas that experienced a big boom in housing, those that depend on manufacturing and those that already had the highest unemployment rates. (Updated July 7 with May data.) Related Article

Unemployment rate
One-year change

May '09 unemployment rate: **9.1%**
One-year change: **+3.8 pct. pts.**

Unemployment rate

0 5 10 15 20%

FILTER COUNTIES

All counties

Metropolitan areas

... with housing bubbles

Rural areas

Manufacturing centers

Sources: Bureau of Labor Statistics; Ofheo; U.S.D.A.

The New York Times

 STORY**SCAN**

Selection 3.2

Writing about how many people are working or have lost their jobs is one of the most basic of all stories that business/economics reporters have to tackle. The figures are closely watched, yet they are anything but simple to decipher. Most unemployment stories are filled with talking heads that help make sense of the subject. What is different here is how David Leonhardt and Catherine Rampell dive into the numbers, do some independent calculations and then explain how the reported numbers are actually worse than expected. As a result, readers leave with new insights into the unemployment picture— namely, what the numbers aren't telling us.

Grim Job Report Not Showing Full Picture

By DAVID LEONHARDT and CATHERINE RAMPELL

Unemployment hitting a 15-year high is a big story. Everyone will write that story. The writers decide to take us in a different direction—one that explains what the officially reported numbers miss.

Writers do a nice job of breaking this down into very simple terms, explaining what is missing from the formal unemployment rate.

As bad as the headline numbers in Friday's employment report were, they still made the job market look better than it really is.

The unemployment rate reached its highest point since 1993, and overall employment fell by more than a half million jobs. Yet that was just the beginning. Thanks to the vagaries of the way that the government's best-known jobs statistics are calculated, they have overlooked many workers who have been deeply affected by the current recession.

The number of people out of the labor force— meaning that they were neither working nor looking for work and that the government did not consider them unemployed—jumped by 637,000 last month, the Labor Department said. The number of part-time workers who said they wanted full-time work—all counted as fully employed—rose by an additional 621,000.

Take these people into account, and the job market may be in its worst condition since the early 1980s. It is still deteriorating rapidly, too.

Published: December 5, 2008.

Already, the share of men older than 20 with jobs was at its lowest point last month since 1983, and very close to the low point of the last 60 years. The share of women with jobs is lower than it was eight years ago, which never happened in previous decades.

Offers background, context.

Liz Perkins, 24 and the mother of four young children in Colorado Springs, began looking for work in October after she learned that her husband, James, was about to lose his job at a bed-making factory.

Good use of an example. This puts a face on the numbers.

But the jobs she found either did not pay enough to cover child care or required her to work overnight. "I can't do overnight work with four children," she said. She has since stopped looking for work.

The family has paid its bills by dipping into its savings and borrowing money from relatives. But Ms. Perkins said that unless her husband found a job in the next three months, she feared the family would become homeless.

Even Wall Street economists, whose analysis usually comes shaded in rose, seemed taken aback by the report. Goldman Sachs called the new numbers "horrendous." Others said "dreadful" and "almost indescribably terrible." In a note to clients, Morgan Stanley economists wrote, "Quite simply, there was nothing good in this report." HSBC forecasters said they now expected the Federal Reserve to reduce its benchmark interest rate all the way to zero.

Reinforces earlier point. Even the experts, using common language, think the situation is bleak.

Such language may sound out of step with a jobless rate that, despite its recent rise, remains at 6.7 percent; the rate exceeded 10 percent in the early 1980s. But over the last few decades, the jobless rate has become a significantly less useful measure of the country's economic health.

That is because far more people than in the past fall into the gray area of the labor market—not having a job and not looking for one, but interested in working. This group includes many former factory workers who have been unable to find new work that pays nearly as well and are unwilling to accept a job that pays much less. Some get by with help from disability payments, while others rely on their spouses' paychecks.

This reinforces the early point that the unemployment rate understates the level of joblessness.

For much of the last year, the ranks of these labor force dropouts were not changing rapidly, said Thomas Nardone, a Labor Department economist who oversees the collection of the unemployment data. People who had lost their jobs generally began looking for new work. But that changed in November.

Much as many stock market investors threw in the towel in early October, and consumers quickly followed suit by cutting their spending, job seekers seemed to turn darkly pessimistic about the American economy in November. Unless the numbers turn out to have been a one-month blip, large numbers of people seem to have decided that a job search is, for now, futile.

"It's not only that there's nothing out there," said Lorena Garcia, an organizer in Denver for 9 to 5, National Association of Working Women, a group that helps low-wage women and women who are looking for work. "But it also costs money to job hunt."

Questions can work as transitions, but don't overuse them.

Just how bad is the labor market? Coming up with a measure that is comparable across decades is not easy.

It is always good to point out areas where numbers may be misinterpreted. Readers appreciate such efforts.

The unemployment rate has been made less meaningful by the long-term rise in dropouts from the labor force. The simple percentage of people without jobs—including retirees, stay-at-home parents and discouraged would-be job seekers—can also be misleading, though. It has dropped in recent decades mainly because of the influx of women into the work force, not because the job market is fundamentally healthier than it used to be.

The Labor Department does publish an alternate measure of unemployment, which counts part-time workers who want full-time work, as well as anyone who has looked for work in the last year. (The official rate includes only people who told a government surveyor that they had looked in the last four weeks.)

This alternate measure rose to 12.5 percent in November. That is the highest level since the government began calculating the measure in 1994.

Perhaps the best historical measure of the job market, however, is the one set by the market itself: pay.

During the economic expansion that lasted from 2001 until December 2007, when the recession began, incomes for most households barely outpaced inflation. It was the weakest income growth in any expansion since World War II.

The one bit of good news in Friday's jobs report, economists said, was that pay had not yet begun to fall sharply. Average weekly wages for rank-and-file workers, who make up about four-fifths of the work force, rose 2.8 percent over the last year, only slightly below inflation.

But economists said those pay gains would begin to shrink next year, if not in the next few weeks, given the rapid drop in demand for workers. "Wage increases of this magnitude will be history very soon," said Joshua Shapiro, an economist at MFR Incorporated, a research firm in New York.

Writers use history to put what they are saying in context. Without context, readers have no way to assess the importance of the numbers being presented.

To be sure, things are not all doom and gloom. Present the other side whenever possible.

Always be aware of how you want to end the story. What thought do you want to leave in the reader's mind?

Selection 3.3

Demographic trends examining different population segments provide great fodder for stories that blend marketing, economics and sociology with a pop culture side. In this column, Fred Brock looks at how the retirements of 76 million Americans born as part of a post–World War II baby boom (1946–1962) are going to turn the labor market upside down. Big societal change is nothing new for the boomers. Since its conception this group, which accounts for one-fourth of the U.S. population, has influenced every market it has come into contact with—diapers, food, education, automobiles, clothing, housing. Now, the labor market is getting ready for a new boomer tidal wave: retirements. What's the problem? There simply are not enough replacement workers in the pipeline. Boomers could be asked to stay longer, or employers may be forced to boost their pay to keep them on board.

Who'll Sit at the Boomers' Desks?

By FRED BROCK

During the Clinton boom years of the late 1990s, in one of the tightest labor markets in memory, corporate America was warned that if it did not cultivate older workers, they would take their skills and move on.

One recession and one so-called jobless recovery later, some questions naturally arise: Was that warning ill founded? Was the tight

Published: October 12, 2003.

job market at the end of the '90s an anomaly? Will chronically high unemployment be the norm for the near future?

The answers appear to be no, no and no.

In fact, the current level of unemployment, which has economists and politicians in a lather, is likely to be the real anomaly. Conditions in the late '90s may have been a reflection of job markets to come. And they are coming very quickly.

The reason, of course, is that the big baby-boom generation is starting to retire. Its oldest members are about 57 and will be 65 in 2011. There simply aren't enough workers behind the boomers in the labor supply pipeline to fill their jobs. Employers will have to try to retain older workers in some capacity or lure retired workers back into the work force. Companies that have treated their workers badly or engaged in even the subtlest forms of age discrimination will regret it.

So will companies that just ignore the problem. "It's stunning how many corporations and chief executives have no idea what's coming; they're so focused on their next quarter's numbers," said Paul Kaihla, a senior writer for the magazine Business 2.0. Mr. Kaihla wrote the cover article, "The Coming Job Boom," in the September issue.

"Some smart companies that know this is coming are treating their workers well during this downturn and trying to retain older workers," he said.

Mr. Kaihla calls the situation a "retirement time bomb" that will gut the ranks of managers and skilled workers, particularly in technology. He cited two companies—Intel and SAS Institute—that are likely to be hit hard but are preparing to cope with the problem. "SAS, where 25 percent of its workers will hit retirement age this decade, is a poster child of how to treat workers well," he said. "It is designing policies to come up with contracts or flexible hours for older workers. Intel, where 15 percent will reach retirement age this decade, is retaining links with its retired workers, knowing that it may have to turn to them when the crisis strikes."

The wedge of this labor crisis is opening now, as some boomers take early retirement. In fact, Mr. Kaihla says these early retirees are one reason the unemployment rate is in the 6 percent range, instead of 8 percent as in some previous downturns.

"The labor shortage has been masked by recession," he said. "By 2005 it'll be in full swing. By 2010 there will be a gap of five to seven million workers, depending on whose projections you accept." He said some projections show that gap swelling to a canyon of 14 million by 2020.

"You can't have the vast majority of your prime-age work force retire and not have it have an effect," Mr. Kaihla said. "Always before, the generation coming in was larger than the previous one. That's not the case now. The feeder pool isn't providing the kind of natural growth we've always had in the work force."

He also noted that the growth rate for education among workers has leveled off at about 60 percent—meaning that this share of workers has some college education. "This is likely to get only marginally higher," he added.

Nowhere is the potential worker shortage more pronounced, Mr. Kaihla said, than at federal agencies like the Defense Department, where half the civilian workers are scheduled to retire this decade.

He says that the coming labor shortage will put an end to outsourcing as a contentious labor issue, and that Congress will increase the number of skilled foreign workers allowed into the country. But neither outsourcing nor immigration will make a big dent in the problem, he added.

What does all this mean for the economy? "It means we're probably going to have to settle for slower economic growth," Mr. Kaihla said.

Some economists, however, aren't so sure. Henry J. Aaron and Gary Burtless, senior fellows at the Brookings Institution in Washington, cite the flexibility of the American work force as a factor that may soften the effects of boomer retirements. "Workers may take higher-level jobs at a younger age than we have traditionally seen," Mr. Burtless said.

Both economists, though, agreed that the leveling off of the education rate among workers could be a problem as employers try to fill positions for skilled workers and managers.

Much of this, of course, is good news for workers—especially older, skilled ones—and bad news for employers. "This will surely put an end to any forms of age discrimination," Mr. Kaihla said. "Companies that engage in it are so blind; they are shooting themselves in the foot. Within a couple of years or so they will be fighting for many of these workers and have to pay a premium for them."

For example, he said, the current jobless recovery has really been a productivity recovery. "There are a lot of angry workers, because instead of hiring new workers, many companies have worked existing workers—many of them older—harder and longer," he said. "The minute the labor market rebounds, they're gone—just at the time we're entering this period of labor shortage."

"There has never been," he added, "a clear example in modern economic times of what we are facing."

Beverly Goldberg, a vice president of the Century Foundation, a research institute in New York, says the projections for labor shortages are likely to be pretty much on target. "Demographics don't change," she said.

Ms. Goldberg, the author of "Age Works: What Corporate America Must Do to Survive the Graying of the Work Force" (Free Press, 2002), said Europe would have more difficulty than the United States because its immigration policies are more restrictive and its birth rates lower. She added, however, that one problem in trying to import workers was that they often lacked the necessary skills to replace older workers.

She said the shortage was already painfully evident in occupations like teaching, where people often retire after 30 years. "Teachers are retiring in astounding numbers," she said. "New York City is combing the world looking for teachers."

She added: "At the moment, more companies than not are lulled into a false sense of security. They have to face the fact that they're next."

Selection 3.4

Few demographic trends have had a more profound cultural and economic impact than women entering the work force in record numbers, a movement that stretches back to the 1960s. Household incomes benefitted from two wage earners, but the birth rate slowed as more women waited until later in life to marry and have children. Now, labor-force participation rates are declining for women for a variety of reasons. Eduardo Porter examines the factors behind this trend and finds women to discuss the conflicts they face between raising a family, running a household and working a full-time job. This is the rare business story in which every source, expert and otherwise is a woman.

Stretched to Limit, Women Stall March to Work
By EDUARDO PORTER

For four decades, the number of women entering the workplace grew at a blistering pace, fostering a powerful cultural and economic transformation of American society. But since the mid-1990s, the growth in the percentage of adult women working outside the home has stalled, even slipping somewhat in the last five years and leaving it at a rate well below that of men.

While the change has been under way for a while, it was initially viewed by many experts as simply a pause in the longer-term movement of women into the work force. But now, social scientists are engaged in a heated debate over whether the gender revolution at work may be over.

Is this shift evidence for the popular notion that many mothers are again deciding that they prefer to stay at home and take care of their children?

Maybe, but many researchers are coming to a different conclusion: women are not choosing to stay out of the labor force because of a change in attitudes, they say. Rather, the broad reconfiguration of

Published: March 2, 2006.

women's lives that allowed most of them to pursue jobs outside the home appears to be hitting some serious limits.

Since the 1960s, tens of millions of women rejiggered bits of their lives, extracting more time to accommodate jobs and careers from every nook and cranny of the day. They married later and had fewer children. They turned to labor-saving machines and paid others to help handle household work; they persuaded the men in their lives to do more chores.

At the peak in 2000, some 77 percent of women in the prime ages of 25 to 54 were in the work force.

Further changes, though, have been proving harder to achieve, stretching the daily challenge facing many mothers at nearly all income levels toward a breaking point.

"What happened on the road to gender equality?" said Suzanne M. Bianchi, a sociologist at the University of Maryland. "A lot of work happened."

Consider Cathie Watson-Short, 37, a former business development executive at high-technology companies in Silicon Valley. She pines to go back to work, but has not figured out how to mesh work with caring for her three daughters.

"Most of us thought we would work and have kids, at least that was what we were brought up thinking we would do—no problem," Ms. Watson-Short said. "But really we were kind of duped. None of us realized how hard it is."

Professor Bianchi, who studies time-use surveys done by the Census Bureau and others, has concluded that contrary to popular

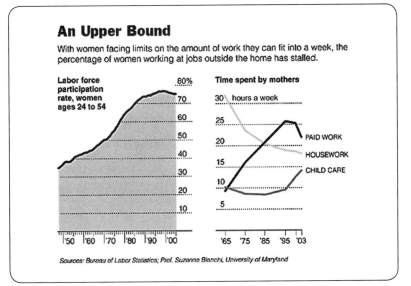

An Upper Bound

With women facing limits on the amount of work they can fit into a week, the percentage of women working at jobs outside the home has stalled.

Labor force participation rate, women ages 24 to 54

Time spent by mothers

PAID WORK
HOUSEWORK
CHILD CARE

Sources: Bureau of Labor Statistics; Prof. Suzanne Bianchi, University of Maryland

belief, the broad movement of women into the paid labor force did not come at the expense of their children. Not only did fathers spend more time with children, but working mothers, she found, spent an average of 12 hours a week on child care in 2003, an hour more than stay-at-home mothers did in 1975.

Instead, mothers with children at home gained the time for outside work by taking it from other parts of their day. They also worked more over all. Professor Bianchi found that employed mothers, on average, worked at home and on the job a total of 15 hours more a week and slept 3.6 fewer hours than those who were not employed.

"Perhaps time has been compressed as far as it will go," she suggested. "Kids take time, and work takes time. The conflicts didn't go away."

Indeed, the research suggests that women may have already hit a wall in the amount of work that they can pack into a week. From 1965 to 1995, Professor Bianchi found, the average time mothers spent doing paid work jumped to almost 26 hours a week from 9 hours. The time spent on housework fell commensurately, to 19 hours from 32.

Then the trend stalled. From 1995 to 2003, mothers, on average, spent about the same amount of time on household chores, but their work outside the home fell by almost four hours a week.

"Looking toward the future," said Francine D. Blau, a professor of economics at Cornell University, "one can question how much further increases in women's participation can be had without more reallocation of household work."

This is having broad repercussions for the economy. Today, about 75 percent of women 25 to 54 years old are either working or actively seeking a job, up from around 40 percent in the late 1950s. That expansion helped fuel economic growth for decades.

But the previous trend flattened in the early 1990s. And since 2000, the participation rate for women has declined somewhat; it remains far below the 90 percent rate for men in the same age range.

There is one big exception to the trend: while the rate of labor participation leveled off for most groups of women, the percentage of single mothers in the work force jumped to more than 75 percent from 63 percent. That of high school dropouts rose to 53 percent from 48 percent.

Economists say that these women were pushed into work with the help of changes in government policy: the expansion of the earned-income tax credit and the overhaul of welfare in the mid-1990s, which replaced long-term entitlements with temporary aid.

To be sure, mothers' overcrowded lives have not been the only factor limiting their roles in the work force. The decline in participation rates for most groups of women since the recession of 2001 at least partly reflects an overall slowdown in hiring, which affected men and women roughly equally.

"The main reason for women's declining labor-force participation rates over the last four years was the weakness of the labor market," said Heather Boushey, an economist at the Center for Economic and Policy Research, a liberal research institute in Washington. "Women did not opt out of the labor force because of the kids."

But even if the recent decline was driven more by economic factors, other experts note that the leveling off began well before the economic slump a few years ago. And whatever the mixture of causes, the changing pace of women's participation in the work force has recently risen to the top of the agenda among scholars and policy makers.

A report by the White House Council of Economic Advisers, presented to Congress in February, contended that the slowdown in the rate of women moving into the workplace, was weighing on the nation's potential for economic growth.

"The new factor at play," the report said, "is the change in the trend in the female participation rate, which has edged down on balance since 2000 after having risen for five decades."

Claudia Goldin, an economics professor at Harvard University, said in a keynote speech to the annual meeting of the American Economic Association in Boston in January that the trend across nearly all groups of women had "led many to wonder if a 'natural rate' of labor force participation has been reached."

A broad set of social and economic forces pushed women into the work force. From the 1960s onward, women flooded into higher education and began to marry later.

Professor Goldin said that a typical female college graduate born in the mid-1960s married at 26, three years later than the typical female college graduate born in the early 1950s.

This alone had large-scale implications for women's ability to work. Many families delayed the arrival of their first child. Today, only about 43 percent of women 25 to 29 have children under 6, compared with about 71 percent of women in that group in the 1960s.

Chinhui Juhn, an economics professor at the University of Houston, pointed out that women in their mid-to-late 20s accounted for most of the increase in work force participation from 1970 onward. But now, she said, "the increase in participation of women in their prime child-bearing years is largely over."

Women's participation in the labor force is being restrained by a side effect of delayed motherhood: a jump in 30-something mothers with toddlers.

"The childbirth effects are coming later," said Janice Madden, a sociologist at the University of Pennsylvania.

By 2004, about 37 percent of women ages 33 to 37 had children under 6, compared with 28 percent in 1979.

At midcareer, these women had to deal with more child care chores. "There have been a lot more household responsibilities in this group," Professor Goldin, the Harvard economist, said. "The fact that their participation rate has not declined much is what is surprising—not that there is a plateau."

Most women, even those with young children, need to work. Many more want to. Ms. Watson-Short, the former California executive who is now a mother of three, said that her stay-at-home-mom friends, like her, felt blindsided by the demands of motherhood.

"They had a totally different idea of where they would be," Ms. Watson-Short said. "They thought they would be in the workplace and have someone help them raise the kids."

But those who kept working are also torn. Catherine Stallings, 34, returned to her job in the communications department of New York University's medical center last month because she could not afford not to. Dealing with work and her 5-month-old daughter, Riley, has been stressful for her and her husband, the marketing director of a sports magazine.

Usually, we are so tired we pass out around 10 or so," Ms. Stallings said. "And my job is not a career-track job. If I were climbing the ladder, it would be a no-win situation."

Some economists argue that it is premature to conclude that the gender revolution in the workplace has reached its limit.

Yet for the participation rates of women to rise significantly, they agree, mothers may have to give up more of the household burden.

Professor Blau of Cornell noted that in Scandinavian countries, where laws provide for more generous parental leave and subsidize day care, women have higher rates of labor participation than in the United States.

Ms. Watson-Short, whose husband is a patent lawyer, expects to go back to some sort of paid work but sees a full-time job as well off in the future. Making the transition back into the work force, even through part-time jobs, will not be as easy as she and her contemporaries once hoped.

"We got equality at work," Ms. Watson-Short said. "We really didn't get equality at home."

Selection 3.5

Job hunting is always hard, but hunting for your first job is toughest of all. This story was written several years ago, but it remains relevant today—young workers and college graduates are having a tougher time than ever before finding jobs. Even workers who get a job are having trouble making ends meet. Wages haven't kept pace with inflation. Those fortunate enough to graduate from college face large debt loads from school in addition to all the costs related to starting a household. Steven Greenhouse does an excellent job of bringing these factors together in a story about yet another segment of the labor market—the entry-level worker. His reporting shows that covering the labor market can be complicated by many factors: wages, inflation, interest rates and the vagaries of the economy. Labor writing offers an opportunity to look at why some people get jobs while others go begging, but doing the job well requires understanding how these different factors are related.

Many Entry-Level Workers Feel Pinch of Rough Market

By STEVEN GREENHOUSE

This Labor Day, the 45 million young people in the nation's work force face a choppy job market in which entry-level wages have often trailed inflation, making it hard for many to cope with high housing costs and rising college debt loads.

Entry-level wages for college and high school graduates fell by more than 4 percent from 2001 to 2005, after factoring in inflation, according to an analysis of Labor Department data by the Economic Policy Institute. In addition, the percentage of college graduates receiving health and pension benefits in their entry-level jobs has dropped sharply.

Some labor experts say wage stagnation and the sharp increase in housing costs over the past decade have delayed workers ages 20 to 35 from buying their first homes.

"People are getting married later, they're having children later, and they're buying houses later," said Cecilia E. Rouse, an economist at Princeton University and a co-editor of a forthcoming book on the economics of early adulthood. "There's been a lengthening of the transition to adulthood, and it is very possible that what has happened in the economy is leading to some of these changes."

Census Bureau data released last week underlined the difficulties for young workers, showing that median income for families with at least one parent age 25 to 34 fell $3,009 from 2000 to 2005, sliding to $48,405, a 5.9 percent drop, after having jumped 12 percent in the late 1990's.

Worsening the financial crunch, far more college graduates are borrowing to pay for their education, and the amount borrowed has jumped by more than 50 percent in recent years, largely because of soaring tuition.

In 2004, 50 percent of graduating seniors borrowed some money for college, with their debt load averaging $19,000, Dr. Rouse said. That was a sharp increase from 1993, when 35 percent of seniors borrowed for college and their debt averaged $12,500, in today's dollars.

Published: September 4, 2006.

Even though the economy has grown strongly in recent years, wages for young workers, especially college graduates, have been depressed by several factors, including the end of the high-tech boom and the trend of sending jobs overseas. From 2001 to 2005, entry-level wages for male college graduates fell by 7.3 percent, to $19.72 an hour, while wages for female graduates declined 3.5 percent, to $17.08, according to the Economic Policy Institute, a liberal research group.

"In a weak labor market, younger workers do the worst," said Lawrence Mishel, the institute's president. "Young workers are on the cutting edge of experiencing all the changes in the economy."

Lawrence F. Katz, a labor economist at Harvard, said plenty of slack remained in the job market for young workers.

The percentage of young adults who are working has dropped since 2000 largely because many have grown discouraged and stopped looking for work. This has happened even though the unemployment rate, which counts only people looking for work, has fallen to 4.4 percent for those ages 25 to 34. It is 8.2 percent for workers ages 20 to 24.

"Any way you slice the data, the labor market has been pretty weak the past five years," Dr. Katz said. "But hotshot young people coming out of top universities have done fine, just like top-notch executives have."

In a steep drop over a short time, 64 percent of college graduates received health coverage in entry-level jobs in 2005, down from 71 percent five years earlier. As employers grapple with fast-rising health costs, many companies have reduced health coverage, with those cutbacks sharpest among young workers.

Partly because of the decline in manufacturing jobs that were a ticket to middle-class life, just one-third of workers with high school diplomas receive health coverage in entry-level jobs, down from two-thirds in 1979.

After an extensive job search, Katey Rich, who graduated from Wesleyan University in June, landed a part-time, $14-an-hour job in Manhattan as an editorial assistant at Film Journal International. With one-bedroom apartments often renting for $2,000 a month, Ms. Rich is looking to share an apartment but is staying with a friend's parents for now. And while she is excited about her new job, she said she was concerned that it did not come with health insurance.

"I'll have to fend for myself," said Ms. Rich, who is from Aiken, S.C. "I have parents who will back me up if things get really rough."

Mark Zandi, chief economist at Moody's Economy.com, said it was surprising how deeply young workers were going into debt to maintain the living standards they want.

The nation's personal savings sank below zero last year for the first time since the Depression, meaning Americans spent more than they earned. But for households under 35, the saving rate has plunged to minus 16 percent, which means they are spending 16 percent more than they are earning.

"The post-boomer generation feels very cavalier about saving," Mr. Zandi said. "They've been very aggressively dis-saving and have borrowed significantly."

John Arnold, 28, a materials-handling specialist at a Caterpillar factory in Morton, Ill., said he was having a hard time making ends meet. At his factory, Caterpillar has pressured the union to accept a two-tier contract in which newer workers like him will earn a maximum of $13.26 an hour—$27,000 a year for a full-time worker—no matter how long they work. For longtime Caterpillar workers in the upper tier, the wage ceiling is often $20 or more an hour.

"A few people I work with are living at home with their parents; some are even on food stamps," said Mr. Arnold, a Caterpillar worker for seven years. "I was hoping to buy a house this year, but there's just no way I can swing it." With just a high school diploma, he said it was hard to find jobs that paid more.

For men with high school diplomas, entry-level pay fell by 3.3 percent, to $10.93, from 2001 to 2005, according to the Economic Policy Institute. For female high school graduates, entry-level pay fell by 4.9 percent, to $9.08 an hour.

Labor Department officials voiced optimism for young workers, noting that the Bureau of Labor Statistics had projected that 18.9 million net new jobs would be created by 2014.

"The future is bright for young people because the opportunities are out there," said Mason Bishop, deputy assistant labor secretary for employment and training. "We want to help them get access to the postsecondary education that enables them to take advantage of the opportunities."

The wage gap between college-educated and high-school-educated workers has widened greatly, with college graduates earning 45 percent more than high school graduates, up from 23 percent in 1979.

Professor Rouse of Princeton said a college degree added $402,000 to a graduate's lifetime earnings.

Alex Shayevsky, who graduated from New York University last year, said majoring in business had paid off. Mr. Shayevsky got a job in the bond department of a major investment bank in New York. He earns $65,000, not including a bonus that could be at least half his salary.

"Getting my degree was very valuable," said Mr. Shayevsky, a 23-year-old from Buffalo Grove, Ill.

Martin Regalia, chief economist for the United States Chamber of Commerce, said young workers would be helped greatly if strong economic growth continued and the labor market tightened further, as happened in the late 1990's.

Sheldon H. Danziger, a professor of public policy at the University of Michigan, sees a bifurcated labor market for young workers.

"You're much better off as a young worker today if you're the child of the well-to-do and you get a good education," Professor Danziger said, "and you're much worse off if you're a child of a blue-collar worker and you don't go to college. There's increasing inequality among young people just as there is increasing inequality among their parents."

Selection 3.6

In a paradox of globalization, U.S. employers are sending jobs to Asia and Mexico, but at the same time, just as many workers are migrating to the United States from Mexico in search of work. The jobs they seek are low-paying, low-skill positions many Americans avoid. The result is a two-tier blue-collar work force in the United States. Hispanic immigrants—many hired through temporary staffing agencies that offer no vacation pay or health coverage—are on the very bottom, taking jobs picking vegetables or working in dirty and sometimes dangerous factories processing chicken or beef. This story, one in a seven-part series about immigration and its impact on America,[4] combines personal detail and narrative writing along with lots of hard, cold facts.

REMADE IN AMERICA
A Slippery Place in the U.S. Work Force
By JULIA PRESTON

MORRISTOWN, Tenn.—The faithful stand and hold their hands high, raising a crescendo of prayer for abundance and grace. In the evangelical church where they are gathered, the folding chairs are filled with immigrants from Latin America.

Balbino López Hernández, who came here illegally from Mexico, closes his eyes to join the hallelujahs. But after the service Mr. López, 28, a factory worker who has been unemployed since June, shares his worries about jobs and immigration raids with other worshipers.

Like many places across the United States, this factory town in eastern Tennessee has been transformed in the last decade by the arrival of Hispanic immigrants, many of whom are in this country illegally. Thousands of workers like Mr. López settled in Morristown, taking the lowest-paying elbow-grease jobs, some hazardous, in chicken plants and furniture factories.

Published: March 21, 2009. Full text available at: www.nytimes.com/2009/03/22/us/22immig.html

Now, with the economy spiraling downward and a crackdown continuing on illegal immigrants, many of them are learning how uncertain their foothold is in the work force in the United States.

The economic troubles are widening the gap between illegal immigrants and Americans as they navigate the job market. Many Americans who lost jobs are turning for help to the government's unemployment safety net, with job assistance and unemployment insurance. But immigrants without legal status, by law, do not have access to it. Instead, as the recession deepens, illegal immigrants who have settled into American towns are receding from community life. They are clinging to low-wage jobs, often working more hours for less money, and taking whatever work they can find, no matter the conditions.

Despite the mounting pressures, many of the illegal immigrants are resisting leaving the country. After years of working here, they say, they have homes and education for their children, while many no longer have a stake to return to in their home countries.

"Most of the things I got are right here," Mr. López said in English, which he taught himself to speak. "I got my family, my wife, my kids. Everything is here."

Americans who are struggling for jobs move in a different world. Here, it revolves around the federally financed, fluorescent-lighted career center on Andrew Johnson Highway, a one-stop market for unemployment insurance and job retraining.

One worker who frequents the center is Joe D. Goodson Jr., 46, who was laid off more than a year ago from his job at a nearby auto parts plant. Born and raised in Morristown, Mr. Goodson said his savings had run low but his spirits were holding up, so far.

Through the career center, Mr. Goodson enrolled in retraining at a technology college. He believes that the government aid system, though inefficient and overwhelmed, will give him just enough support to survive the economic storm.

"I just try to look on the positive side always," Mr. Goodson said. "Work hard. Things get bad? Work harder."

What help there is for illegal immigrants in Morristown comes mainly from churches, like Centro Cristiano Betel Internacional, where Mr. López connects with a word-of-mouth network to find odd jobs.

Nationwide, Hispanic immigrants, both legal and illegal, saw greater job loss in 2008 than did Hispanics born in the United States or black workers, according to the Pew Hispanic Center. Nearly half of foreign-born Hispanics are illegal immigrants, according to the center, a nonpartisan research group in Washington.

Some illegal immigrants who lost jobs here, mostly workers with families back home, have left the country. Most are determined to stay. Employers, wary of immigration agents, now insist workers have valid Social Security numbers. Mr. López, who does not have one, said, "Without the number, you are nothing in this country."

Gaining a Foothold

In a paradox of globalization, immigrant workers moved from Mexico to Morristown just as many jobs were migrating from here to Mexico.

The influx here came as Hispanic immigrants were spreading across the United States, moving beyond traditional destinations in California and the Southwest to take jobs in the Northern Plains and deep into the South.

As recently as 2006 and 2007, more than 300,000 Hispanic immigrants, legal and illegal, were joining the United States labor force each year, drawn by jobs in meatpacking, construction and agriculture. They now make up nearly 8 percent of the work force.

In Morristown, a manufacturing city set among Appalachian farmland, the loss of jobs to Mexico and other countries with lower wages depressed local factory pay long before the immigrants appeared. But while the poorest American factory workers watched jobs leave, Americans with skills found new jobs in plants making auto parts, plastics and printing supplies.

The 1960 census did not record a single immigrant in Hamblen County, of which Morristown is the seat. By 2007, Hispanic immigrants and their families made up almost 10 percent of the county population of 61,829, having nearly doubled their numbers since 2000, census data show.

The immigrants started in tomato fields nearby, but by the late 1990s labor contractors were bringing migrant crews into town, to fill jobs in construction and at factories like two poultry plants belonging to Koch Foods, a company based in Illinois.

The result was a two-tier blue-collar work force. Hispanic immigrants—many hired through temporary staffing agencies that offered no vacation pay or health coverage—were on the bottom, in jobs where they faced little competition from Americans.

Prof. Chris Baker, a sociologist at Walters State Community College in Morristown, said many factories in the region had been able to hang on because of the immigrant workers. "The employers hire Latinos, and after that, they leave," he said. "It goes from white to black to Latino to—gone."

Some residents did not take kindly to the immigrants, especially the illegal ones. But their ire was not about jobs; it was mainly directed at the school board, for devoting tax money to an international center to help Spanish-speaking students learn English.

In the summer of 2006, one member of the Hamblen County Commission, Thomas E. Lowe, organized a demonstration against illegal immigrants in front of City Hall. It fizzled after the police, fearing disorder, turned out in a show of force.

Then the friction abated. The United Food and Commercial Workers won an organizing drive at Koch Foods by gaining the support of immigrants.

Mr. Lowe did not win re-election. The city chose a mayor, Barbara C. Barile, who describes herself as "an inclusive kind of person." She created a diversity task force and proposed an annual immigrant fiesta. In December, she sent police officers to accompany a midnight procession through downtown honoring the Virgin of Guadalupe, the Mexican patroness.

But an immigration crackdown by state and federal authorities stirred the waters again.

A few years ago, even illegal immigrants in Tennessee could obtain driver's licenses, buy cars, open bank accounts and take out mortgages. In 2006, the state canceled a program that authorized immigrants who were not legal residents to drive.

Cooperation increased between state and local police and federal immigration agents. For illegal immigrants, minor traffic stops could escalate and end in deportation. After immigration raids in the region, employers and temporary agencies started to give closer scrutiny to identity documents.

An Immigrant's Life

One immigrant whose Morristown welcome ended abruptly was Balbino López Hernández.

After sneaking across the Arizona border at 17, he joined a brother who lived in Morristown. In 2004 he landed a job at Berkline, a furniture company known for reclining chairs whose headquarters are in town.

Mr. López earned a minimum of $8.85 an hour assembling heavy metal frames for chairs and sofas. But, like other immigrants here, he measured the job against pushing a plow in Mexico. By that standard, he said, it was a "blessing."

At Berkline, seasoned American employees tended to avoid the physically demanding position in which Mr. López was placed, at the head of an assembly line. Mr. López loved the job, and before long he was one of the more productive workers on the floor. The high productivity of new immigrant workers was one reason employers like those in Morristown were glad to hire them, economists said.

Mr. López's task was to swing metal bars into place, then use a noisy drill, over and over, to secure dozens of screws, nuts and washers. The bars had sharp edges, and his arms are covered with scars. Still, he was content because he set his own pace.

"Always," he said, "I go to work and do my job and come home, to make myself happy and make them happy too."

Though he is not a legal resident, Mr. López allowed his name and photograph to be published because his status is known to immigration authorities.

The assembly floor operated on an incentive system: the more frames Mr. López made, the more he earned. But his energy put pressure on others on the line, including some Americans who were not interested in doing more work without a raise.

Mr. López, shy and soft-spoken, did well at work but poorly in love. One girlfriend, an American, three weeks after giving birth to his son, Jacob, left Mr. López to raise the boy alone. Another took to drugs and was frequently in trouble with the police.

His luck changed when he met Brittany Martin, 18, a tall blonde with a level head. Last January, he decided to spruce up his cottage in preparation for marriage, so he picked up his speed at Berkline.

"I would get my sandwich and just eat there, eat and work," Mr. López said. "I never stopped for nothing." Soon he was producing three times his weekly quota of chair frames, sometimes making more than $1,000 a week, pay stubs show. Some Americans started to taunt him, calling him "money man."

"Why does that Mexican make so much money?" Mr. López said one worker asked within earshot.

Not long after, on June 11, a senior manager summoned Mr. López, saying Berkline had been alerted that he might be an illegal immigrant. He confessed and was fired.

Mr. López believes that someone, perhaps a co-worker, turned him in. Two days later, the Morristown police, citing the false Social Security number he had presented at Berkline, arrested him on charges of criminal impersonation. Although those charges were soon dismissed for lack of evidence, the police reported Mr. López to federal immigration agents.

Dennis Carper, senior vice president for human resources at Berkline, confirmed that Mr. López had been terminated because of his invalid Social Security number. He said Berkline did not report Mr. López to the police.

Mr. López is now fighting deportation. He and Ms. Martin married in July and are expecting a child in May. He was released from detention to care for his wife and son, but since he was ordered deported before the wedding, it is not certain he will be able to stay.

While his immigration case proceeds, he remains unauthorized to apply for a job. He is scrounging for bits of work, fixing cars and patching roofs, and praying at Centro Betel. It is bad, he said, but

Mexico would be worse. "In my country," he said, "I'm just going to feed my family salt and tortillas."

The Shadows

In some ways, since Mr. López no longer has to hide, he has advantages over many immigrants in Morristown.

Enrique C., 48, and his wife, Rita, 38, both illegal immigrants from Mexico, learned how vulnerable their livelihood here was when both of them lost their jobs in recent months. The couple, neither of whom speaks English, asked that their full names and photographs not be published because they feared detection by immigration authorities.

During the long nights of winter, after their sons, 12 and 13, finished their homework, they turned off all the lights in the cottage they own except one bulb and gathered around a space heater. On some nights cockroaches emerged, seeking the heat.

Rita had held night-shift jobs in sweltering factories and on the chilly deboning line in a Koch chicken plant. Since she worked mainly through temporary agencies, when the crunch came she was one of the first to go.

Her husband worked from 2001 until last August at Hardwoods of Morristown, a wood-floor maker, earning $8.75 an hour splitting planks with a whirring saw. For years Enrique liked his job, and his bosses praised him, he said, for doing the work of two men.

But over time he had run-ins with supervisors, starting when they disagreed over the treatment of a wrist injury.

He complained that splinters tore his gloves. Bathrooms were filthy, he said, and the plant posted a rule limiting when workers could use them. He took photographs of clogged toilets and collected bagfuls of ragged gloves.

After seven years, Enrique, who admits he can be ornery, lost his temper one day and insulted the plant manager. The official separation notice states that he was fired for insubordination. Tim Elliott, a top executive at Hardwoods, wrote in an e-mail message that a worker who "refuses to do a task assigned to him" would disrupt the teamwork the company requires.

"They fired me because I started to make demands," Enrique said.

Once defiant, Enrique now lives looking over his shoulder and avoiding confrontation. Although his driver's license has expired, he drives a carpool with three other workers for an hour twice a day to a job he found through a temporary agency in a furniture factory for $7 an hour.

It is a job he cannot lose. He has a mortgage to pay, and he is determined to see his sons go to college. "We're going to go along very quietly," Enrique said. "We don't want to be deported."

* * *

Selection 3.7

One of the hottest job topics being debated is whether the United States is sending its best jobs overseas, leaving the stinkers behind. It is almost impossible to report on jobs and labor without the issue coming up. First to leave were the high-paying, low-skill blue-collar steel and manufacturing jobs, and then companies began outsourcing service, software and technology jobs. So is the United States on the verge of losing millions of white collar jobs? In this story, Eduardo Porter examines that question by digging deeper into the research, finding that the threat of global outsourcing is greatly overstated. Some of the most interesting stories are those that poke holes in conventional wisdom. Porter does just that here.

True or False: Outsourcing Is a Crisis

By EDUARDO PORTER

If you read only the headlines, the future of globalization may seem scary, indeed.

American jobs have already been heading abroad. And as telecommunications and more powerful computers enable companies to take even more jobs overseas, the service sector, which accounts for about 85 percent of the United States work force, will be increasingly vulnerable to competition from the cheap labor pools of the developing world.

So the question looms: Is America on the verge of losing oodles of white-collar jobs?

Probably not. The threat of global outsourcing is easily overstated.

The debate over the global competition for jobs is awash in dire projections. All those legal assistants in New York and Washington, for example, could be replaced with smart young graduates from Hyderabad. Office support occupations—jobs like data entry assistant, file clerk and the entire payroll department—could also be carried out in remote locations. "We are really at the beginning stages of this, and it is accelerating rapidly," said Ron Hira, assistant professor of public policy at the Rochester Institute of Technology.

In a study published this year, two economists at the Organization for Economic Cooperation and Development in Brussels estimated that 20 percent of the developed world's employment could be "potentially affected" by global outsourcing. That could include all American librarians, statisticians, chemical engineers and air traffic controllers, the study said.

Published: June 19, 2005.

What does "potentially affected" mean? Even if offshoring didn't drain away all these jobs, global competition for employment— including workers in developing countries who earn so little by comparison—could severely dent the livelihoods of American workers. "It isn't going to hurt in terms of jobs," said William J. Baumol, an economics professor at New York University who has studied the costs of globalization. "It is going to hurt in terms of wages."

But even if millions of tasks can be done by cheaper labor on the other side of the planet, businesses won't rush to move every job they can to wherever the cost is lowest. The labor market isn't quite that global, and it's unlikely to be anytime soon.

In a new set of reports, the McKinsey Global Institute, a research group known for its unabashedly favorable view of globalization, argued that 160 million service jobs—about 10 percent of total worldwide employment—could be moved to remote sites because these job functions don't require customer contact, local knowledge or complex interactions with the rest of a business.

Yet after surveying dozens of companies in eight sectors, from pharmaceutical companies to insurers, it concluded that only a small fraction of these jobs would actually be sent away.

The report estimates that by 2008, multinational companies in the entire developed world will have located only 4.1 million service jobs in low-wage countries, up from about 1.5 million in 2003. The figure is equivalent to only 1 percent of the total number of service jobs in developed countries.

Some sectors, like retail and health care, are likely to put very few jobs in poor countries. McKinsey estimated that less than 0.07 percent of health care jobs in 2008 would be outsourced to low-wage countries. But even designers of packaged software, whose work can easily be done abroad, will outsource only 18 percent of their jobs, the report said.

Moving tasks to faraway sites isn't simple. According to McKinsey's study, many business processes are difficult to separate into discrete chunks that can be sent away. Many insurance companies use information technology systems that have been cobbled together over time and would be difficult to manage remotely. Managers can be unwilling or unprepared to work overseas. And sometimes the tasks that can be sent offshore are too small to make the move worthwhile.

To top it off, there aren't that many suitable cheap workers available. Human-resources managers interviewed for the McKinsey study said that for reasons ranging from poor language skills to second-rate education systems, only about 13 percent of the young, college-educated professionals in the big developing countries are suitable to work for multinationals. And competition from local companies reduces this pool.

Sure, there are a billion Indians, but only a tiny percentage of the Indian work force have the appropriate qualifications. "Only a fraction have English as a medium of instruction, and only a fraction of those speak English that you or I can understand," said Jagdish N. Bhagwati, a professor of economics at Columbia University.

Of course, many of these obstacles can be overcome with time. The pool of adequate workers in poorer countries will grow, and companies will eventually iron out many of the logistical complications.

But that is likely to take a while. "The rate at which companies are willing and able is much slower than you would realize," said Diana Farrell, director of the McKinsey Global Institute. "We see this as being evolutionary, continuous but measured change."

MAKING**CONNECTIONS**

1 The fourth story in this chapter explains how after four decades of women entering the work force, some women are choosing to leave. Discuss the reasons why and what stories you could see writing about this trend.

Baby boomers are reaching retirement age. What implications might this have for employers, and what stories could you propose to your editor about retirement? **2**

3 Immigration is a hotly debated policy issue in the United States. How is the topic of immigration relevant to business news? **4**

Outsourcing is often blamed for job losses. Is this a problem or not? Suggest two stories you could see doing about outsourcing and its impact. What types of stories would they be—straight news, a column, a series? Pick one of your ideas. What would you write as a lede?

BUSINESS CONCEPTS REVIEW

Baby boomers	Refers to the 76 million Americans born between 1946 and 1962—currently the largest demographic group in the United States.
Great Recession of 2007–2009	Global recession spurred by a collapse in housing prices. Financial institutions failed, General Motors went bankrupt and the U.S. government was forced to pump billions into the U.S. economy to stave off another Great Depression.
Immigration	Migration to a place that is not your native country of origin.
Labor force	The number of people employed and unemployed in the economy.
Labor-force participation rate	The percentage of the adult population in the United States who are in the labor force.
Labor market drop-outs	Laid-off workers who become discouraged and stop looking for work but are still interested in working. They are no longer counted as unemployed and are also known as "discouraged workers."
Outsourcing	Subcontracting work to an outside third party or supplier to trim costs.
Unemployment rate	Includes workers not employed, available for work and who have tried to find work during the previous four weeks. The percentage is calculated by dividing the number of unemployed by the number of workers in the labor force. The rate does not include persons who have stopped looking for work, students, homemakers or retirees.

wages

IT'S HARD TO WRITE ABOUT THE ECONOMY without coming face to face with the question of whether U.S. living standards are eroding. This is one of those complex issues that won't go away: Is the United States falling behind?

By some measures, the answer is yes. A lot of $20-per-hour jobs have left the United States in recent years, and the people who lost those jobs haven't found new ones with a comparable wage. But if you look at other factors, such as the cost of clothing, food, taxes—even gasoline—compared with other regions of the world, the United States doesn't look so bad. Answering big questions is an issue of finding the right context. In this instance, falling behind in relation to what?

Big-picture stories like this need a frame of reference. Without a frame, the danger is the reporter will hopelessly thrash around in the weeds for weeks or months. Often, history offers a good way to start. One frame that can help you focus your reporting on wages is what has happened to wages and living standards over a wide span of time.

A century ago, America was an industrial outpost. It offered an abundance of cheap, raw materials and inexpensive labor. America's factories were dangerous and dirty places. Workers toiled for little pay, digging coal, making steel and slaughtering cattle. After much labor strife, laws were passed and conditions improved. U.S. factories became the most productive in the world, producing large quantities of homogenous goods at low cost.

Workers were rewarded with higher pay and benefits. Living standards rose. But as pay rose, so did the cost of the goods being produced. Meanwhile, less-industrialized nations began laying the infrastructure for their own manufacturing economy. In these countries, taxes, land, utilities and labor all cost less. The advent of computers, satellite communication and fast cargo ships made it economical to ship goods long distances. U.S. companies began building factories in places like China, India and Malaysia, sending jobs overseas.

Today, the United States imports more goods than it exports. This trend has had a major impact on the U.S. job market. New jobs are being created, but they are not equal in pay to the jobs lost, particularly in manufacturing. Wal-Mart may hire sales clerks at $10 per hour to ring up the flat-screen TVs that are selling for $500, half what they sold for two years ago. But the wage Wal-Mart workers make is a far cry from the $20 per hour some workers earned manufacturing TVs when they were made in the United States.

The cost of goods has fallen, but in some cases wages have fallen faster. As a result, Americans today are facing big challenges to their standard of living. The middle class, once the bedrock of American society, is shrinking. Meanwhile, wealth is becoming concentrated among the upper 1 percent of Americans. Tax policy and legislation enacted by Congress over the past decade favor big business and the very rich.

As we learned in Chapter 3, jobs are far less stable than they were a generation ago. So is the pay that accompanies those jobs. Competition from abroad has put tremendous downward pressure on wages, which have failed to keep pace with inflation. There is nothing sinister in all this; American businesses are simply battling to lower their costs. During the 2007–2009 recession, employers slashed jobs in a disproportionate number to the magnitude of the economy's decline.[1]

Most new jobs are expected to come on the lower end of the pay scale. According to the Labor Department, five of the 10 occupations expected to add the most jobs through 2016 would be "very low paying," meaning earning no more than $22,000 per year.[2]

Those are some interesting numbers. What makes those figures interesting? Context. The figures are offered in the context of a larger statement that gives the reader useful information about the subject you are writing about. Used correctly, numbers help people draw meaningful comparisons. Otherwise, they are just numbers.

Selection 4.1

Extreme opposites help drive a point home. Eric Dash uses this tactic to show the depth of the gulf between worker and chief executive pay. James "Skinny" Smith earns $6.40 per hour and works as a meat grinder. ConAgra Foods chief executive Bruce C. Rohde earned $45 million over eight years, plus a huge retirement package and bonuses, despite the company's sub-par performance. Notice how Dash brings the story back around to Smith at the end, drawing a sharp contrast between how Smith and ConAgra's new CEO, Gary M. Rodkin, commute to work.

EXECUTIVE PAY: A SPECIAL REPORT
Off to the Races Again, Leaving Many Behind
By ERIC DASH

OMAHA—In 1977, James P. Smith, a shaggy-haired 21-year-old known as Skinny, took a job as a meat grinder at what is now a ConAgra Foods pepperoni plant. At $6.40 an hour, it was among the best-paying jobs in town for a high school graduate.

Published: April 9, 2006. Full text available at: www.nytimes.com/2006/04/09/business/businessspecial/09pay.html

Nearly three decades later, Mr. Smith still arrives at the same factory, shortly before his 3:30 A.M. shift. His hair has thinned; he has put on weight. Today, his union job pays him $13.25 an hour to operate the giant blenders that crush 3,600-pound blocks of pork and beef.

His earnings, which total about $28,000 a year, have not kept pace even with Omaha's low cost of living. The company eliminated bonuses about a decade ago. And now, almost 50, Mr. Smith is concerned that his $80,000 retirement nest egg will not be enough—especially since his plant is on a list of ones ConAgra wants to sell.

"I will probably have to work until I die," Mr. Smith said in his Nebraskan baritone.

Not so for Bruce C. Rohde, ConAgra's former chairman and chief executive, who stepped down last September amid investor pressure. He is set for life.

All told, Mr. Rohde, 57, received more than $45 million during his eight years at the helm, and was given an estimated $20 million retirement package as he walked out the door.

Each year from 1997 to 2005, when Mr. Rohde led ConAgra, he was awarded either a large cash bonus, a generous grant of stock or options, or valuable benefits, such as extra years' credit toward his guaranteed pension.

But the company, one of the nation's largest food companies with more than 100 brands, struggled under his watch. ConAgra routinely missed earnings targets and underperformed its peers. Its share price fell 28 percent. The company cut more than 9,000 jobs. Accounting problems surfaced in every one of Mr. Rohde's eight years.

Even when ConAgra restated its financial results, which lowered earnings in 2003 and 2004, Mr. Rohde's $16.4 million in bonuses for those two years stayed the same.

Mr. Rohde turned down repeated requests for an interview. Chris Kircher, a ConAgra spokesman, said that Mr. Rohde received no bonuses in 2001 and 2005, evidence that his compensation was based in part on performance. He added that Mr. Rohde's severance was negotiated 10 years ago, when he was first hired, not as he left. The whole package was "negotiated under a different board, a different point in the company's history, and in a different environment," Mr. Kircher said.

The disparity between Mr. Rohde's and Mr. Smith's pay packages may be striking, but it is not unusual. Instead, it is the norm.

Even here in the heartland, where corporate chieftains do not take home pay packages that are anywhere near those of Hollywood moguls or Wall Street bankers, the pay gap between the boss and the rank-and-file is wide.

New technology and low-cost labor in places like China and India have put downward pressure on the wages and benefits of the average American worker. Executive pay, meanwhile, continues to rise at an astonishing rate.

The average pay for a chief executive increased 27 percent last year, to $11.3 million, according to a survey of 200 large companies by Pearl Meyer & Partners, the compensation practice of Clark Consulting. The median chief executive's pay was somewhat lower, at $8.4 million, for an increase of 10.3 percent over 2004. By contrast, the average wage-earner took home $43,480 in 2004, according to Commerce Department data. And recent wage data from the Labor Department suggest that workers' weekly pay, up 2.9 percent in 2005, failed to keep pace with inflation of 3.3 percent.

Many forces are pushing executive pay into the stratosphere. Huge gains from stock options during the 1990's bull market are one major reason. So is the recruitment of celebrity C.E.O.'s, which has bid up the compensation of all top executives.

Compensation consultants, who are hired to advise boards, are often motivated to produce big paydays for managers. After all, the boss can hand their company lucrative contracts down the road.

Compensation committees, meanwhile, are often reluctant to withhold a bonus or stock award for poor performance. Many big shareholders, such as mutual funds and pension plans, have chosen not to cast votes critical of management. The results have been a growing gap between chief executives and ordinary employees, and often between the boss and managers one layer below.

The average top executive's salary at a big company was more than 170 times the average worker's earnings in 2004, up from a multiple of 68 in 1940, according to a study last year by Carola Frydman, a doctoral candidate at Harvard, and Raven E. Saks, an economist at the Federal Reserve.

"We need to bring some reality back," said John C. Bogle Sr., the founder and former chairman of the Vanguard Group, the mutual fund company, and an outspoken critic of executive compensation practices. "That is something that in the long run is not good for society. We have the haves and the have-nots."

Supersized salaries, bonuses and benefits, long controversial, are now drawing scrutiny from the Securities and Exchange Commission and have become part of the national political debate. About 81 percent of Americans say they think that the chief executives of large companies are overpaid, a percentage that changes little with income level or political party affiliation, according to a Los Angeles Times/ Bloomberg survey in February. Many shareholders, moreover, are just plain angry.

"It's not just ConAgra—it is really in most corporations that executives are paid too much," said Don D. Hudgens, a small investor in Omaha who has submitted shareholder proposals to rein in executive pay at ConAgra and other companies. "I am a conservative Republican. I believe in the free market. But sometimes the payment of the chief executive isn't involved in that free market."

The divide between executives and ordinary workers was not always so great. From the mid-1940's through the 1970's, the pay of both groups grew at about the same rate, 1.3 percent, according to the study by Ms. Frydman and Ms. Saks. They analyzed the compensation of top executives at 102 large companies from 1936 to 2003.

But starting in the 1980's, executive compensation began to accelerate. In 1980, the average chief executive made about $1.6 million in today's dollars. By 1990, the figure had risen to $2.7 million; by 2004, it was about $7.6 million, after peaking at almost twice that amount in 2000. In other words, executive pay rose an average of 6.8 percent a year.

At the same time, the growth rate slowed for the average worker's pay. That figure rose to about $43,000 in 2004 from about $36,000 in 1980, an increase of 0.8 percent a year in inflation-adjusted terms.

Corporations, meanwhile, projected that their own earnings would grow by an average of 11.5 percent a year during that 24-year stretch, by Mr. Bogle's calculations. In reality, he said, they delivered growth of 6 percent a year, slightly less than the growth rate of the entire economy, as measured by gross domestic product.

Chief executives "aren't creating any exceptional value, so you would think that the average compensation of the C.E.O. would grow at the rate of the average worker," Mr. Bogle said. "When you look at it in that way, it is a real problem."

The problem was certainly real at ConAgra. Mr. Rohde's arrival there in 1996 coincided with three of the most powerful forces propelling executive pay and hourly workers' wages in opposite directions. Stock options were being used to reward managers richly, the food industry's rapid consolidation pushed down workers' pay and the introduction of new machinery improved productivity but cost many jobs.

ConAgra, whose products include Chef Boyardee canned goods, Hunt's ketchup and Healthy Choice dinners, began in 1919 as a small food processor, grew rapidly under Charles M. Harper, a former Pillsbury executive who went by the name Mike. In the mid-1970's, he drew up an ambitious expansion strategy to establish ConAgra as a major player from "dirt to dinner," as a corporate slogan later put it. ConAgra would snap up more than 280 businesses in the next two decades. From 1980 to 1993, investors saw total returns of over 1,000 percent, or 22 percent a year.

Wall Street fell in love with ConAgra's growth story. And the pay of Mr. Harper, who consistently hit the board's performance targets, reflected the admiration. In 1976, his pay was $1.3 million in today's dollars. By the end of his tenure, in the early 1990's, it was about $6 million a year.

"Under Mike Harper, they were a company that paid very little cash and a lot of long-term stock," said Frederic W. Cook, who was a compensation consultant to ConAgra's board until 2002. "There were rules you could never sell the stock. They lived poor and they died rich."

By the mid-1990's, though, ConAgra's growth strategy was running out of steam. Its market share and sales were flat. And its decentralized approach—essentially letting its 90 subsidiaries operate like independent companies—no longer worked in an industry dominated by Wal-Mart and other large supermarket buyers.

Mr. Rohde—who had been ConAgra's chief outside lawyer, advising Mr. Harper on more than 200 deals—was hired in 1996 to help the company reorganize. He became chief executive the next year.

ConAgra's stock price was near a record high, and Mr. Rohde was paid handsomely. His first year's total compensation was $7.9 million, including an initial $4.3 million restricted stock grant, vested over 10 years, and a $500,000 long-term performance payout.

Mr. Rohde tried to centralize many of ConAgra's main operations and integrate dozens of its businesses. But analysts said he let the company's brands stagnate and struggled to execute his plans.

From mid-1999 to mid-2001, ConAgra struggled amid a sweeping overhaul. The company incurred $1.1 billion in restructuring charges. It terminated more than 8,450 employees and closed 31 plants. And analysts began complaining that ConAgra did not invest enough in its brands to keep profits up.

Mr. Rohde continued to be well-compensated. During that two-year period, he received cash and stock option grants of more than $8.7 million, even as ConAgra's board withheld his annual bonus and all long-term equity awards for 2001 because of weak results.

But what the board took away with one hand, it gave back with the other. In July 2001, it granted Mr. Rohde 300,000 stock options. The reason, according to proxy filings, was that an unnamed independent consultant's compensation report indicated that his equity-based pay was not competitive. "There's nothing wrong at all conceptually with giving someone options after a bad year," said Mr. Cook, who was the unnamed consultant. "An option is an incentive for the future. It is not a reward for the past."

Still, Mr. Cook said he recognized that people say "they rewarded him for failure."

"Financially," he added, "it's hard to argue with that."

Two months later, ConAgra's compensation committee piled on 750,000 more stock options. Based on a review of option grants, a proxy filing said, Mr. Rohde's option position had been "below com-petitive levels for a number of years." And the board wanted to recog-nize "the results achieved in repositioning the company for the future."

Then Mr. Rohde hit the jackpot in 2003 and 2004, with the board awarding him $16.4 million in bonus money and the part of his long-term incentive plan he had earned. The payments were based largely on earnings targets. But in March 2005, ConAgra announced that it would have to restate earnings for 2003 and 2004, reducing them by a total of up to $200 million for the two years after poor internal controls led to income tax errors.

"That works out to nearly 20 cents per share annually, or between 10 percent and 15 percent of earnings," John M. McMillin, an analyst at Prudential Equity Group, wrote at the time. ConAgra "is in the process of restating earnings for both years and we ask, why not restate the bonus for the C.E.O.?"

Mr. Kircher, the ConAgra spokesman, said the restatement did not have a material impact on the way Mr. Rohde's bonuses were calculated.

With the accounting issues clouding the company's future and more layoffs and financial challenges ahead, Mr. Rohde announced last May that he planned to step down. In 2005, the board gave him only his $1.2 million salary.

But through it all, Mr. Rohde managed to take home more than $45 million in pay, including salary, bonuses and restricted stock grants. He did not sell any of his stock while chief executive but stands to benefit if he sells his shares now.

Carl E. Reichardt, the former head of Wells Fargo, led the com-pensation committee that approved Mr. Rohde's pay every year of his tenure, and continues in that role today. Mr. Reichardt also declined to comment.

One former member of the compensation committee found it difficult to explain the pay-for-performance link. Looking back, said Clayton K. Yeutter, a former United States trade representative who served on the compensation committee from 1997 to 2001, "I can understand what you are getting to, because the compensation became pretty generous, because the stock did not perform very well." He said he could not recall any meeting details.

Mr. Smith, the meat grinder, can only dream about such generos-ity. His wages have grown at a pace of 2.7 percent a year for the last 28 years. But, adjusted for inflation, his $13.25 an hour salary today is roughly two-thirds his $6.40-an-hour starting wage.

Mr. Rohde's salary alone rose at 8 percent a year, and he col-lected more than $22 million in cash compensation during almost nine years at the company. Since stepping down in September, he started collecting $2.4 million in severance pay, twice his most recent sal-ary, as well as full health benefits, which he will have through 2009.

ConAgra shareholders are footing the bill for a secretary and an office near his home. And that $984,000 annual pension? It reflects 20 years of service, even though he was a ConAgra executive for not quite nine. In July, Mr. Rohde told The Omaha World-Herald that he hoped to spend part of his retirement flying his helicopter between his home and his family's Minnesota getaway home.

Mr. Smith, on the other hand, envisions spending his golden years hunting mallards and casting for catfish at a nearby riverfront cabin. He will have to make do on the $80,000 in his 401(k) plan, as well as his Social Security checks and a pension of $106 a month that was frozen almost a decade ago. But to hear Mr. Smith tell it, he is not angry at Mr. Rohde or, more broadly, at the widening gap between executive and worker pay. Instead, his feelings are somewhere between disappointment and disbelief.

"If the stock keeps going up, maybe they deserve it. If the stock is going down to the bottom, they should get nothing," Mr. Smith said. "My opinion."

Last May, ConAgra directors began looking for a new chief executive. In a few months, they identified their man: Gary M. Rodkin, a 53-year-old PepsiCo executive with 25 years of food-industry experience, including more than a decade overseeing PepsiCo's core brands. But he did not come cheap.

Even before his first day of work, Mr. Rodkin was given a $1 million salary and a guaranteed $2 million bonus for this year, according to his employment contract. He was granted 1.48 million stock options, with a projected value of $5.8 million today, exercisable over the next three years. "We wanted to get him aligned with the interests of shareholders of the company," Steven F. Goldstone, ConAgra's chairman and the former chief executive of RJR Nabisco, told Bloomberg News at the time. "The idea is to increase shareholder value. If he increases shareholder value, he makes money, too."

If Mr. Rodkin does not increase shareholder returns, his stock options will decline in value, as will the $1.6 million in ConAgra stock he recently bought with his own cash.

Still, ConAgra has already agreed to take care of Mr. Rodkin when he leaves. Based on his employment agreement, he will walk away with at least $6 million in severance, a prorated bonus and a $129,000 pension supercharged with three years of credit for each year he worked.

And though he took the job at ConAgra, PepsiCo is still honoring a $4.5 million, two-year consulting contract it gave him when he left. "If the new guy is the right guy, he is worth his weight in gold," said Brian Foley, an independent compensation consultant in White Plains, who reviewed Mr. Rohde's and Mr. Rodkin's employment agreements and other compensation documents. "If he is the wrong guy, you have a severance package that is substantially more expensive."

ConAgra's board, in the meantime, agreed to ease Mr. Rodkin's transition by flying him each week, for up to two years, from his home in White Plains to its Omaha headquarters.

Mr. Smith commutes to work in his green 1998 pickup truck.

* * *

Amanda Cox contributed reporting.

Selection 4.2

Louis Uchitelle gives readers an idea of what happens to people's lives when an employer like Maytag decides to pull up stakes. We meet Guy and Lisa Winchell, who both depended on Maytag and lost their jobs. Next we hear from Steve Schober, who now makes a fourth of the six-figure salary he made as an industrial designer at Maytag—and half of his current salary goes toward health care. Uchitelle sprinkles in nice details about Newton, Iowa, where Maytag was based before Whirlpool bought the company. Reporters always get a better story when they can travel to the locale where the story is centered. Details acquired through reporting help bring people and places to life. And sources are always more willing to talk to someone face to face than over the telephone or through e-mail.

Is There (Middle Class) Life After Maytag?
By LOUIS UCHITELLE

NEWTON, Iowa—The last of the Maytag factories that lifted so many people into the middle class here will close on Oct. 26. Guy Winchell and his wife, Lisa, will lose their jobs that day. Their combined income of $43 an hour will disappear and, soon after, so will their health insurance. Most of the pensions they would have received will also be gone.

The Winchells are still in their 40s. They can retrain or start a business, choices promoted by city leaders in a campaign to "reinvent" Newton without its biggest employer. But as they ponder their futures, the Winchells are uncertain about how to deal with a lower standard of living. "I'm not wanting to go waitress," said Mrs. Winchell, who, at 41, drives a forklift and earns $19 an hour, "but I can do what I have to to make money."

Mr. Winchell, 46, having earned $24 an hour as a skilled electrician, seems paralyzed by the disappearance of his employer. He imagines that there is work for electricians in central Iowa but he hasn't looked. "Lisa is always on me because I'm so angry," he said.

Published: August 26, 2007.

Matthew Holst for The New York Times

Lisa and Guy Winchell will lose their jobs at the Maytag plant in Newton, Iowa, when it shuts down on Oct. 26. Above, they worked on his bus, converted into a recreational vehicle.

"She says, 'What would your mom have said?' My mom would have said, 'Worrying is not going to help.'"

Newton's last day as a manufacturing mecca comes a century after Fred L. Maytag built his first mechanical washing machine here. Over time he also located his headquarters, research center and most production in Newton, changing it from a rural county seat into a prosperous city of 16,000. Absent Maytag's high pay, overall hourly earnings last year for other workers in the county would have been $3 an hour less, according to Iowa Workforce Development, a state agency.

And then the Whirlpool Corporation bought Maytag in the spring of 2006 and began shutting down its operations here, eliminating jobs and depressing wages. Those caught in this process around the country are gradually swelling what Katherine S. Newman, a Princeton sociologist, describes as "The Missing Class," the title of a soon-to-be-published book (Beacon Press), of which she is co-author.

Ms. Newman calculates that 54 million adults and children occupy a "nether region" of family incomes well above the poverty line—but well short of the middle class. Either they fall out of the middle class, as the Winchells are in danger of doing, or they have never earned enough at one job to get a family of four into the middle class.

"We are caught in a never-ending cycle of de-industrialization in which the best jobs disappear," Ms. Newman said. "It is amazing to me how much we have come to accept that there is nothing to be done about this loss of income."

Here in Newton, Maytag's fortress-like headquarters building, its beige-colored bulk looming over the downtown, has been emptied of 1,200 white-collar workers. Of nearly 900 unionized blue-collar workers still left last December in the sprawling factory, 400 were laid off and the rest got a reprieve, including the Winchells.

But theirs is a dead-end task: keeping retailers supplied until Whirlpool can start production of redesigned Maytag models built on the chassis of Whirlpool machines at the company's existing factories in Monterrey, Mexico, and Clyde, Ohio. In Clyde, top pay for nearly all of the 3,700 non-union blue-collar workers is $17 an hour, several dollars less than Maytag paid in Newton. But as Bill Townsend, the plant manager, put it, "whenever we advertise for employment, it is not difficult finding folks."

Nor is it difficult to recruit workers in Newton anymore. Absent Maytag, a good wage in central Iowa is $12 or $13 an hour. The trick is to get that much as well as health insurance—and if not the wage, then at least the health insurance, even if that means commuting 40 to 50 miles, as more than a few ex-Maytag workers are now doing.

The downshift is reflected in the Labor Department's national data. Median family income has risen at an average annual rate of only six-tenths of a percent, adjusted for inflation, since the mid-1970s—in sharp contrast to the 2.8 percent growth rate in the preceding 26 years.

Hardship, however, is initially postponed in Newton. Local 997 of the United Automobile Workers, representing Maytag's blue-collar staff, negotiated a severance package with Whirlpool last fall that extends each departing worker's health insurance for five or six months and pays at least $850 for each year worked, up to 30 years.

For the Winchells, who have five children, all but one from previous marriages—their smiling faces on display in oval-shaped photographs grouped together on a living-room wall—the severance packages translate into more than 20 weeks of pay for the couple. The delayed impact helps to explain, as Mr. Winchell put it, why he and his wife won't be forced until early next spring to face the inevitable distress of shrunken incomes and uncertain health care.

"I'll find work," he declared, "but I really don't know what I am going to do. I've thought about applying to hospitals because they have health insurance. One of us will have to take a job with health insurance."

Whatever the damage to living standards, from Whirlpool's point of view, its strategy in acquiring Maytag was impeccable. Make the same number of washing machines in two plants—Clyde and Monterrey—instead of three, achieving economies of scale. Add 1,000 workers in Clyde to accommodate the increased output, but non-union workers earning less, with fewer benefits, than the unionized work force in Newton.

The State of Iowa offered numerous incentives to Whirlpool to stay in Newton. Gov. Tom Vilsack suggested publicly that he would build for Whirlpool "the most energy-efficient plant in the world."

As a lure, the city said it would give full college scholarships to children who went through the public schools. "It was part of a retention strategy; here's the benefit we can provide if you stay," said Kim Didier, executive director of the Newton Development Corporation.

But for Jeff M. Fettig, Whirlpool's chairman, leaving Newton was, in the end, a no-brainer. Staying, he said in an interview, was "not economically viable." He explained: "It was two companies doing the same thing that you needed one company doing very well."

Given such realities, Steve Schober, an industrial designer at Maytag for 25 years, with a fistful of patents to his credit, applied to Whirlpool's research department in Benton Harbor, Mich., and was turned down, partly because he acknowledged in a job interview that he was unhappy about moving his family from Newton.

So, at 52, with six months of severance as a cushion, he went out on his own last year, starting Schober Design and working from his home—a large, handsome Tudor-style with a sloping front lawn in an elegant neighborhood, a few blocks from the brick mansion where Fred Maytag once lived. As a freelancer, however, Mr. Schober's annual income plunged in the first year from the low six figures he had earned at Maytag to $25,000.

Half now goes to pay for health insurance for himself and his children, Katie, 18, and Ben, 16. His wife, Sarah, 51, a special education teacher earning $30,000 a year, has coverage for herself from the public school system. Adding the family would cost $800 a month, slightly less than Mr. Schober now pays, so the couple will probably drop his coverage for hers.

"Health insurance was one of those invisible benefits of working for a corporation," he said. "You didn't have to think about it."

He and his wife invited a reporter to their home on a summer afternoon, offering refreshments and describing their situation matter-of-factly, as if talking of a less fortunate family's situation, not their own. Their children were present at first, but soon Katie, who will be a college freshman in the fall, partly on scholarship, drifted out of the living room, and then Ben, a strapping high school athlete, abruptly excused himself, departing to meet his friends, his parents explained.

"I have three options," Mr. Schober said. "I could get a job in a different field that doesn't approach what I made at Maytag, but has a benefits package. I've thought about working for the post office. Or I could send out my résumé to design studios. One of the issues in doing this is my age, which works against me. Or I can continue to do what I am doing, building a client base from Newton."

He is embarked on the third option. While the pay is still sparse, the work is interesting, he said, citing as an example a contract with a winery to design small utensils to open wine bottles. But each month to cover expenses, including a $1,000 mortgage payment, the family cuts into its savings. "We never did that before," Mrs. Schober said.

The Schobers think differently now about money. They shop more cautiously. As a family, they organized a garage sale, taking in $580 by selling castoffs that would have accumulated in the basement. And the couple have taken part-time weekend jobs.

They work at Newton's recently opened auto speedway. On race weekends, Mrs. Schober is at an information booth, answering questions, and he shuttles handicapped patrons in a six-passenger golf cart. Each job pays $10 an hour.

"It helps the cash flow," Mrs. Schober said.

Tim and Rhonda Saunders, in their mid-40s, have taken a different route. He went back to school, while she took a full-time job.

While Mr. Saunders put in 20 years at Maytag, mostly shaping sheet metal into cabinets and doors, she raised their two children and worked part-time as a bookkeeper. His layoff last December forced her into the full-time job, at $12 an hour in the accounts-payable department of a small manufacturer, so the family could have health insurance. She took the new job without giving up the part-time work and the $220 a week it brings in. That work is now done at home on evenings and weekends.

"We have to pay more for her health insurance than I did at Maytag: $300 a month versus $50," Mr. Saunders said. "And the coverage is not quite as good. But without it, I could not have gone back to school."

What pushed him into school was the job market. He found that he could not replace, or even approach, his $23-an-hour Maytag wage, not with only a high school diploma. A cousin steered him toward computer programming as a good source of future income, and he enrolled at the Des Moines Area Community College, attending classes full-time on the Newton campus. He turned out to be an A student.

More than 450 other ex-Maytag employees are also enrolled in full-time schooling, their expenses paid by the federal government as part of its Trade Adjustment Assistance program.

Maytag first qualified in 2003. The company was faltering then, losing market share to imports and whittling down its blue-collar staff from a high of 2,500 in 2000. The Labor Department ruled that the import competition qualified the laid-off workers for up to $15,000 each in tuition, along with book and transportation subsidies, and unemployment insurance for two years.

The extended unemployment pay has been a lure. For a number of ex-Maytag workers, it comes to about $360 a week, or $9 an hour—not much below what many jobs pay in Iowa. In his own initial effort to land work, Mr. Saunders found that the best he could do was $11 an hour.

So he went to school, and the family tightened its belt. He listed the economies he and his wife have imposed: no more weekend camping trips, cooking hamburgers instead of steaks on the grill, paying less of the college tuition for their children, who are turning more to student loans.

But then he inadvertently mentioned a planned excursion to New York with their daughter, and acknowledged that the $3,000 trip was hardly belt-tightening.

"My son always wanted a used racing car," he explained. "And when he turned 18 a couple of years ago, we gave him one, knowing then that my daughter would want to go to New York when she was 18 and see a couple of shows. So we saved the money and it was put away before this ever happened. It was something I wanted to do for her. She was so easy to raise and she worked so hard in school."

Tootie Samson, a 47-year-old mother of three, and a grandmother, is also going back to school with federal aid, but with a different goal in mind. Having already earned a two-year degree in interior design on her own, she'll now go for a bachelor's and maybe open her own shop.

Ms. Samson joined Maytag on the assembly line in 1997 after working 20 years as a bookkeeper at less than $10 an hour. She came for the wage, $20 an hour today, and to qualify for a pension, lost now in the buyout. She was laid off in 2003, allowing her time to study interior design. Then, to her surprise, she was called back last March. Whirlpool had underestimated how many workers it would need to keep the plant running through October.

"For me, it is fortunate to be back at Maytag as it closes," she said. "You need that closure. It's done. It's over. You always think that maybe you'll get called back and now you know it is over and you can move on with your life."

With Maytag gone, the Newton Development Corporation scrambled to find buyers for the headquarters building and the factory—the great concern being that once shuttered, these buildings would become giant eyesores. Iowa Telecom finally bought the headquarters building, and the Industrial Realty Group of Los Angeles, the factory, with Whirlpool subsidizing both purchases as a goodwill gesture.

But Maytag fulfilled one function that can't be finessed. As the biggest employer paying the best wages, it put upward pressure on the pay of other employers, who sought to prevent their best workers from jumping to Maytag. Now that pressure is gone. The loss is seen in the development corporation's effort to persuade a fiberglass company to put a plant here employing 700 people at $12 to $13 an hour, and health insurance.

Ms. Didier, an ex-Maytag employee earning less herself as the development corporation's executive director, put the best face on it she could. "With Maytag," she said, "it was difficult for companies to get good people at a lower wage, and now they can."

Selection 4.3

Louis Uchitelle reaches back into history to offer a perspective on the loss of $20-an-hour jobs. Uchitelle shows how manufacturing wages like those paid to steelworkers in Braddock, Penn., helped establish the middle class. With that wage, workers bought cars and homes and sent their kids to college. Business and society flourished. But those jobs are leaving the United States. This story is part of a broader look at the problems related to the loss of high-wage jobs here and in Newton, Iowa, where the Maytag plant closed. Uchitelle is building on his previous reporting here to approach the same subject from a broader perspective.

THE NATION
The Wage That Meant Middle Class
By LOUIS UCHITELLE

Whatever Senator Barack Obama meant by his less than art-ful remarks about small-town Pennsylvanians "bitter" over lost jobs, he certainly turned a lot of attention last week to the decline of the American worker, bitter or not.

The talk most often has been of shuttered factories, layoffs, out-sourcing and other effects of globalization, especially in a state like Pennsylvania, which has lost tens of thousands of industrial jobs. But there is another way to look at blue-collar workers or their counter-parts in the service sector.

Leaving aside for a moment those who have lost their jobs, what of those who still have them? Once upon a time, a large number earned at least $20 an hour, or its inflation-adjusted equivalent, and now so many of them don't.

The $20 hourly wage, introduced on a huge scale in the middle of the last century, allowed masses of Americans with no more than a high school education to rise to the middle class. It was a marker, of sorts. And it is on its way to extinction.

Americans greeted the loss with anger and protest when it first began to happen in big numbers in the late 1970s, particularly in the steel industry in Western Pennsylvania. But as layoffs persisted, in Pennsylvania and across the country, through the '80s and '90s and right up to today, the protests subsided and acquiescence set in.

Hourly workers had come a long way from the days when employers and unions negotiated a way for them to earn the prizes of the middle class—houses, cars, college educations for their chil-dren, comfortable retirements. Even now a residual of that golden age remains, notably in the auto industry. But here, too, wages are falling

Published: April 20, 2008.

below the $20-an-hour threshold—$41,600 annually—that many experts consider the minimum income necessary to put a family of four into the middle class.

The nation's political leaders—Democrats and Republicans alike—have argued that education and training are a route back to middle-class wages for those who have fallen out. But the demand isn't sufficient to absorb all the workers that the leaders would educate. Even now, roughly 15 percent of college-educated workers find themselves in jobs for which they are overqualified, the Economic Policy Institute reports, and many of these jobs pay less than $20 an hour.

"People are mainly worried about having a job and only secondly what it pays and whether they are gaining ground," said Frank Levy, a labor economist at the Massachusetts Institute of Technology, trying to explain the absence of an outcry and a political debate in which the candidates do not quantify the decline. "If you aren't gaining ground," Mr. Levy added, "then you look for other ways to pay for consumption, going into debt or, until recently, refinancing your home."

Still, the erosion haunts the presidential campaign. Mr. Obama, competing against Hillary Rodham Clinton in the Pennsylvania primary to be held on Tuesday, touched this nerve in his description of small-town voters who "cling" to their guns and their religion in their resentment over lost jobs. It was a description that prompted John McCain, the Republican candidate, to label Mr. Obama an "elitist," and Mrs. Clinton to portray him as out of touch with small-town sentiment. But like Mr. Obama, neither spoke of dollars missing from paychecks, or of the disappearing $20-an-hour wage.

That basic wage blossomed first in the auto industry in 1948 and served, in effect, as a banner in the ideological struggle with the Soviet Union. As the news media frequently noted, salt-of-the-earth American workers were earning enough to pay for comforts that their counterparts behind the Iron Curtain could not afford.

As the years passed, unions succeeded in negotiating this basic wage not as an ultimate goal but as an early rung in their wage ladders. That was the union standard, particularly in heavy industries, and in the early postwar decades nonunion employers fell into line, spreading middle-class incomes broadly through the service sector.

"The most important model that rolled off the Detroit assembly lines in the 20th century," said Harley Shaiken, a labor economist at the University of California at Berkeley, "was the middle class for blue-collar workers."

The high point came in the 1970s, just as the United States was beginning to lose its controlling grip on the economies of the non-Communist world. Since then the percentage of people earning at least $20 an hour has eroded in every sector of the economy, falling last year to 18 percent of all hourly workers from 23 percent in 1979—a gradual unwinding of the post–World War II gains.

The decline is greatest in manufacturing, where only 1.9 million hourly workers still earn that much. That's down nearly 60 percent since 1979, the Bureau of Labor Statistics reports.

The shrinkage is sometimes quite open. The Big Three automakers are currently buying out more than 25,000 employees who earn above $20 an hour, replacing many with new hires tied to a "second tier" wage scale that never quite reaches $20. A similar buyout last year removed 80,000 auto workers. Many were not replaced, but many were, with the new hires paid today at the non-middle-class scale, and with fewer benefits.

The United Auto Workers agreed to this arrangement, accepting management's argument that it must have labor cost relief to rebound and prosper. Whatever the justification, the new accord in effect abandoned the 1948 contract. That agreement is still hailed as historic. In contrast, the 2007 contract that reversed it is hardly recognized as a significant event in labor history. "It is significant," Mr. Shaiken insisted, referring to last year's contract. "The Big Three and the U.A.W. were the model for industrial America at its zenith."

This time the auto workers weren't first. They ratified a practice that had spread to tire makers, heavy-equipment manufacturers, parts plants, groceries, retailers and longshoremen, diluting older workers' resistance by preserving their status, while lowering earning power for new hires.

Two tiers is one tactic. Another is filling middle-income jobs with temporary workers earning less. Add outsourcing to the list, and the off-shoring of such middle-income work as computer programming and radiology. Then there are the manufacturers who close a union plant and shift production to a nonunion one, often in the South but also in the Midwest.

When Whirlpool, for example, acquired Maytag last year it closed a Maytag washing machine factory in Newton, Iowa, that had employed hundreds of workers at more than $20 an hour and shifted production to its plant in Clyde, Ohio, adding hundreds of workers at $17 an hour.

Put givebacks on the list as well. Tens of thousands of workers have accepted wage cuts pressed on them by embattled employers, cuts that in many cases pushed their wages below middle-class levels. Flight attendants are a notable example. And as each new group acquiesces, the standard for what constitutes an acceptable wage comes down in America.

"You can't have an economy heavily invested in tradable goods and services that is completely oblivious to global wages," said Ron Bloom, special assistant to the president of the United Steelworkers.

The decline is most significant in the data that the Bureau of Labor Statistics collects for the nation's hourly work force, which totals 76 million, or 52 percent of all workers, and ranges from managers and professionals to factory and construction workers to technicians, educators and sales people. The wages of many salaried workers show a similar trend, although the bureau does not convert their pay into hourly amounts.

The trend in the hourly work force is striking. Take only the peak years in each business cycle, starting in 1979. The proportion earning at least $20 an hour declined from 23 percent that year, to 20 percent in 1980, to 18 percent in 1989, and to 16 percent in 2000. Manufacturing was hit the hardest.

The current business cycle brought some relief. It reached its peak last year, before plunging into what now appears to be the opening months of a stiff recession. In 2007, before the plunge, the percentage of middle-income hourly workers earning at least $20 an hour had risen, to 18 percent. The improvement came mainly from a rising proportion of women in higher-end hourly work.

Wages also held up in the public sector. Strip out that sector, and only 16 percent of privately employed hourly workers took home at least $20 an hour, just fractionally above the 2000 level.

Selection 4.4

If the days of the $20-an-hour job are gone, should this era's big employers—companies like Wal-Mart—play the role that General Motors once did in helping foster a middle class? Wal-Mart workers are paid poverty-level wages—a common complaint lodged against retailers, restaurants and other service industries whose employees can't live on what they are paid. The writer effectively frames this story by talking to people who question whether Wal-Mart should be doing more for workers, and by offering proponents who support the company.

At Wal-Mart, Choosing Sides Over $9.68 an Hour
By STEVEN GREENHOUSE

BENTONVILLE, Ark.—With most of Wal-Mart's workers earning less than $19,000 a year, a number of community groups and lawmakers have recently teamed up with labor unions in mounting an intensive campaign aimed at prodding Wal-Mart into paying its 1.3 million employees higher wages.

Published: May 4, 2005.

A new group of Wal-Mart critics ran a full-page advertisement on April 20 contending that the company's low pay had forced tens of thousands of its workers to resort to food stamps and Medicaid, costing taxpayers billions of dollars. On April 26, as part of a campaign called "Love Mom, Not Wal-Mart," five members of Congress joined women's advocates and labor leaders to assail the company for not paying its female employees more.

And in a book to be published this fall, a group of scholars will argue that Wal-Mart Stores, having replaced General Motors as the nation's largest company, has an obligation to treat its employees better.

Among workers at Wal-Mart's 3,700 stores across the United States, the debate is also heating up.

Frances Browning, for example, once earned $15 an hour, but now at Wal-Mart, where she is a cashier in Roswell, Ga., she is paid $9.43. She says she is happy to have the job.

"I was unemployed for two and a half years before I found my job at Wal-Mart," Ms. Browning, 57, said. "Like everybody else I'd love to make a lot more, but I have to be realistic."

But Jason Mrkwa, 27, a high school graduate who stocks frozen food at a Wal-Mart in Independence, Kan., maintains that he is underpaid. "I make $8.53, even though every one of my evaluations has been above standard," Mr. Mrkwa (pronounced MARK-wah) said. "You can't really live on this."

Labor groups and their allies are focusing on Wal-Mart because they say that the campaign will not just benefit its workers but also reduce the existing pressure on unionized competitors to reduce their own wages and benefits.

"Wal-Mart should pay people at a minimum enough to go above the U.S. poverty line," said Andrew Grossman, executive director of Wal-Mart Watch, the coalition of community, environmental and labor groups running the series of ads criticizing Wal-Mart. "A company this big and this wealthy has the ability to pay higher wages."

H. Lee Scott Jr., Wal-Mart's chief executive, vigorously defends his company, arguing that wages are primarily determined by market forces and that Wal-Mart pays more than most retailers and provides better opportunities for advancement.

"If people tell you that Wal-Mart is leading the so-called 'race to the bottom' in terms of job quality or pay, they're not only wrong, they're dead wrong," he said to journalists at a company-sponsored conference here in April, the first time Wal-Mart has gone out of its way to invite a number of reporters to its headquarters to hear its views. "We are instead creating a better workplace with more opportunity and more benefits than have been available in retail."

Mr. Scott contends that the critics, including competitors, are defenders of an outdated status quo, intent on upholding a retailing system full of inefficiency and inflated prices.

Erik S. Lesser for The New York Times

Frances Browning, who had been unemployed, is happy to have her Wal-Mart cashier's job in Roswell, Ga.

He said that if Wal-Mart were as greedy as its detractors say, it would never have attracted 8,000 job applicants for 525 places at a new store in Glendale, Ariz., or 3,000 applicants for 300 jobs in outlying Los Angeles.

Michael T. Duke, chief of the company's stores division, said, "Wal-Mart is a very good place to work for our associates, and every day we make it even better."

Mr. Mrkwa, the food stocker, does not see it that way. With pay that brings him about $20,000 a year, he said he could not afford a decent apartment or a vehicle better than his 1991 Dodge Dakota. "I don't see why Wal-Mart can't pay more," Mr. Mrkwa said. "Unfortunately, in the market we live in there just aren't many jobs available."

Wal-Mart says its full-time workers average $9.68 an hour, and with many of them working 35 hours a week, their annual pay comes to around $17,600. That is below the $19,157 poverty line for a family of four, but above the $15,219 line for a family of three.

Wal-Mart critics often note that corporations like Ford and G.M. led a race to the top, providing high wages and generous benefits that other companies emulated. They ask why Wal-Mart, with some $10 billion in profit on about $288 billion in revenue last year, cannot act similarly.

"Henry Ford made sure he paid his workers enough so that they could afford to buy his cars," said William McDonough, executive vice president of the United Food and Commercial Workers union. "Wal-Mart is doing the polar opposite of Henry Ford. Wal-Mart brags about how its low prices help poor Americans, but its low wages are helping increase the number of Americans in poverty."

Mr. Scott argues that retailers, with narrow profit margins, face a different competitive situation and cannot afford to be as generous to their workers as automakers and other capital-intensive companies.

"Some well-meaning critics," he said, "believe that Wal-Mart, because of our size, should play the role that General Motors played after World War II, and that is to establish the post-world-war middle class that the country is so proud of. The facts are that retailing doesn't perform that role in the economy as G.M. does or did. Retailing doesn't perform that role in any country in the world."

Many of those assailing Wal-Mart argue that the company can, and should, pay its workers at least $2 more an hour and add $1 or $2 an hour beyond that to improve its health benefits. A Harvard Business School study found that Wal-Mart paid $3,500 a year for each employee for health care, while the typical American corporation paid $5,600.

If Wal-Mart spent $3.50 an hour more for wages and benefits of its full-time employees, that would cost the company about $6.5 billion a year. At less than 3 percent of its sales in the United States, critics say, Wal-Mart could absorb these costs by slightly raising its prices or accepting somewhat lower profits.

But company executives dismiss such proposals, saying they would largely wipe out Wal-Mart's profit or its price advantage over competitors. Wal-Mart had a profit margin on sales last year around 3.5 percent. If "we raised prices substantially to fund above-market wages, as some critics urge," the company argued in a recent two-page ad in The New York Review of Books, "we'd betray our commitment to tens of millions of customers, many of whom struggle to make ends meet."

Here in Bentonville, Mr. Scott pursued that theme. "If you're telling me because you're Wal-Mart and you're going to pay $12 an hour and this other retailer is going to pay $5.15 an hour, the federal minimum wage, and they're not going to provide any benefits at all and somehow the consumer is rewarded in all this, all you're doing is perpetuating the status quo," he said. "You're driving inefficiencies into the system. It doesn't make any sense."

Wal-Mart argues that, as retailing companies go, it treats its workers better than average. It says 74 percent of its employees work full time, compared with fewer than 40 percent at many other retailers. But critics note that a leading competitor, Costco, pays $16 an hour—65 percent more than the average wage at Wal-Mart stores and 33 percent more than the $12 average at its Sam's Club stores.

At Costco, 82 percent of the workers are covered by company health insurance, compared with 48 percent at Wal-Mart.

George Whalin, president of Retail Management Consultants in San Marcos, Calif., said that Wal-Mart should ignore the attacks. "Retail has always paid poorly and it probably always will," he said. "Wal-Mart has a responsibility to serve their customers—to give them a good product—and to their shareholders. They don't have a responsibility to society to pay a higher wage than the law says you have to pay."

But Burt Flickinger, another retailing consultant, said it would be in Wal-Mart's long-run interest to pay better. "Wal-Mart's turnover will be close to half a million workers this year," he said. "By paying higher wages, Wal-Mart will make its employees happier and will reduce turnover. A lot of its new workers, for instance, don't know where to stock things. Higher wages will mean more productivity per person, and that should help raise profits."

The debate is far from over. LaTasha Barker, a single mother who worked for two years as a cashier at a Sam's Club in Cicero, Ill., said she earned so little that she could not afford the $1,860 a year for family health insurance.

"They don't pay a living wage," said Ms. Barker, who quit her $8.40-an-hour job in 2004 to take a $15-an-hour social work job. While at Sam's, she said, she qualified for Medicaid and $139 a month in food stamps.

By contrast, Jamie Schifferer, manager of the health and beauty aids department at a Wal-Mart in Algonquin, Ill., said Wal-Mart was a terrific employer. She quit her $25,000-a-year post running a Cingular wireless shop to go to Wal-Mart.

After 20 months, she earns $12.50 an hour—close to her previous pay—but now works 40 hours a week rather than the 60 hours at Cingular.

"I was very miserable," she said. "As soon as I heard about this store opening, I jumped. It's perfect for me right now."

Selection 4.5

Outrage always makes for a great story. And what could be more outrageous than bankers who are paid big bonuses while being bailed out by the federal government? This story provides another example of the growing rift in society over the widening gap between highly paid executives and average workers. Businesses defend these and other pay packages, saying they are needed to attract and retain talent. Justified or not, the size of the pay packages has caused public outrage. This will continue to be a hot-button issue that should be watched closely.

Bankers Reaped Lavish Bonuses During Bailouts

By LOUISE STORY and ERIC DASH

Thousands of top traders and bankers on Wall Street were awarded huge bonuses and pay packages last year, even as their employers were battered by the financial crisis.

Nine of the financial firms that were among the largest recipients of federal bailout money paid about 5,000 of their traders and bankers bonuses of more than $1 million apiece for 2008, according to a report released Thursday by Andrew M. Cuomo, the New York attorney general.

At Goldman Sachs, for example, bonuses of more than $1 million went to 953 traders and bankers, and Morgan Stanley awarded seven-figure bonuses to 428 employees. Even at weaker banks like Citigroup and Bank of America, million-dollar awards were distributed to hundreds of workers.

The report is certain to intensify the growing debate over how, and how much, Wall Street bankers should be paid.

In January, President Obama called financial institutions "shameful" for giving themselves nearly $20 billion in bonuses as the economy was faltering and the government was spending billions to bail out financial institutions.

On Friday, the House of Representatives may vote on a bill that would order bank regulators to restrict "inappropriate or imprudently risky" pay packages at larger banks.

Mr. Cuomo, who for months has criticized the companies over pay, said the bonuses were particularly galling because the banks survived the crisis with the government's support.

"If the bank lost money, where do you get the money to pay the bonus?" he said.

All the banks named in the report declined to comment.

Mr. Cuomo's stance—that compensation for every employee in a financial firm should rise and fall in line with the company's overall results—is not shared on Wall Street, which tends to reward employees based more on their individual performance. Otherwise, the thinking goes, top workers could easily leave for another firm that would reward them more directly for their personal contribution.

Many banks partly base their bonuses on overall results, but Mr. Cuomo has said they should do so to a greater degree.

At Morgan Stanley, for example, compensation last year was more than seven times as large as the bank's profit. In 2004 and 2005, when the stock markets were doing well, Morgan Stanley spent only two times its profits on compensation.

Published: July 30, 2009.

Robert A. Profusek, a lawyer with the law firm Jones Day, which works with many of the large banks, said bank executives and boards spent considerable time deciding bonuses based on the value of workers to their companies.

"There's this assumption that everyone was like drunken sailors passing out money without regard to the consequences or without giving it any thought," Mr. Profusek said. "That wasn't the case."

Mr. Cuomo's office did not study the correlation between all of the individual bonuses and the performance of the people who received them.

Congressional leaders have introduced several other bills aimed at reining in the bank bonus culture. Federal regulators and a new government pay czar, Kenneth Feinberg, are also scrutinizing bank bonuses, which have fueled populist outrage. Incentives that led to large bonuses on Wall Street are often cited as a cause of the financial crisis.

Though it has been known for months that billions of dollars were spent on bonuses last year, it was unclear whether that money was spread widely or concentrated among a few workers.

The report suggests that those roughly 5,000 people—a small subset of the industry—accounted for more than $5 billion in bonuses. At Goldman, just 200 people collectively were paid nearly $1 billion in total, and at Morgan Stanley, $577 million was shared by 101 people.

All told, the bonus pools at the nine banks that received bailout money was $32.6 billion, while those banks lost $81 billion.

Some compensation experts questioned whether the bonuses should have been paid at all while the banks were receiving government aid.

"There are some real ethical questions given the bailouts and the precariousness of so many of these financial institutions," said Jesse M. Brill, an outspoken pay critic who is the chairman of Compensation Standards.com, a research firm in California. "It's troublesome that the old ways are so ingrained that it is very hard for them to shed them."

The report does not include certain other highly paid employees, like brokers who are paid on commission. The report also does not include some bank subsidiaries, like the Phibro commodities trading unit at Citigroup, where one trader stands to collect $100 million for his work last year.

Now that most banks are making money again, hefty bonuses will probably be even more common this year. And many banks have increased salaries among highly paid workers so that they will not depend as heavily on bonuses.

Banks typically do not disclose compensation figures beyond their total compensation expenses and the amounts paid to top five highly paid executives, but they turned over information on their bonus pools to a House committee and to Mr. Cuomo after the bailout last year.

The last few years provide a "virtual laboratory" to test whether bankers' pay moved in line with bank performance, Mr. Cuomo said. If it did, he said, the pay levels would have dropped off in 2007 and 2008 as bank profits fell.

So far this year, Morgan Stanley has set aside about $7 billion for compensation—which includes salaries, bonuses and expenses like health care—even though it has reported quarterly losses.

At some banks last year, revenue fell to levels not seen in more than five years, but pay did not. At Citigroup, revenue was the lowest since 2002. But the amount the bank spent on compensation was higher than in any other year between 2003 and 2006.

At Bank of America, revenue last year was at the same level as in 2006, and the bank kept the amount it paid to employees in line with 2006. Profit at the bank last year, however, was one-fifth of the level in 2006.

Still, regulators may have limited resources for keeping pay in check. Only banks that still have bailout money are subject to oversight by Mr. Feinberg, the pay czar. He will approve pay for the top 100 compensated employees at banks like Citigroup and Bank of America as well as automakers like General Motors.

A Conversation with . . . **Louis Uchitelle**

ECONOMICS WRITER

© The New York Times

Louis Uchitelle covers economics for The New York Times, specializing in macro, labor and fiscal trends. He has written extensively about the unwinding of job security and the spread of layoffs. He shared a George Polk Award for a series of seven stories published in 1996 titled "The Downsizing of America." Uchitelle is the author of "The Disposable American: Layoffs and Their Consequences," published by Knopf in 2006. Before joining The Times in 1980, first as an editor and then as an economics writer, he worked for the Associated Press as a reporter, an editor and a foreign correspondent in Latin America. The following is an edited transcript of a telephone interview.

How did you get started?
I started with a small newspaper in Mount Vernon, New York, and I wrote every type of story. Two years later I joined the Associated Press, and there I covered

everything—sports, economics, guerilla movements in South America, national stories, every conceivable story. I also worked as an editor at the AP. I was a foreign correspondent, an editor and then I joined The Times 29 years ago. In 1987 I became a full-time economics writer. At the time, the only economics writer outside the Washington bureau was Leonard Silk, and he was doing a column.

Why did you decide to cover economics?

No one was doing general economics, and I interpreted that broadly to mean labor issues of all sorts, corporate globalization, outsourcing, business economics, the Federal Reserve. I sort of defined it for The Times.

How did you develop your expertise?

You start with the technical stuff. You do a story about investment and you learn all you can about investment. You do stories about the monthly jobs reports and in the process you learn everything you can. You go on to income inequality and you try to find out how that works. Labor issues are very much part of it. You go across labor fields. You don't become a labor writer covering the unions. You get into retail. Wal-Mart became the biggest company in the country in terms of annual employment, so I got into the issues of how a company like that works.

Where do you come up with your story ideas?

Reading is extremely important. So is talking to a lot of people. Once you start doing these stories, people suggest stories. I just did a story about jobs that go begging. We don't train people in skills like welding, and I wondered if there was a demand for skilled workers even in the recession and whether there were shortages. It turned out there were, particularly for skilled workers with experience. In nursing, if you were looking for someone with 10 years' experience doing critical care in recovery rooms—that person is in short supply.

You ask, "What is the common denominator?" In the worker shortage story, the common denominator is someone who got an education—not college, necessarily, but high school always. They typically went through an apprenticeship and then accumulated years of on-the-job experience. Those people with that experience aren't there in sufficient numbers. I was talking to one company that was hiring 80 welders who could do flawless welds for oil refineries. For every 20 applicants, only one could do it. I find that fascinating in a culture where we insist on a college education without knowing how that prepares you to work.

How do you frame a story?

I try to find a subject that typifies trends that are out there. It is a conceptual thing. I think a lot of that comes from my years in Argentina, Uruguay and Paraguay for the Associated Press. There wasn't a lot of straight news from those countries that interested American readers. You had to learn to find stories that would interest Americans—that is "conceptualization."

Can you give me an example?

I did something early in the recession on how the recession was affecting Savannah, Georgia, and I used that to tell the larger story, trying to be as anecdotal as possible. I often try to find a subject that typifies trends that are out there.

Which do you like better, reporting or writing?

The writing comes out of the reporting. As you report, the story frames itself in your head. By the time the reporting is over, you have the first three or four paragraphs. I don't make a distinction between reporting and writing. I find myself writing the story as I report it and beginning to see what the main lines are. I don't sit down with a bunch of notes and then say, "Now what do I do with this?" I find that you have to do a lot of interviewing, and when you sit down, you have your interviews organized in your head. So you go to the pertinent parts.

Who reads what you write?

I am writing for the general public. I never write for so-called knowledgeable readers, thinking they know what I am writing about. I start with the idea that I have to explain everything.

What recommendations do you have for beginners?

Do a wide variety of general reporting. Just explain what is going on and synthesize it. I mean you sit through a board of education meeting and you have to come up, at the end, with what it is they did. If they had a long discussion, what was the thrust of that conversation? The synthesis part of it, to me, is crucial.

How has economics reporting changed over the course of your career?

It has gone from covering spot news to explaining broad phenomenon and trends. We have gone from economics as recitation of statistics to the type of reporting I am describing.

I love the reporting. I do a great deal of reporting and only then, after I have done the reporting, do I draw conclusions based on the reporting. I hope we don't lose that—conclusions and observations grounded in detailed reporting— and veer off into opinion. I think blogging pushes people this way. I have tried blogging. Every time I try it, I think I can just spin something off. It turns out I can't. I need to call a half-dozen people before I can do something I am pleased with. That's the danger: opinion insufficiently grounded in reporting.

Will Twitter replace what you do?

It's a tool. Journalism should require a great deal of reporting, and Twitter can help in that process. The unemployment rate rose or fell today. That can be done quickly. The broader piece that explains trends requires a broader mix of reporting—20 interviews, 30 interviews, 40 interviews. I don't skimp on gathering information and viewpoints.

MAKING**CONNECTIONS**

1

What are the implications for a town like Newton, Iowa, when a company pulls up stakes?
What kinds of stories could you pursue if something like this happened in the area you cover?

Does Wal-Mart have a corporate
responsibility to pay its workers wages
above the poverty level? Explain your
reasoning. What do you see as the role
of the media on an issue like this one?

2

3

If the middle class is disappearing,
what might that mean for society?
What interesting story on that subject
have you not seen published, and
how would you report it?

4

The gap between rich and poor is getting
larger. What are some ways you could show
this in a slideshow or interactive graphic that
you would produce for the Web?

BUSINESS CONCEPTS REVIEW

Base compensation
Refers to the base salary paid to an employee. Usually used in relation to executives who receive several types of compensation.

Bonus
Used by employers to reward employees for meeting performance goals. Bonuses have come under attack because incentive pay agreements require they be paid even when a company loses money.

Layoff
Eliminating or dismissing a worker from his or her job.

Middle class
A group of individuals who fall between the lower or working class and upper classes in society. The term is poorly defined, but is often used in reference to the bedrock of the U.S. population.

Minimum wage
The minimum amount of compensation an employee must receive for performing labor as prescribed by federal law.

Poverty rate
Income threshold set by the U.S. government. The level is adjusted for inflation using the consumer price index.

Productivity
The amount of output in goods and services for each hour of a worker's time.

Standard of living
Generally measured by income in relation to the poverty rate, a level of comfort afforded individuals who are able to maintain a certain level of consumption.

Stock options
A contractual right to purchase stock at a given price. Awarded to executives as an incentive to drive earnings and the stock price higher.

CHAPTER 5

debt

YOU'VE BORROWED MONEY FROM FRIENDS, money to buy a car, money to pay tuition. You have felt the pain of being in debt—but do you know enough to write about it? And even if you did, where would you start?

It is often said that the entire world can be divided into two types of people—those who own and those who owe. That being the case, the United States definitely falls into the debtor column. U.S. consumers are in hock more than $2.5 trillion. And the U.S. federal government is the biggest borrower. It owes $12 trillion.[1] Financing that debt is a huge expense—Uncle Sam pays roughly $1.2 billion in interest every day.[2]

But wait a minute. That government figure understates the U.S. debt problem, says David Walker, president and CEO of the Peter G. Peterson Foundation, an anti-deficit group. Walker, who formerly was U.S. Comptroller General, says the United States owes closer to $56.4 trillion when taking into account underfunded obligations like Medicare and Social Security.[3]

Holy cow. Just how big is $56.4 trillion?

Let's say you have just interviewed Walker and have to write a story. You turn on your calculator and find that it doesn't even carry the decimal point that high. Try this: Figure out how much each American owes by dividing the figure by the U.S. population. The result: Each man, woman and child owes $184,000 in federal debt, by Walker's calculations. That amount would buy a nice three-bedroom house in many mid-size cities.[4]

The best way to write about big numbers is to describe the figures in relation to something else. Break them down so they make sense to the average person. Another example: A Los Angeles nuclear-powered attack submarine stretches 362 feet, the equivalent of one football field spanning from end zone to end zone. That is one B-I-G submarine, cruising under the ocean's surface at about 25 knots (29 mph).[5]

Let's get back to debt. Why should we care? History shows us that most financial disasters are debt related. Debt is blamed as a cause of the Great Depression. Most businesses that fail had too much debt. (They also had too little in the way of cash to meet those debt payments, but that is another story.)

So how do you write about such a subject? You start by breaking it down, using simple language. Next, you humanize this abstract concept by finding people who can serve as examples of what you are trying to convey. Bankruptcy court is a great place to find the numbers and the statistics. But to make the reader care about those numbers, you need to put a face on the dollar sign.

The opening story on General Motors (GM) shows one way to write about bankruptcy—spinning a story off the news. GM was the largest industrial company to file for bankruptcy. It is doubtful that as a young cub reporter you will be covering such a beast of a business failure. But the issues are the same. Readers want to know what is happening to the company and its employees, and whether creditors who lent the company money are going to be paid back.

Debtors used to be incarcerated or sold into slavery. That practice has since been outlawed, but as you will see later in this chapter, big financial companies have fought and won tougher laws making it hard to file bankruptcy and extinguish debts.

It is only appropriate in a chapter on debt that we look at the biggest debtor of all—the federal government. It is unlikely that the United States will file bankruptcy, but the crushing debt load that it faces in coming years could greatly change its economic fortunes.

Three stories appearing later in the chapter deal with not only how consumers are struggling with debt, but how companies have profited handsomely by offering them easy credit. Most business stories have a villain and a victim. Deciding who is right or wrong is up to the reader. But writers can use conflict to help pull readers through the story. And few topics create more conflict than money and debt—except maybe sex. We'll save that for another book.

STORY**SCAN**

Selection 5.1

What elements need to be in a bankruptcy story? This is a second-day story that looks at the General Motors bankruptcy. It looks forward and tries to answer questions most people would like to know once the dust has settled: Will GM survive? Sure, the government is cheerful about the company's prospects, but you would expect that from Obama and Co., the people bankrolling the deal with billions in federal government aid. This story includes a lot of information any reporter covering even a much smaller bankruptcy would want to pay attention to, such as: What will the company be like post-bankruptcy? How many people will it employ? Will divisions or products be sold? And probably most important of all: Will the company make money post-bankruptcy? Bill Vlasic and Nick Bunkley do a notable job of reporting the basics, but they also add a healthy dose of skepticism about GM's future. Good business reporting doesn't buy the party line.

Obama Is Upbeat for G.M.'s Future

By BILL VLASIC and NICK BUNKLEY

President Obama marked the lowest point in General Motors' 100-year history—its bankruptcy filing on Monday—by barely mentioning it, instead focusing his remarks on the second chance G.M. will have to become a viable company with more government aid.

"I'm confident that the steps I'm announcing today will mark the end of an old G.M., and the beginning of a new G.M.," Mr. Obama said.

While the moment had been anticipated for weeks, the bankruptcy filing nevertheless included more crushing news to G.M.'s home state, Michigan, which is already reeling from waves of layoffs and plant closings.

Shortly after filing for Chapter 11 in Federal Bankruptcy Court in Manhattan, G.M. said it would close 14 more American factories—including seven in Michigan—and cut up to 21,000 more jobs.

"This is a ton of bricks hitting us," said Senator Carl Levin, Democrat of Michigan. "These are real jobs, real families and real communities, with real names of real factories that are going to be closed."

Among the Michigan plants facing shutdown are its Willow Run transmission factory in Ypsilanti, which was built in 1943 to assemble B-24 bombers during World War II.

"I was angry at first, then I cried, then I got angry again," said Don Skidmore, the president of United Automobile Workers Local 735, which represents the plant's 1,100 workers. "I'm hurt for the people. The looks on their faces are horrible."

When a company files for bankruptcy, it is always important to ask how many jobs will be cut and how many plants or stores will be closed. You also want to know how big the bankruptcy is in relation to others. See "By the Numbers" story that follows.

Filed at the bankruptcy court will be a list of creditors and how much they are owed. The company does not have to pay its debts while in bankruptcy, but these debts will have to be settled before it emerges from Chapter 11 protection.

Companies will often ask a judge to set aside union contracts and other obligations in bankruptcy.

Published: June 2, 2009.

This is often the case. Companies have a better chance of twisting creditors' arms in bankruptcy.

After the factory closings, which will leave 12 in Michigan, G.M. will have fewer than 40,000 workers building cars in the United States—one-tenth of a work force that in the 1970s numbered 395,000 people.

Mr. Obama acknowledged the pain associated with G.M.'s drastic downsizing, but said that he saw no option other than bankruptcy to fix the company's bloated cost structure.

"I will not pretend that the bad times are over," he said. "Difficult days are ahead."

The White House and G.M. hope a speedy trip through bankruptcy, in 90 days or fewer, will limit further damage to the company, its employees, dealers and suppliers.

Debt holders (bondholders, banks) usually get paid back only cents on every dollar of debt they are owed. One ploy often used is to get bondholders to accept less in exchange for stock in the new company.

A quick restructuring appears possible because of new agreements with the U.A.W. and a majority of G.M.'s bondholders who agreed to swap their debt for equity in what is being referred to as the "new G.M."

The expectations for an accelerated court process were buoyed by the quick proceedings in the Chrysler bankruptcy. Chrysler, which entered bankruptcy on April 30, could now emerge shortly as a new corporate entity owned by a U.A.W. health care trust, the Italian automaker Fiat, and the American and Canadian governments.

If a company has filed for bankruptcy, it is always important to ask what assets will be sold as part of the reorganization.

On Monday morning, lawyers representing a group of Indiana pension funds appealed a bankruptcy judge's approval of Chrysler's sale to Fiat. But the judge, Arthur J. Gonzalez, later that day entered his final approval of the sale and agreed to shorten a customary 10-day stay of such a sale to 4 days. That would allow the Chrysler deal to take effect at noon on Friday.

We always like to know who will be running the company. Sometimes CEOs quit. If the company can't agree on a reorganization plan, the court appoints a trustee to help oversee the reorganization.

Fritz Henderson, who will stay on as G.M.'s chief executive at least until a new board is formed later this summer, said he was eager to exit bankruptcy.

"We're confident we will move fast," Mr. Henderson said at a news conference in New York. "Not with a sense of urgency, but with pure, unadulterated speed."

The company is hoping to spread a sense of optimism. It created a new Web site, GMReinvention.com, where it posted the first ad in a new campaign.

The company filed first-day motions in court Monday to allow it to keep paying employees and suppliers while in bankruptcy. The plan from the president's auto task force calls for G.M. to receive $30.1 billion in federal aid, in addition to the $19.4 billion it has already received. The governments of Canada and Ontario will contribute $9.5 billion more.

GM was lucky. It received government aid to help speed the reorganization. Most companies have to work to find a bank willing to lend them money so they can keep going.

A reconstituted G.M. is expected to emerge from bankruptcy with its best assets, including its Chevrolet, Cadillac, Buick and GMC brands, and with 60 percent government ownership. The remaining stock will be split among a U.A.W. health care trust, bondholders and the Canadian governments.

Yes, keep the best assets, but this doesn't necessarily mean the company will make money.

But closed plants and discontinued brands—Saturn, Pontiac, Saab and Hummer—will be among the assets that will not remain with the company. Mr. Henderson said the bankruptcy represented a "defining moment" for the automaker that would allow it to "permanently" unshackle itself from the cost of supporting hundreds of thousands of retirees and the $27 billion in debt held by investors.

Good detail: What is GM dumping? And who might buy it? Often plans for asset sales are overly optimistic. After all, this is bankruptcy—the bargain bin of discount sales.

Still, it will take more than a restructuring to stem G.M.'s decades-long slide in market share, from more than 50 percent in the 1960s to about 20 percent now. Fixing the balance sheet is only the beginning, said Joseph Phillippi, an industry consultant. "The second half is going to be cultural," he said. "G.M. was No. 1 for so long, and now it's going to be another carmaker in the middle of the pack."

Companies always trumpet how they are going to sell off assets such as brands, plants, equipment. One problem: Assets help produce revenue and profit. If you shrink the company, what do you have left?

Mr. Henderson promised a renewed commitment to its customers, and even offered an apology of sorts for the poor quality of past G.M. products. "The G.M. which let too many of you down is history," he said.

Stockholders are wiped out in bankruptcy, so the common stock is worthless. New shares are issued when the company emerges from Chapter 11 protection.

The fall of G.M. was also marked by its removal from the group of 30 blue-chip companies that comprise the Dow Jones industrial average.

Mr. Obama said the government would take a hands-off approach to managing G.M., and would divest its stock in the company as soon as it could. But that is likely years away.

Meanwhile, the Ford Motor Company—the only member of Detroit's Big Three to not require federal assistance—expressed concern that it could be hurt by the level of aid given to G.M.

"We look forward to working with the Obama administration to ensure that the government's majority ownership of G.M. will not change the industry's competitive dynamics and that a level playing field will be maintained," Ford said Monday in a statement.

Remember to keep an eye on how big the company will be after it reorganizes. This could influence its success.

Once G.M. has finished cutting jobs, brands and models, it could fall behind Ford in terms of sales.

The cuts at G.M. include two assembly plants in Michigan, and two in Delaware and Tennessee. Other large plants that stamp metal parts or build engines will be shut in Indiana, Ohio, Virginia and New York.

Workers at the Willow Run plant in Michigan learned their factory was closing when they arrived at the union hall at 7:30 A.M. They were told that some production would stop immediately, and all but 300 of 1,100 workers would be laid off within months.

Great walk-off quote.

"It's like being at a funeral," said Mr. Skidmore, the plant's union leader.

Selection 5.2

So how does GM compare when it comes to the size of other bankruptcies? It will definitely go down in the record books for two reasons: GM was once the country's largest automaker, and its bankruptcy marks the biggest failure of a major industrial company. What is the biggest bankruptcy in history? That distinction goes to Lehman Brothers, which reported about $691 million in assets when it collapsed in September 2008, sending shockwaves through the rest of the U.S. economy. Quick action by the Department of the Treasury and the Federal Reserve Board kept the economy from collapsing into another depression.

DEALBOOK
G.M.'s Big Bankruptcy, by the Numbers
By ANDREW ROSS SORKIN

Measured by the size of its assets, General Motors's Chapter 11 case isn't the largest the nation has ever seen. That dubious honor belongs to the investment bank Lehman Brothers, which reported about $691 billion in assets when it collapsed into bankruptcy protection in mid-September.

Even excluding financial companies—which generally have bigger balance sheets than industrial companies—G.M. isn't the reigning Chapter 11 heavyweight. The largest nonfinancial bankruptcy in United States history is that of WorldCom: when it filed in 2002, it reported about $104 billion in assets. (Many of those "assets" vanished, however, when WorldCom's accounting fraud was straightened out.)

Nevertheless, G.M.'s reorganization will have its place in the record books.

With more than $82 billion in assets, G.M. on Monday became the largest industrial company to file for Chapter 11 protection. Its assets are more than double what Chrysler reported when it, G.M.'s smaller rival, filed for Chapter 11 protection in late April.

Other numbers give a broader sense of how huge and complicated G.M.'s case will be.

For example, G.M. reported total liabilities of $172.8 billion on Monday. That's more than four times the $41 billion in debt that WorldCom reported in its Chapter 11 petition.

Or consider this: G.M. has about 235,000 employees, which is nearly 10 times the number of employees at Lehman when that company sought protection from creditors. G.M. also does business

Published: June 1, 2009.

with nearly 6,100 G.M. dealers—an amount it hopes to prune in bankruptcy court—as well as 11,500 suppliers in North America.

The chart below, based on figures from BankruptcyData.com, shows how G.M.'s Chapter 11 case stacks up against some other big bankruptcies:

Largest U.S. bankruptcy filings

Company	Date	Assets
Lehman Brothers Holdings	9/15/2008	$691
Washington Mutual	9/26/2008	328
WorldCom	7/21/2002	104
General Motors	6/1/2009	82
Enron	12/2/2001	66
Conseco	12/17/2002	61
Chrysler	4/30/2009	39
Thornburg Mortgage	5/1/2009	37
Pacific Gas and Electric	4/6/2001	36
Texaco	4/12/1987	35

Source: BankruptcyData.com and G.M.'s Chapter 11 petition. Data includes public company bankruptcy filings since 1980; assets in billions.

The New York Times

Selection 5.3

Good business writing involves uncovering not just the story, but how to best tell it. One method is to find an anecdote, or short story that typifies the point you are trying to drive home to the reader. Gretchen Morgenson effectively uses this technique as she shows us how otherwise rational people are seduced by financial institutions pitching credit cards as desirable and risk free. In reality, consumers are digging themselves into a hole with each ring of the cash register. Finding the right anecdote isn't easy—it can take dozens of interviews. But the search is well worth the effort. The correct anecdote can be extremely powerful. Look at Diane McLeod in this story. She is so under the gun from collection agencies that she puts her phone in the dishwasher. Saying things are "bad" is one thing, but telling somebody you store your phone in the dishwasher immediately creates an image in the reader's mind of just how bad the situation has become.

The Debt Trap
Given a Shovel, Americans Dig Deeper Into Debt

By GRETCHEN MORGENSON

The collection agencies call at least 20 times a day. For a little quiet, Diane McLeod stashes her phone in the dishwasher.

But right up until she hit the wall financially, Ms. McLeod was a dream customer for lenders. She juggled not one but two mortgages, both with interest rates that rose over time, and a car loan and high-cost credit card debt. Separated and living with her 20-year-old son, she worked two jobs so she could afford her small, two-bedroom ranch house in suburban Philadelphia, the Kia she drove to work, and the handbags and knickknacks she liked.

Then last year, back-to-back medical emergencies helped push her over the edge. She could no longer afford either her home payments or her credit card bills. Then she lost her job. Now her home is in foreclosure and her credit profile in ruins.

Ms. McLeod, who is 47, readily admits her money problems are largely of her own making. But as surely as it takes two to tango, she had partners in her financial demise. In recent years, those partners, including the financial giants Citigroup, Capital One and GE Capital, were collecting interest payments totaling more than 40 percent of her pretax income and thousands more in fees.

Years of spending more than they earn have left a record number of Americans like Ms. McLeod standing at the financial precipice. They have amassed a mountain of debt that grows ever bigger because of high interest rates and fees.

While the circumstances surrounding these downfalls vary, one element is identical: the lucrative lending practices of America's merchants of debt have led millions of Americans—young and old, native and immigrant, affluent and poor—to the brink. More and more, Americans can identify with miners of old: in debt to the company store with little chance of paying up.

It is not just individuals but the entire economy that is now suffering. Practices that produced record profits for many banks have shaken the nation's financial system to its foundation. As a growing number of Americans default, banks are recording hundreds of billions in losses, devastating their shareholders.

To reduce the risk of a domino effect, the Bush administration fashioned an emergency rescue plan last week to shore up Fannie Mae and Freddie Mac, the nation's two largest mortgage finance companies, if necessary.

Published: July 20, 2008.

Todd Heisler/The New York Times

In the series "The Debt Trap," The Times presents articles and multimedia, including an interview with Diane McLeod of Selection 5.3, examining why so many people fall into debt and cannot escape. The series is available at: http://www.nytimes.com/interactive/2008/07/20/business/20debt-trap.html#

To be sure, the increased availability of credit has contributed mightily to the American economy and has allowed consumers to make big-ticket purchases like homes, cars and college educations.

But behind the big increase in consumer debt is a major shift in the way lenders approach their business. In earlier years, actually being repaid by borrowers was crucial to lenders. Now, because so much consumer debt is packaged into securities and sold to investors, repayment of the loans takes on less importance to those lenders than the fees and charges generated when loans are made.

Lenders have found new ways to squeeze more profit from borrowers. Though prevailing interest rates have fallen to the low single digits in recent years, for example, the rates that credit card issuers routinely charge even borrowers with good credit records have risen, to 19.1 percent last year from 17.7 percent in 2005—a difference that adds billions of dollars in interest charges annually to credit card bills.

Average late fees rose to $35 in 2007 from less than $13 in 1994, and fees charged when customers exceed their credit limits more than doubled to $26 a month from $11, according to CardWeb, an online publisher of information on payment and credit cards.

Mortgage lenders similarly added or raised fees associated with borrowing to buy a home—like $75 e-mail charges, $100 document preparation costs and $70 courier fees—bringing the average to $700 a mortgage, according to the Department of Housing and Urban Development. These "junk fees" have risen 50 percent in recent years, said Michael A. Kratzer, president of FeeDisclosure.com, a Web site intended to help consumers reduce fees on mortgages.

"Today the focus for lenders is not so much on consumer loans being repaid, but on the loan as a perpetual earning asset," said Julie L. Williams, chief counsel of the Comptroller of the Currency, in a March 2005 speech that received little notice at the time.

Lenders have been eager to expand their reach. They have honed sophisticated marketing tactics, gathering personal financial data to tailor their pitches. They have spent hundreds of millions of dollars on advertising campaigns that make debt sound desirable and risk-free. The ads are aimed at people who urgently need loans to pay for health care and other necessities.

It is not just financial conglomerates that are profiting on consumer debt loads. Some manufacturers and retailers can generate more income from internal financing arms that lend to their customers than from their primary businesses.

Tallying what the lenders have made off Ms. McLeod over the years is revealing. In 2007, when she earned $48,000 before taxes, she was charged more than $20,000 in interest on her various loans.

Her first mortgage, originated by the EquiFirst Corporation, charged her $14,136 a year, and her second, held by CitiFinancial, added $4,000. Capital One, a credit card company that charged her 28 percent interest on her balances, billed $1,400 in annual interest. GE Money Bank levied 27 percent on the $1,500 or so that Ms. McLeod owed on an account she had with a local jewelry store, adding more than $400.

Olde City Mortgage, the company that arranged one of Ms. McLeod's loans, made $6,000 on a single refinancing, and EquiFirst received $890 in a loan origination fee.

Such fees and interest rates are a growing burden on Americans, especially those who rely on credit cards to make ends meet.

And recent changes in the bankruptcy laws, supported by financial services firms, make it all the harder for consumers, especially those with modest incomes, to get out from under their debt by filing for bankruptcy.

But with so many borrowers in trouble, some bankruptcy experts and regulators are beginning to focus on the responsibilities of lenders, like requiring them to make loans only if they are suitable to the borrowers applying for them.

The Federal Reserve Board, for instance, recently put into effect rules barring a lender from making a loan without regard to the borrower's ability to repay it.

Henry E. Hildebrand III, a Bankruptcy Court trustee in Nashville since 1982 and one of the nation's busiest, has seen at first hand what happens when lenders do not take some responsibility for loans that go bad. "I look across the table at people who are right out of school and have more debt than they can handle, and they are starting out life in a bankruptcy," he said.

Ms. McLeod used debt to keep going until she was fired from her job in March for writing inappropriate e-mail messages. Since then, she has been selling her coveted handbags and other items on eBay to raise money while waiting to be evicted from her home.

"I think a lot of people in this country have a lot more debt than they let the outside world know," Ms. McLeod said. "I worked in retail for five years. And men, women would open up their wallets to pay and the credit cards that were in some of the wallets just amazed me."

Borrowing to Shop

For decades, America's shift from thrift could be summed up in this familiar phrase: When the going gets tough, the tough go shopping. Whether for a car, home, vacation or college degree, the nation's lenders stood ready to assist.

Companies offered first and second mortgages and home equity lines, marketed credit cards for teenagers and helped college students to amass upward of $100,000 in debt by graduation.

Every age group up to the elderly was the target of sophisticated ad campaigns and direct mail programs. "Live Richly" was a Citibank message. "Life Takes Visa," proclaims the nation's largest credit card issuer.

Eliminating negative feelings about indebtedness was the idea behind MasterCard's "Priceless" campaign, the work of McCann-Erickson Worldwide Advertising, which came out in 1997.

"One of the tricks in the credit card business is that people have an inherent guilt with spending," Jonathan B. Cranin, executive vice president and deputy creative director at the agency, said when the commercials began. "What you want is to have people feel good about their purchases."

Mortgage lenders took to cold-calling homeowners to persuade them to refinance. Done to reduce borrowers' monthly payments, serial refinancings allowed lenders to charge thousands of dollars in loan processing fees, including appraisals, credit checks, title searches and document preparation fees.

Not surprisingly, such practices generated dazzling profits for the nation's financial companies. And since 2005, when the bankruptcy law was changed, the credit card industry has increased its earnings 25 percent, according to a new study by Michael Simkovic, a former James M. Olin fellow in Law and Economics at Harvard Law School.

The "2005 bankruptcy reform benefited credit card companies and hurt their customers," Mr. Simkovic concluded in his study. He said that even though sponsors of the bankruptcy bill promised that consumers would benefit from lower borrowing costs as delinquent borrowers were held more accountable, the cost of borrowing from credit card companies has actually increased anywhere from 5 percent to 17 percent.

Among the most profitable companies were Ms. McLeod's creditors.

For Capital One, which charges her 28 percent interest on her credit card, net interest income, after provisions for loan losses, has risen a compounded 25 percent a year since 2002.

GE Money Bank, which levied a 27 percent rate on Ms. McLeod's debt and is part of the GE Capital Corporation, generated profits of $4.3 billion in 2007, more than double the $2.1 billion it earned in 2003.

Because many of these large institutions pool the loans they make and sell them to investors, they are not as vulnerable when the borrowers default. At the end of 2007, for example, one-third of Capital One's $151 billion in managed loans had been sold as securities.

Officials at General Electric declined to comment. Capital One did not return phone calls.

As the profits in this indebtedness grew, financial companies moved aggressively to protect them, spending millions of dollars to lobby against any moves lawmakers might take to rein in questionable lending.

But consumers are voicing anger over lending practices. A recent proposal by the Federal Reserve Board to limit some abusive practices has drawn more than 11,000 letters since May. Most are from irate borrowers.

A Rising Tide of Bills

Just two generations ago, America was a nation of mostly thrifty people living within their means, even setting money aside for unforeseen expenses.

Today, Americans carry $2.56 trillion in consumer debt, up 22 percent since 2000 alone, according to the Federal Reserve Board. The average household's credit card debt is $8,565, up almost 15 percent from 2000.

College debt has more than doubled since 1995. The average student emerges from college carrying $20,000 in educational debt.

Household debt, including mortgages and credit cards, represents 19 percent of household assets, according to the Fed, compared with 13 percent in 1980.

Even as this debt was mounting, incomes stagnated for many Americans. As a result, the percentage of disposable income that consumers must set aside to service their debt—a figure that includes monthly credit card payments, car loans, mortgage interest and principal—has risen to 14.5 percent from 11 percent just 15 years ago.

By contrast, the nation's savings rate, which exceeded 8 percent of disposable income in 1968, stood at 0.4 percent at the end of the first quarter of this year, according to the Bureau of Economic Analysis.

More ominous, as Americans have dug themselves deeper into debt, the value of their assets has started to fall. Mortgage debt stood at $10.5 trillion at the end of last year, more than double the

$4.8 trillion just seven years earlier, but home prices that were rising to support increasing levels of debt, like home equity lines of credit, are now dropping.

The combination of increased debt, falling asset prices and stagnant incomes does not threaten just imprudent borrowers. The entire economy has become vulnerable to the spending slowdown that results when consumers like Ms. McLeod hit the wall.

That First Credit Card

Growing up in Philadelphia, Diane McLeod never knew financial hardship, she said. Her father owned six pizza shops and her mother was a homemaker.

"There was always money for everything, whether it was bills or food shopping or a spur-of-the-moment vacation," Ms. McLeod recalled. "If they worried about money, they never let us know."

Hers was a pay-as-you-go family, she said. Although money was not discussed much around the dinner table, credit card debt was not a part of her parents' financial plan, and sometimes personal purchases were put off.

When Ms. McLeod married at 18, she and her husband carried no credit cards. She stayed at home after her son was born, but when she was 27 her husband died.

She remarried a few years later and continued as a homemaker until her son turned 13. Between her husband's job laying carpets and her own, money was not exactly tight.

In the mid-'90s, Ms. McLeod got several credit cards. When the marriage began to founder, she said, she shopped to make herself feel better.

Earning a livable wage at Verizon Yellow Pages, Ms. McLeod finally decided to leave her marriage and buy a home of her own in February 2003. The cost was $135,000, and her mortgage required no down payment because her credit history was good.

"I was very proud of myself when I bought the house," Ms. McLeod explained. "I thought I would live here till I died." Adding to her burden, however, was about $25,000 in credit card debt she had brought from her marriage. Because her husband did not have a regular salary, all the cards were in her name.

After she had been in the house for a year, a friend who was a mortgage broker suggested she consolidate her debts into a new home loan. The property had appreciated by about $30,000, and once again she put no money down for the loan. "It was amazing how easy it was," she recalled. "But that's a trap, and I didn't know it then."

Naturally, the refinance had costs. There was an $8,000 penalty to pay off the previous mortgage early as well as roughly $1,500 in closing costs on the new loan.

To cover these fees, Ms. McLeod dipped into her retirement account. Only later did she realize that she had to pay an early-withdrawal penalty of $3,000 to the Internal Revenue Service. Short on cash, she put it on a credit card.

Soon she had racked up another $19,000 in credit card debt. But because her home had appreciated, she once again refinanced her mortgage. Although she was making $50,000 a year working two jobs, her income was not enough to support the new $165,000 loan. She asked her son to join her on the loan application; with his income, the numbers worked.

"Boy, would I regret that," she said. The decision would drive a wedge between mother and son and damage his credit profile as well.

Almost immediately after she refinanced, in late 2005, the department store where she worked her second job, as a jewelry saleswoman at night and on weekends, cut back her hours. She quit altogether, and her son moved out of the house, where he had been helping with the rent, to live with a girlfriend. Ms. McLeod was on her own and paying $1,500 a month on her mortgage.

Because the house had been recently appraised at $228,000, she said, she felt sure she could refinance again if she needed to pay off her credit card. "You felt like you had a way out," she said.

But as happens with many debt-laden Americans, an unexpected illness helped push Ms. McLeod over the edge. In January 2006, her doctor told her she needed a hysterectomy. She had health care coverage, but she could no longer work at a second job.

She made matters worse during her recovery, while watching home shopping channels. "Eight weeks in bed by yourself is very dangerous when you have a TV and credit card," Ms. McLeod said. "QVC was my friend."

Later that year, Ms. McLeod realized she was in trouble, squeezed by her mortgage and credit card payments, her $350 monthly car bill, rising energy prices and a stagnant salary. She started to sell knickknacks, handbags, clothing and other items on eBay to help cover her heating and food bills. She stopped paying her credit cards so that she could afford her mortgage.

A year ago she was back in the hospital, this time with a burst appendix. Her condition worsened, and she lost the use of one kidney. She spent 19 days in the hospital and six weeks recuperating. Her prescription-drug costs added to her expenses, and by September she could no longer pay her mortgage.

When her father died in early January, she was devastated. About a month later, on Feb. 14, Ms. McLeod was suspended and soon afterward fired from Verizon.

Toting up her financial obligations, Ms. McLeod said she owed $237,000 on her home mortgage. Of that, sheriff's costs are $4,350, and "other" fees related to the foreclosure come to $3,000. A house of similar size down the street from Ms. McLeod sold for $153,000 in January.

Her credit card debt totals around $34,000, she said. Each month the late fees and over-limit penalties add to her debt. Ms. McLeod said she would probably file for bankruptcy.

Patricia A. Hasson, president of the Credit Counseling Service of Delaware Valley, said Ms. McLeod would probably wind up having to repay 40 percent to 60 percent of her credit card debt. The owner of her mortgages could come after her for the difference between what she owes on her loan and what her house ultimately sells for. The first mortgage was sold to investors; Citigroup declined to say whether it held onto the second mortgage or sold it to investors.

A sheriff's auction of her home on June 12 received no bidders, Ms. McLeod said. The bank will soon evict her.

"Oh, I definitely have regrets," Ms. McLeod said. "I regret not dealing with my emotions instead of just shopping. And I regret involving my son in all this because that has affected him and his finances and his self-esteem."

Ms. McLeod says she hopes to be living in an apartment she can afford soon and to get back to paying her bills on time.

She does not want another credit card, she said. But even though her credit profile is ruined, she still receives come-ons.

Recently an envelope arrived offering a "pre-qualified" Salute Visa Gold card issued by Urban Bank Trust. "We think you deserve more credit!" it said in bold type.

A spokeswoman at Urban Bank said the Salute Visa is part of a program "designed to provide access to credit for folks who would not otherwise qualify for credit."

The Salute Visa offered Ms. McLeod a $300 credit line. But a closer look at the fine print showed that $150 of that would go, as annual fees, to Urban Bank.

Selection 5.4

There are two sides to every debate. Often the side with the loudest megaphone wins. In this case, the banking industry lobbied Congress and won the battle. Congress toughened bankruptcy laws, making it harder for consumers to wipe their debts out by filing bankruptcy. The banks' argument was simple: The laws were too lenient. This practice was raising the cost of credit for good customers since banks had to cover debtors' losses. This story turns the entire argument on its head. It does so by focusing on one practice most people would find ridiculous—the practice of credit card companies flooding people who have filed for bankruptcy with new credit cards. To say the banking industry looks foolish is an understatement. Never underestimate the power of using the ridiculous or humor to drive home a point to the reader.

Newly Bankrupt Raking In Piles of Credit Offers

By TIMOTHY EGAN

TACOMA, Wash., Dec. 9—As one of more than two million Americans who rushed to a courthouse this year to file for bankruptcy before a tough new law took effect, Laura Fogle is glad for her chance at a fresh start. A nurse and single mother of two, she blames her use of credit cards after cancer surgery for falling into deep debt.

Ms. Fogle is broke, and may not seem to be the kind of person to whom banks would want to offer credit cards. But she said she had no sooner filed for bankruptcy, and sworn off plastic, than she was hit with a flurry of solicitations from major banks.

"Every day, I get at least two or three new credit card offers— Citibank, MasterCard, you name it—they want to give me a credit card, at pretty high interest rates," said Ms. Fogle, who is 41 and lives here. "I've got a stack of these things on my table. It's tempting, but I've sworn them off."

If it seems odd to Ms. Fogle that banks would want to lend money to the newly bankrupt, it is no mystery to the financial community, which charges some of the highest interest rates to these newly available customers.

*   *   *

"The theory is that people who have just declared bankruptcy are a good credit risk because their old debts are clean and now they won't be able to get a new discharge for eight years," said John D. Penn, president of the American Bankruptcy Institute, a nonprofit clearinghouse for information on the subject.

Credit card companies have long solicited bankrupt people, on a calculated risk that income from the higher interest rates and late fees paid by those who are trying to get their credit back will outweigh the losses from those who fail to make payments altogether. The companies also directed many of those customers toward so-called secured cards, which require a cash deposit.

But the new law makes for an even better gamble for lenders, consumer groups say. It not only makes bankrupt debtors wait eight years to clear their debts again, but it also requires many of those who do go back into bankruptcy to pay previous credit card bills that may have been excused under the old law.

Bankers defend the practice of soliciting the newly bankrupt, saying it gives them a chance to build a new credit history.

Published: December 11, 2005. Full text available at: www.nytimes.com/2005/12/11/national/11credit.html

"The people coming out of bankruptcy need an opportunity to get back on their feet," said Laura Fisher, a spokeswoman for the American Bankers Association, the industry's largest trade group.

"If you take away the opportunity to get credit," Ms. Fisher said, "it's like taking away the want ads from a job-seeker."

But consumer groups say the new law has put millions of Americans at risk of being in a continuous debt loop through their credit cards. And while the banks have taken a short-term financial hit because of the new filings—leaving banks holding the bills—they will benefit in the long run because the new law makes it much easier to make money on people who live near the edge every month on their credit cards, some consumer groups say.

Credit cards are the most profitable part of the banking industry, with late fees and high interest charges helping make them so. Last year, more than five billion solicitations for new cards were sent out, nearly double the number from eight years ago.

"The whole business model of the credit card industry is built around outstanding debt," said Ellen Schloemer, a researcher at the Center for Responsible Lending, a nonprofit group that tracks lower-middle-class financial issues, based in Durham, N.C. "This is the only industry that calls people deadbeats when they pay all their bills every month."

Among bankers, policies differ in how to approach the newly bankrupt. Bank of America does not give credit cards to people who have filed for debt protection, said Betty Riess, a bank spokeswoman.

However, because there is a delay between a bankruptcy petition filing and a credit report showing the debt consolidation, the bank may still be sending offers to someone who has filed, Ms. Riess said.

Citigroup, whose credit card offers have piled up in Ms. Fogle's home, has its own internal credit rating system that does not always rule out the bankrupt.

"We use direct mail to find many of our new customers," said Samuel Wang, a Citigroup spokesman, in an e-mail message.

As of the end of October, 2,010,567 people had filed for bankruptcy protection this year, a modern record, federal bankruptcy court officials say. In just over two weeks of October, more than 600,000 people filed petitions, leading to long lines outside courthouses across the country, and clerks swamped with petitions.

The debtors were rushing to beat an Oct. 17 deadline when the most sweeping changes in bankruptcy law in a quarter-century took effect.

Most of the newly bankrupt filed under Chapter 7 of the code, which allows them to expunge many unsecured debts. The new law makes it much more difficult to erase debt; it increases the cost of filing and adds requirements like credit counseling.

The banking industry worked in Congress for nearly 10 years to pass the law, and critics say it gave them everything they wanted to increase profits from people prone to debt. Bankers say the law makes it harder for people to abuse the system.

"The hidden agenda of those who wrote the new law was death by a thousand cuts," said Travis B. Plunkett, legislative director of the Consumer Federation of America, which opposed the law.

Opponents, including a group of bankruptcy law professors, argued that the changes gave the banking industry too much of an advantage.

"In our view, the fundamental change over the last 10 years has been the way that credit is marketed to consumers," the bankruptcy professors wrote in a letter to the Senate this year.

"Credit card lenders have become more aggressive in marketing their products, and a large, profitable market has emerged in subprime lending. Increased risk is part of the business model."

Ms. Fogle would seem to be a perfect candidate for long-term debt to credit cards. Though she works regularly as a nurse at Good Samaritan Hospital here, earning $16 an hour, and has health insurance, she said a health emergency pushed her into debt. Last year, she needed surgery for uterine cancer, which caused her to lose days of work and income. Credit cards made up the difference, and soon she was $15,000 in debt.

She filed for protection of the courts in late August, and her debts are now removed. "My plan is to lay off credit cards until I can really afford them," she said. "But it's tempting. I would like to have one in case of emergency."

Ms. Fogle said she was trying to stick to a disciplined new pattern with her finances. "I try to buy only what I need, instead of what I want," she said. "But there are small things that I want—a latte, every now and then, taking my kids to the movies."

The credit card offers inform Ms. Fogle that she is pre-approved, but at higher interest rates—23 percent or more, which is typical for offers to the newly bankrupt.

"It's obvious what they're trying to do here—start people off with a fresh credit card at a much higher rate than before," she said.

Nearly 60 percent of all credit card holders, about 85 million Americans, carry a balance—that is, they do not pay off the entire debt, according to the bankers' association.

The average debt among those with a monthly balance is $9,000, said the Consumer Federation of America in a recent report. Paying just the monthly minimum—usually 2 percent of the balance—on

$9,000, it would take 42 years to pay off the debt, at a typical 18 percent interest rate, the consumer group calculated. Since that study, some banks have raised the minimum to 4 percent.

Opponents of the new bankruptcy law argue that it did not put new restrictions on credit solicitation and will turn the courts and the government into private collection agencies for bankers.

While bankruptcy filings increased 17 percent over the last eight years, credit card profits went up 163 percent to $30.2 billion, according to a report filed with the House Judiciary Committee by opponents of the new law.

"In the eight years since the credit industry first came to Congress seeking relief from the rising rate of personal bankruptcy filings, the extent of credit has not been curtailed, nor have the industry profits been diminished due to bankruptcy filings," Congressional opponents wrote in their report while the bill was under consideration.

Americans owe $800 billion in credit card debt, more than triple the amount from 1989, and a 31 percent increase from five years ago, according to a recent report, "The Plastic Safety Net," by the Center for Responsible Lending, and Demos, a research group based in New York.

The study found that a third of low- and middle-income American households used credit cards for basic expenses—rent, groceries and utilities—in any 4 of the last 12 months.

Those with the worst credit card debt were people ages 50 to 64, who owed $9,124 on average, the study found.

"The people I'm seeing right now, they're mostly middle or lower middle class," said Jack Burtch, a bankruptcy lawyer in Washington State. "In a good many of the cases, credit cards are what got them into trouble. And I don't see how credit cards will get them out of it."

Selection 5.5

This story offers two benefits. First, it does a decent job of explaining something complicated—the difference between a Chapter 13 bankruptcy and a Chapter 7 bankruptcy. It offers examples and then clearly explains how the law works. Second, reporters Tara Siegel Bernard and Jenny Anderson enlist bankruptcy attorneys' help to make sense of the law. The reporters take the added step of finding homeowners and consumers struggling with financial troubles. This puts a face on the problem and helps them drive a major point behind their story: Changes in the law have made filing bankruptcy more complicated, but they haven't stopped people from filing as the law intended.

Downturn Drags More Consumers Into Bankruptcy

By TARA SIEGEL BERNARD and JENNY ANDERSON

The economy's deep troubles are pushing a growing number of already struggling consumers into bankruptcy, often with far more debt than those who filed in previous downturns.

Plummeting home values, dwindling incomes and the near disappearance of credit have proved a potent mixture. While all the usual reasons that distressed borrowers seek bankruptcy—job loss, medical bills, divorce—play significant roles, new economic forces are changing the calculus of who can ride out the tough times and who cannot.

The number of personal bankruptcy filings jumped nearly 8 percent in October from September, after marching steadily upward for the last two years, said Mike Bickford, president of Automated Access to Court Electronic Records, a bankruptcy data and management company.

Filings totaled 108,595, surpassing 100,000 for the first time since a law that made it more difficult—and often twice as expensive—to file for bankruptcy took effect in 2005. That translated to an average of 4,936 bankruptcies filed each business day last month, up nearly 34 percent from October 2007.

Robert M. Lawless, a professor at the University of Illinois College of Law, pointed to the tightening of credit by banks as a significant factor in the increase in October. As banks have pulled back on lending, he said, consumers have been finding it more difficult, and in many cases impossible, to use credit cards, refinance their home mortgages or fall back on their home equity lines to get them through a rough period.

"A credit crunch can drive people into bankruptcy today rather than later as sources of lending dry up," Professor Lawless said. "With the consumer credit tightening and the economy in a nosedive, this pop could just be the beginning of a long-term rise in the bankruptcy filing rate to levels that are even higher than we had before the 2005 bankruptcy law."

Not only are filings up, but recent filers have had much more credit card debt, often run up in an attempt to keep current on a mortgage that now exceeds the value of their home, bankruptcy lawyers said in interviews.

A recent study found that the typical family who filed for bankruptcy in 2007 was carrying about 21 percent more in secured debts, like mortgages and car loans, and about 44 percent more in unsecured debts, like credit cards and medical and utility bills, than filers in 2001.

Published: November 15, 2008.

Their incomes, meanwhile, remained static over those six years, according to the study, which used data from the 2007 Consumer Bankruptcy Project, a joint effort of law professors, sociologists and physicians. Researchers surveyed 2,500 households nationwide that filed for bankruptcy in February and March 2007.

"Earlier downturns followed strong booms, so families went into recessions with higher incomes and lower debt loads," said Elizabeth Warren, a professor at Harvard Law School and, along with Professor Lawless, part of the Bankruptcy Project team. "But the fundamentals are off for families even before we hit the recession this time, so bankruptcy filings are likely to rise faster."

Not surprisingly, filings are increasing most rapidly in states where real estate values skyrocketed and then crashed, including Nevada, California and Florida. In Nevada, bankruptcy filings in October were up 70 percent compared with last year. In California, bankruptcies jumped 80 percent in the same period, while Florida's filings rose 62 percent.

In those regions, some people are trying to rescue their homes through bankruptcy proceedings, but many are just as relieved to walk away, shedding layers of debt that otherwise would have taken decades to pay off.

Tony and Carrie Forsyth, both 30, chose not to walk away from their house in Florida. The couple said they thought their financial situation would improve in 2006, when Mr. Forsyth accepted a promotion from his employer, a Michigan food distributor, that required them to move to Florida. But they could not sell their home in Ypsilanti, Mich., so they decided to rent it out.

In June 2006, the couple headed south and bought a house for $220,000 in Tamarac, Fla., with no money down. Five months later, their tenants in Michigan stopped paying, and the family had to carry two mortgage payments, just as the adjustable-rate mortgage on their Michigan home reset to a higher interest rate. They lost the Michigan home to foreclosure in February 2007.

By that time, however, the couple, who have two young daughters, were using credit cards to pay for food, utilities and clothes. After accumulating about $20,000 in debt, they said, they realized that bankruptcy was the only way they could remain in their Florida home, whose value, meanwhile, had plunged 25 percent. They filed for Chapter 13 bankruptcy protection this year, which permitted them to keep the house, and they agreed to repay a portion of their debts over the next three years.

A Chapter 7 bankruptcy, by contrast, provides filers with what is known as a "fresh start" because debts are forgiven. In this case, assets are liquidated, though the states allow for various exemptions. To qualify for a Chapter 7, filers need to pass a means test to determine whether they are unable to repay their debts.

Filers who are deemed able to repay a portion of their debts must file for Chapter 13 bankruptcy. Some debtors choose Chapter 13 because it permits them to save their primary homes from foreclosure, though they are required to catch up on their mortgage payments.

Mr. Forsyth said declaring bankruptcy was a difficult step. "Because of our Christian background, it didn't feel right," he said. "But there was no other way for us to live and support our family unless we went that route."

Mrs. Forsyth added: "We are just rolling with life. You have to eat. You have to have diapers."

The Forsyths are emblematic of the new forces that have led to the sharp rise in bankruptcy filings. "Historically, a person would get behind in his mortgage because of a temporarily catastrophic financial event, such as job loss, divorce, illness," said Chip Parker, a bankruptcy lawyer in Jacksonville, Fla. "However, when these adjustable-rate mortgages started resetting from their teaser rate and clients couldn't refinance their way out of trouble, they were getting behind even though there was no catastrophic event."

Bankruptcy lawyers report that they have been having more consultations with middle-class families with six-figure incomes—including many who either bought a home during the boom or pulled out most or all of their available home equity just keep to up with the cost of living. Also caught up in the bankruptcies are real estate investors, who hoped to flip properties they had bought near the height of the market.

"There are a lot of foreclosures that haven't taken place yet because people still have available credit," said Jeffrey H. Tromberg, a bankruptcy lawyer in Fort Lauderdale, Fla. "We don't see them until they've maxed out their credit cards."

A similar pattern has emerged in Las Vegas, where more people are filing for Chapter 7 bankruptcy protection because it makes more financial sense to walk away from their homes. Real estate values have plummeted, and now the local economy is also suffering. Car salesmen and casino dealers are being laid off. Valet parking attendants and masseuses are collecting less in tips.

"My clients are basically good people that got into a home the best way they could and can no longer meet their obligations because their income has gone down," said Roger P. Croteau, a lawyer in Las Vegas who concentrates on bankruptcy. "There is no equity to pay off their credit cards, and they are maxed out. They haven't saved enough because of housing costs."

Ellen Stoebling, a bankruptcy lawyer in Las Vegas, added: "People are using their cards to try and hold onto their property for as long as possible in hopes they can somehow talk some sense into their lender and stay in the property."

The problems are not limited to people with adjustable-rate mortgages and homes that are now worth less than they owe. Job losses are also playing a role. Bankruptcies are also up sharply in Delaware, Rhode Island and Indiana, where the unemployment rates have been climbing.

And, of course, some people continue to seek bankruptcy for the usual reasons.

Lisa Marquis, a 35-year-old mother of five in Indiana, has no medical insurance but has undergone 21 operations in the last nine years, some related to emphysema and other respiratory diseases, and others related to accidents and several miscarriages.

Mrs. Marquis cannot work, but her husband earns $13.50 an hour as a truck driver—a salary that makes them ineligible for Medicaid but unable to pay their medical bills. Earlier this year, the family had to leave the mobile home they owned because the mold there was making it hard for her to breathe; they moved into a house where they paid more than $600 a month in rent. Mr. Marquis was spending three days a week in court fending off angry creditors, cutting down on the number of hours he could work.

In April, facing more than $114,000 in medical bills and less available overtime work, the Marquises filed for Chapter 13 bankruptcy—the third time in less than 10 years that Mrs. Marquis had to file for protection because of medical bills. Because the latest filing is a Chapter 13, they have agreed to pay some of their debts.

"We could have waited to do a 7," Mrs. Marquis said. "I want to pay my debts. I didn't want to cheat people who helped to save my life."

Despite the rise in bankruptcies, academics and lawyers say they believe that many others have been discouraged from filing because of the 2005 bankruptcy law.

Ms. Warren, the Harvard law professor, said many borrowers had been left with the mistaken impression that they could no longer file. And, she argued, "the widespread perception that bankruptcy is not available to help families makes this economic crisis worse."

Selection 5.6

The enormous budget deficits the federal government will run in the coming years could constrain the country's choices for years and end up doing serious economic damage if foreign lenders become unwilling to finance the debt. The United States has run big budget deficits before, but how did it dig itself into what amounts to a $2 trillion hole? In this column, David Leonhardt examines what factors caused the country to swing from a projected $800 billion annual *surplus in 2001 to a $1.2 trillion annual budget gap. So how did Leonhardt get the story? By talking to lots of people and by analyzing the numbers—in this case 10 years of Congressional Budget Office reports. Leonhardt organizes his column using a timeline approach. The reader is taken back to where the problem started. Note the fifth paragraph: "The story of today's deficits starts in January 2001, as President Bill Clinton was leaving office." This stylistic feature immediately captures the reader's attention by giving the message a sense of both time and place.*

ECONOMIC SCENE
America's Sea of Red Ink Was Years in the Making
By DAVID LEONHARDT

There are two basic truths about the enormous deficits that the federal government will run in the coming years.

The first is that President Obama's agenda, ambitious as it may be, is responsible for only a sliver of the deficits, despite what many of his Republican critics are saying. The second is that Mr. Obama does not have a realistic plan for eliminating the deficit, despite what his advisers have suggested.

The New York Times analyzed Congressional Budget Office reports going back almost a decade, with the aim of understanding how the federal government came to be far deeper in debt than it has been since the years just after World War II. This debt will constrain the country's choices for years and could end up doing serious economic damage if foreign lenders become unwilling to finance it.

Mr. Obama—responding to recent signs of skittishness among those lenders—met with 40 members of Congress at the White House on Tuesday and called for the re-enactment of pay-as-you-go rules, requiring Congress to pay for any new programs it passes.

The story of today's deficits starts in January 2001, as President Bill Clinton was leaving office. The Congressional Budget Office estimated then that the government would run an average annual surplus of more than $800 billion a year from 2009 to 2012. Today, the government is expected to run a $1.2 trillion annual deficit in those years.

You can think of that roughly $2 trillion swing as coming from four broad categories: the business cycle, President George W. Bush's policies, policies from the Bush years that are scheduled to expire but that Mr. Obama has chosen to extend, and new policies proposed by Mr. Obama.

Published: June 9, 2009.

The first category—the business cycle—accounts for 37 percent of the $2 trillion swing. It's a reflection of the fact that both the 2001 recession and the current one reduced tax revenue, required more spending on safety-net programs and changed economists' assumptions about how much in taxes the government would collect in future years.

About 33 percent of the swing stems from new legislation signed by Mr. Bush. That legislation, like his tax cuts and the Medicare prescription drug benefit, not only continue to cost the government but have also increased interest payments on the national debt.

Mr. Obama's main contribution to the deficit is his extension of several Bush policies, like the Iraq war and tax cuts for households making less than $250,000. Such policies—together with the Wall Street bailout, which was signed by Mr. Bush and supported by Mr. Obama—account for 20 percent of the swing.

About 7 percent comes from the stimulus bill that Mr. Obama signed in February. And only 3 percent comes from Mr. Obama's agenda on health care, education, energy and other areas.

If the analysis is extended further into the future, well beyond 2012, the Obama agenda accounts for only a slightly higher share of the projected deficits.

How can that be? Some of his proposals, like a plan to put a price on carbon emissions, don't cost the government any money. Others would be partly offset by proposed tax increases on the affluent and spending cuts. Congressional and White House aides agree that no large new programs, like an expansion of health insurance, are likely to pass unless they are paid for.

Alan Auerbach, an economist at the University of California, Berkeley, and an author of a widely cited study on the dangers of the current deficits, describes the situation like so: "Bush behaved incredibly irresponsibly for eight years. On the one hand, it might seem unfair for people to blame Obama for not fixing it. On the other hand, he's not fixing it."

"And," he added, "not fixing it is, in a sense, making it worse."

When challenged about the deficit, Mr. Obama and his advisers generally start talking about health care. "There is no way you can put the nation on a sound fiscal course without wringing inefficiencies out of health care," Peter Orszag, the White House budget director, told me.

Outside economists agree. The Medicare budget really is the linchpin of deficit reduction. But there are two problems with leaving the discussion there.

First, even if a health overhaul does pass, it may not include the tough measures needed to bring down spending. Ultimately, the only way to do so is to take money from doctors, drug makers and insurers, and it isn't clear whether Mr. Obama and Congress have the stomach for that fight. So far, they have focused on ideas like preventive care that would do little to cut costs.

Second, even serious health care reform won't be enough. Obama advisers acknowledge as much. They say that changes to the system would probably have a big effect on health spending starting in five or 10 years. The national debt, however, will grow dangerously large much sooner.

Mr. Orszag says the president is committed to a deficit equal to no more than 3 percent of gross domestic product within five to 10 years. The Congressional Budget Office projects a deficit of at least 4 percent for most of the next decade. Even that may turn out to be optimistic, since the government usually ends up spending more than it says it will. So Mr. Obama isn't on course to meet his target.

But Congressional Republicans aren't, either. Judd Gregg recently held up a chart on the Senate floor showing that Mr. Obama would increase the deficit—but failed to mention that much of the increase stemmed from extending Bush policies. In fact, unlike Mr. Obama, Republicans favor extending all the Bush tax cuts, which will send the deficit higher.

Republican leaders in the House, meanwhile, announced a plan last week to cut spending by $75 billion a year. But they made specific suggestions adding up to a meager $5 billion. The remaining $70 billion was left vague. "The G.O.P. is not serious about cutting down spending," the conservative Cato Institute concluded.

What, then, will happen?

"Things will get worse gradually," Mr. Auerbach predicts, "unless they get worse quickly." Either a solution will be put off, or foreign lenders, spooked by the rising debt, will send interest rates higher and create a crisis.

The solution, though, is no mystery. It will involve some combination of tax increases and spending cuts. And it won't be limited to pay-as-you-go rules, tax increases on somebody else, or a crackdown on waste, fraud and abuse. Your taxes will probably go up, and some government programs you favor will become less generous.

That is the legacy of our trillion-dollar deficits. Erasing them will be one of the great political issues of the coming decade.

MAKING**CONNECTIONS**

1

Debtors don't have to pay their bills after filing for bankruptcy protection. Instead, they are given time to come up with a plan to repay creditors.

Explain in your own words why General Motors was forced to file for bankruptcy. Should the U.S. government have helped GM? Or should shareholders be forced to suffer losses for GM's past mistakes?

2

3

List three reasons why debt is favored instead of thrift in U.S. culture. Discuss the impact of advertising and the pressure to consume goods on consumers' borrowing behavior.

4

If you were pursuing a story about the credit card industry, what are some of the issues you would want to include in your story? Credit card companies blame bankruptcy for their losses. Since that is the case, should credit card companies be allowed to market cards to people who have gone bankrupt?

BUSINESS CONCEPTS REVIEW

Chapter 7 bankruptcy
A liquidation—no plan of reorganization is filed. A trustee is appointed by the court to handle the sale of assets to satisfy debts.

Chapter 11 bankruptcy
Typically filed by a business and there is a plan of reorganization. The debtor remains in possession while the business is reorganized.

Chapter 13 bankruptcy
Allows debtors to keep property and pay debts over time, usually three to five years. The biggest advantage is debtors can save their homes from foreclosure.

Collateral
Property or assets that are pledged to secure debt repayment. If the debt is not repaid the lender may seize the asset.

Commercial bank
Commercial institution chartered by federal or state government that accepts deposits, offers checking and savings accounts and makes loans.

Creditor
One who extends credit and to whom funds are owed such as a bank, supplier or lender.

Debt
Obligation that must be repaid to another in the form of goods, services or money. Debt can take many forms. Loans, bonds and commercial paper are all types of debt.

Default
Arises when a debtor fails to make timely payments of principal and interest to a creditor on obligations such as a loan or a bond.

Foreclosure
Legal action filed by a lender against a homeowner who has not made timely payments of principal and interest on a mortgage. The action results in the bank taking title to the home or property.

Home equity loan
A loan where borrowers use the equity or value they own in their homes as collateral for a loan. The loan creates a lien against the home and leads to a reduction in the homeowner's equity value since the mortgage debt has been increased by the size of the loan.

BUSINESS CONCEPTS REVIEW (continued)

Line of credit   A contractual arrangement where a financial institution agrees to lend money to a customer up to a specific limit.

Liquidation   A fire sale of assets at deeply depressed prices to satisfy debts. Creditors usually receive only cents for every dollar of claims.

Loan value   The maximum that may be borrowed, or the amount a lender is willing to lend against a security or collateral.

Mortgage   A debt where the borrower gives the lender a lien against property. The mortgage is repaid over time with a set schedule of payments.

Secured debt   Borrower pledges assets—such as a vehicle the borrower is purchasing—as collateral for the loan. If the loan isn't repaid, the lender has the right to seize the collateral.

Unsecured debt   No collateral is pledged by the borrower. Since unsecured debts are riskier for banks, borrowers are charged higher interest rates.

Write-down   Downward adjustment in the value of an asset for accounting purposes.

Write-off   Reduction in the value of an asset as a loss.

taxes

● TAXES ARE ONE OF THOSE SUBJECTS that reporters often malign as being too boring or too difficult to comprehend. Writers shun the subject. Editors turn a deaf ear. If you tell your editor you have an interesting story about taxes, you might not get far without a sexy murder or other scandal to liven things up.

Pulitzer Prize winner David Cay Johnston made a career out of covering taxes for one reason: No one else was doing it well. In his view, the usual dull, uninspired stories about taxes point to a fundamental flaw in journalism. "The problem is most journalists really don't deeply know what they are writing about," Johnston says. "I call it 'he said' journalism. You report the story, but you are not questioning fundamentally what is going on."

To ask good questions about taxes and not just accept what people tell you (or some such thing), you'll need to do some homework—read about the theory of taxes, learn about Tax Court filings and get acquainted with statistical data. But most important of all, don't accept things on face value—check them out. Covering taxes isn't all that different from anything else, whether the story involves a school board, a police department or the jetliner that just crashed. There is a language to be learned, terminology used by lawyers, accountants and bureaucrats that needs to be understood.

The importance of taxes can't be overstated. They affect just about everything. Businesses look closely at taxes when deciding where to expand, what to buy and when to sell. All these decisions have tax consequences. In the end, a company may decide to move its operations outside the United States to get more favorable tax treatment.

Individuals react much the same way: They modify their behavior based on the taxes they have to pay. Whether you're buying a house or selling a share of stock, taxes affect just about every financial move you make. One example is cigarettes: They are among the most heavily taxed items a consumer can buy. In New York City, a pack of cigarettes costs more than $9. More than half that amount, or $5.26, is taxes.[1] With cigarette taxes so high, some smart capitalists have figured out how to buy up cigarettes in low-tax states, truck them off to New York City and sell them at a profit. As a result, states like New York are losing billions in revenue to bootleggers. This chapter looks at some of the issues surrounding taxes that you will inevitably face as a reporter, ranging from tax rates and problems with the tax code to how some companies skip town after getting tax breaks without ever creating the jobs they promised.

The important thing to remember as you enter the world of business journalism is this: Taxes matter.

Selection 6.1

In only 1,100 words, this piece by Edmund L. Andrews does a remarkable job of debunking the age-old myth that U.S. corporations pay exorbitant taxes. Because this is a column, the writer is given more license to voice his opinion, but he still must back up his statements with facts. That means coming up with the numbers that support his points, and also helping his readers go beyond the obvious numbers—tax rates—to show what "actual tax burden" means. Notice how Andrews uses comparisons across time and geography to put the numbers into further perspective.

ECONOMIC VIEW
Why U.S. Companies Shouldn't Whine About Taxes

By EDMUND L. ANDREWS

To hear some people talk, the United States is the scourge of the Fortune 500. Despite all the tax cuts that President Bush and Congress have passed in the last five years, business groups and their supporters in Washington complain that the United States imposes higher tax rates on corporate profits than almost any other industrialized country.

"Foreign-based competitor companies operate under tax rules that are often more favorable than our own," warned R. Glenn Hubbard, a former economic adviser to President Bush and now dean of the Columbia Business School, at a House hearing two weeks ago. "Current law can result in circumstances that harm the competitiveness of U.S. companies."

Around Washington, the rumblings are growing for "reform" of corporate taxes to improve the global competitiveness of American companies.

Henry M. Paulson Jr., the incoming Treasury secretary, declared at his confirmation hearing that he wanted to increase "competitiveness" in the tax code.

Can it be true that the United States, where bare-knuckled capitalism is a romantic ideal and being nouveau riche is a badge of honor, is harder on big corporations than "old Europe" welfare states like Germany, France and Sweden?

Published: July 9, 2006.

Don't believe it. There are plenty of problems with the corporate tax code—rococo complexity, perverse incentives, antique ideas—but overly high taxes is not one of them.

By most measures, the corporate tax burden is lower in the United States than it is in the European Union or in Japan or most other industrialized countries.

The political danger, at least from a fiscal standpoint, is that arguments for corporate tax reform will be hijacked to justify another round of corporate tax cuts. That was what happened with the corporate tax overhaul of 2004, which became a grab bag of tax breaks to almost every corner of business, at a net cost of $60 billion over 10 years.

Those who see the American corporate tax as oppressive point to a striking fact: the standard corporate tax rate of 35 percent is now higher than that of most other industrialized countries. The average top rate is 25.8 percent in the European Union, where most nations have cut rates to attract investment.

But official tax rates are not the same as actual tax burdens. What American companies lose in high tax rates they more than make up in higher tax breaks.

One indicator of the true tax burden is corporate tax revenue as a share of gross domestic product. According to the Organization for Economic Cooperation and Development, a research organization based in Paris and financed by governments of industrialized nations, corporate taxes in 2003 were 2.1 percent of G.D.P. in the United States, 3.2 percent in the European Union and 4.3 percent in industrialized countries in Asia.

Though comparisons of true tax rates are treacherous, the evidence suggests that the United States more than makes up for high statutory rates with generous tax breaks. Robert S. McIntyre, director of Citizens for Tax Justice, has calculated that the average corporation paid taxes of about 18 percent in 2004.

The European Commission, using a more theoretical approach, calculated that the average effective tax rate in 15 Western European nations has hovered between 20 and 22 percent since 1998. When the 10 new Central European members of the European Union are included, the average corporate tax bite was 17.7 percent.

"There is good reason to believe that the corporate tax burden in the United States could be less than the rest of the world because the rest of the world has been broadening their tax bases while we have been cutting ours," said Martin A. Sullivan, an analyst at the journal Tax Notes.

To be sure, many experts contend that the American tax code does impose some competitive disadvantages. One big complaint is that the United States is one of the very few countries that taxes corporate profits worldwide. Almost all other nations use "territorial" systems, taxing only profits inside their borders.

The difference is significant. Thyssen-Krupp, the German steel conglomerate, owes no German taxes on profits from its operations in Brazil, China or Poland. And European value-added tax on domestic sales does not apply to exports to the United States. United States Steel, by contrast, potentially owes American taxes on profits from its subsidiary in Slovakia and must also charge value-added taxes on exports sold in Germany.

In practice, the disadvantage is smaller than it appears. For one thing, American companies receive tax credits for taxes paid in other countries. More important, American companies have proved extremely adept at shifting profits into low-tax countries like Ireland and then deferring the American taxes on those profits by keeping them outside the United States.

Under current federal law, companies can postpone taxes on foreign profits until those profits return to the United States. By some estimates, American multinationals had accumulated more than $400 billion in profits outside the country.

Last year, Congress rewarded that behavior. First, it widened companies' ability to claim tax credits against their foreign taxes, at a cost to the Treasury of almost $40 billion over 10 years. Second, it gave companies a one-time chance to repatriate their vast hoard of overseas profits at a tax rate of only 5.25 percent—a bonanza for many pharmaceutical and electronics businesses.

"The current U.S. rules, while complex, represent the best of all worlds for multinational taxpayers," declared Stephen E. Shay, a former international tax counsel to the Treasury Department, at a hearing last month of a House Ways and Means subcommittee.

Many analysts agree that today's rules are a mess: they do not raise much revenue from foreign profits, they encourage companies to invest outside the United States, they encourage profit-shifting schemes and they probably put some American companies at a competitive disadvantage.

The challenge is to change the system without cutting taxes yet again. Michael J. Graetz, a professor at Yale Law School and a proponent of radical tax overhaul, told lawmakers last month that the top corporate tax rate ought to be cut from 35 percent to as little as 15 percent.

But Mr. Graetz said Congress would have to make up for the lost revenue. "It is not possible to achieve this kind of corporate rate reduction without a major restructuring of our domestic tax system," he said.

President Bush called for exactly such a revenue-neutral restructuring during his re-election campaign. But any overhaul would provoke intense battles between potential winners and losers. With Republicans terrified about losing control of Congress in the midterm elections this year, Mr. Bush has postponed making any proposals until at least next year.

Selection 6.2

*David Cay Johnston says taxes can be covered just like everything else: Study
the numbers. Figure out what they say. And then look for patterns. But there
needs to be a hook to the story—especially when you are talking about a
subject like taxes. Johnston grabs the reader with this news—the richest
people in the United States are getting the biggest tax breaks, a fact that is
making them even richer. Even before you get halfway through the story, you
begin to feel a sense of outrage—unless, of course, you are worth a zillion
bucks. It is "gotcha" journalism at its best.*

Richest Are Leaving Even the Rich Far Behind

By DAVID CAY JOHNSTON

When F. Scott Fitzgerald pronounced that the very rich "are different from you and me," Ernest Hemingway's famously dismissive
response was: "Yes, they have more money." Today he might well add:
much, much, much more money.

The people at the top of America's money pyramid have so
prospered in recent years that they have pulled far ahead of the rest of
the population, an analysis of tax records and other government data
by The New York Times shows. They have even left behind people
making hundreds of thousands of dollars a year.

Call them the hyper-rich.

They are not just a few Croesus-like rarities. Draw a line under
the top 0.1 percent of income earners—the top one-thousandth.
Above that line are about 145,000 taxpayers, each with at least
$1.6 million in income and often much more.

The average income for the top 0.1 percent was $3 million
in 2002, the latest year for which averages are available. That
number is two and a half times the $1.2 million, adjusted for
inflation, that group reported in 1980. No other income group rose
nearly as fast.

The share of the nation's income earned by those in this uppermost category has more than doubled since 1980, to 7.4 percent in
2002. The share of income earned by the rest of the top 10 percent
rose far less, and the share earned by the bottom 90 percent fell.

Next, examine the net worth of American households. The
group with homes, investments and other assets worth more than $10
million comprised 338,400 households in 2001, the last year for which
data are available. The number has grown more than 400 percent since
1980, after adjusting for inflation, while the total number of households has grown only 27 percent.

Published: June 5, 2005.

June 5, 2005

The Wealthiest Benefit More From the Recent Tax Cuts

Under the recent tax cuts, the richest taxpayers get the largest break, in dollars and in the drop in their share of all federal taxes paid. That is because those taxpayers benefit most from lower taxes on dividends and investment gains, and because the alternative minimum tax, which was originally intended to apply only to the very richest people, now takes back a large portion of the tax cuts of people who are not the richest. "Taxpayers" refers to both single and joint filers.

DOWNLOAD THIS GRAPHIC AS A PDF DOCUMENT - CLICK HERE

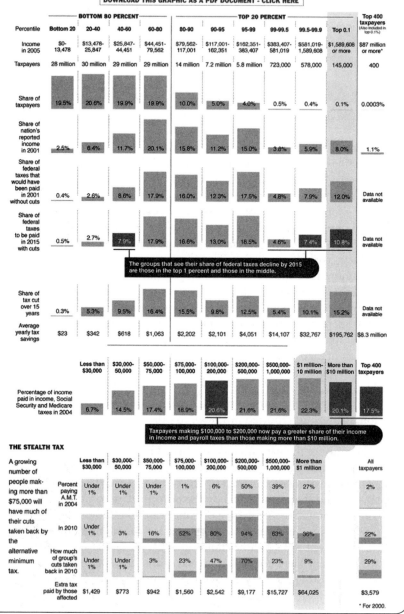

		BOTTOM 80 PERCENT				TOP 20 PERCENT					Top 400 taxpayers (Also included in top 0.1%)
Percentile	Bottom 20	20-40	40-60	60-80	80-90	90-95	95-99	99-99.5	99.5-99.9	Top 0.1	
Income in 2005	$0-13,478	$13,478-25,847	$25,847-44,451	$44,451-79,562	$79,562-117,001	$117,001-162,351	$162,351-383,407	$383,407-581,019	$581,019-1,589,608	$1,589,608 or more	$87 million or more*
Taxpayers	28 million	30 million	29 million	29 million	14 million	7.2 million	5.8 million	723,000	578,000	145,000	400
Share of taxpayers	19.5%	20.6%	19.9%	19.9%	10.0%	5.0%	4.0%	0.5%	0.4%	0.1%	0.0003%
Share of nation's reported income in 2001	2.5%	6.4%	11.7%	20.1%	15.8%	11.2%	15.0%	3.8%	5.9%	8.0%	1.1%
Share of federal taxes that would have been paid in 2001 without cuts	0.4%	2.6%	8.6%	17.9%	16.0%	12.3%	17.5%	4.8%	7.9%	12.0%	Data not available
Share of federal taxes to be paid in 2015 with cuts	0.5%	2.7%	7.9%	17.9%	16.6%	13.0%	18.5%	4.6%	7.4%	10.8%	Data not available

The groups that see their share of federal taxes decline by 2015 are those in the top 1 percent and those in the middle.

Share of tax cut over 15 years	0.3%	5.3%	9.5%	16.4%	15.5%	9.8%	12.5%	5.4%	10.1%	15.2%	Data not available
Average yearly tax savings	$23	$342	$618	$1,063	$2,202	$2,101	$4,051	$14,107	$32,767	$195,762	$8.3 million

	Less than $30,000	$30,000-50,000	$50,000-75,000	$75,000-100,000	$100,000-200,000	$200,000-500,000	$500,000-1,000,000	$1 million-10 million	More than $10 million	Top 400 taxpayers
Percentage of income paid in income, Social Security and Medicare taxes in 2004	6.7%	14.5%	17.4%	18.9%	20.6%	21.6%	21.6%	22.3%	20.1%	17.5%

Taxpayers making $100,000 to $200,000 now pay a greater share of their income in income and payroll taxes than those making more than $10 million.

THE STEALTH TAX

A growing number of people making more than $75,000 will have much of their cuts taken back by the alternative minimum tax.

		Less than $30,000	$30,000-50,000	$50,000-75,000	$75,000-100,000	$100,000-200,000	$200,000-500,000	$500,000-1,000,000	More than $1 million	All taxpayers
	Percent paying A.M.T. in 2004	Under 1%	Under 1%	Under 1%	1%	6%	50%	39%	27%	2%
	In 2010	Under 1%	3%	16%	52%	80%	94%	63%	36%	22%
	How much of group's cuts taken back in 2010	Under 1%	Under 1%	3%	23%	47%	70%	23%	9%	29%
	Extra tax paid by those affected	$1,429	$773	$942	$1,560	$2,542	$9,177	$15,727	$64,025	$3,579

* For 2000.

The New York Times

Source: For more information about the data, please refer to this sources page: http://www.nytimes.com/2005/06/05/national/class/05class_graphic_sources.html

The Bush administration tax cuts stand to widen the gap between the hyper-rich and the rest of America. The merely rich, making hundreds of thousands of dollars a year, will shoulder a disproportionate share of the tax burden.

President Bush said during the third election debate last October that most of the tax cuts went to low- and middle-income Americans. In fact, most—53 percent—will go to people with incomes in the top 10 percent over the first 15 years of the cuts, which began in 2001 and would have to be reauthorized in 2010. And more than 15 percent will go just to the top 0.1 percent, those 145,000 taxpayers.

The Times set out to create a financial portrait of the very richest Americans, how their incomes have changed over the decades and how the tax cuts will affect them. It is no secret that the gap between the rich and the poor has grown, but the extent to which the richest are leaving everyone else behind is not widely known.

The Treasury Department uses a computer model to examine the effects of tax cuts on various income groups but does not look in detail fine enough to differentiate among those within the top 1 percent. To determine those differences, The Times relied on a computer model based on the Treasury Department's model that is owned by the nonpartisan Tax Policy Center. Experts at organizations representing a range of views, including the Heritage Foundation, the Cato Institute and Citizens for Tax Justice, reviewed the projections and said they were reasonable, and the Treasury Department said through a spokesman that the model was reliable.

The analysis also found the following:

- Under the Bush tax cuts, the 400 taxpayers with the highest incomes—a minimum of $87 million in 2000, the last year for which the government will release such data—now pay income, Medicare and Social Security taxes amounting to virtually the same percentage of their incomes as people making $50,000 to $75,000.

- Those earning more than $10 million a year now pay a lesser share of their income in these taxes than those making $100,000 to $200,000.

- The alternative minimum tax, created 36 years ago to make sure the very richest paid taxes, takes back a growing share of the tax cuts over time from the majority of families earning $75,000 to $1 million—thousands and even tens of thousands of dollars annually. Far fewer of the very wealthiest will be affected by this tax.

The analysis examined only income reported on tax returns. The Treasury Department says that the very wealthiest find ways, legal and illegal, to shelter a lot of income from taxes. So the gap between the very richest and everyone else is almost certainly much larger.

The hyper-rich have emerged in the last three decades as the biggest winners in a remarkable transformation of the American economy characterized by, among other things, the creation of a more global marketplace, new technology and investment spurred partly by tax cuts. The stock market soared; so did pay in the highest ranks of business.

One way to understand the growing gap is to compare earnings increases over time by the vast majority of taxpayers—say, everyone in the lower 90 percent—with those at the top, say, in the uppermost 0.01 percent (now about 14,000 households, each with $5.5 million or more in income last year).

From 1950 to 1970, for example, for every additional dollar earned by the bottom 90 percent, those in the top 0.01 percent earned an additional $162, according to The Times analysis. From 1990 to 2002, for every extra dollar earned by those in the bottom 90 percent, each taxpayer at the top brought in an extra $18,000.

President Ronald Reagan signed tax bills that benefited the wealthiest Americans and also gave tax breaks to the working poor. President Bill Clinton raised income taxes for the wealthiest, cut taxes on investment gains, and expanded breaks for the working poor. Mr. Bush eliminated income taxes for families making under $40,000, but his tax cuts have also benefited the wealthiest Americans far more than his predecessors' did.

The Bush administration says that the tax cuts have actually made the income tax system more progressive, shifting the burden slightly more to those with higher incomes. Still, an Internal Revenue Service study found that the only taxpayers whose share of taxes declined in 2001 and 2002 were those in the top 0.1 percent.

But a Treasury spokesman, Taylor Griffin, said the income tax system is more progressive if the measurement is the share borne by the top 40 percent of Americans rather than the top 0.1 percent.

The Times analysis also shows that over the next decade, the tax cuts Mr. Bush wants to extend indefinitely would shift the burden further from the richest Americans. With incomes of more than $1 million or so, they would get the biggest share of the breaks, in total amounts and in the drop in their share of federal taxes paid.

One reason the merely rich will fare much less well than the very richest is the alternative minimum tax. This tax, the successor to one enacted in 1969 to make sure the wealthiest Americans could not use legal loopholes to live tax-free, has never been adjusted for inflation.

As a result, it stings Americans whose incomes have crept above $75,000.

The Times analysis shows that by 2010 the tax will affect more than four-fifths of the people making $100,000 to $500,000 and will take away from them nearly one-half to more than two-thirds of the recent tax cuts. For example, the group making $200,000 to $500,000 a year will lose 70 percent of their tax cut to the alternative minimum tax in 2010, an average of $9,177 for those affected.

But because of the way it is devised, the tax affects far fewer of the very richest: about a third of the taxpayers reporting more than $1 million in income. One big reason is that dividends and investment gains, which go mostly to the richest, are not subject to the tax.

Another reason that the wealthiest will fare much better is that the tax cuts over the past decade have sharply lowered rates on income from investments.

While most economists recognize that the richest are pulling away, they disagree on what this means. Those who contend that the extraordinary accumulation of wealth is a good thing say that while the rich are indeed getting richer, so are most people who work hard and save. They say that the tax cuts encourage the investment and the innovation that will make everyone better off.

"In this income data I see a snapshot of a very innovative society," said Tim Kane, an economist at the Heritage Foundation. "Lower taxes and lower marginal tax rates are leading to more growth. There's an explosion of wealth. We are so wealthy in a world that is profoundly poor."

But some of the wealthiest Americans, including Warren E. Buffett, George Soros and Ted Turner, have warned that such a concentration of wealth can turn a meritocracy into an aristocracy and ultimately stifle economic growth by putting too much of the nation's capital in the hands of inheritors rather than strivers and innovators. Speaking of the increasing concentration of incomes, Alan Greenspan, the Federal Reserve chairman, warned in Congressional testimony a year ago: "For the democratic society, that is not a very desirable thing to allow it to happen."

Others say most Americans have no problem with this trend. The central question is mobility, said Bruce R. Bartlett, an advocate of lower taxes who served in the Reagan and George H. W. Bush administrations. "As long as people think they have a chance of getting to the top, they just don't care how rich the rich are."

But in fact, economic mobility—moving from one income group to another over a lifetime—has actually stopped rising in the United States, researchers say. Some recent studies suggest it has even declined over the last generation.

Selection 6.3

This story examines a ticking time bomb embedded in the tax code—the alternative minimum tax (AMT). Pulitzer Prize winner David Cay Johnston gives us a history of the AMT, pointing out how something that was well intentioned has become viewed as an ugly mess. When Johnston is going to tell us something that could be complicated, he starts off like this: "The tax affects taxpayers in three ways." He keeps his sentences short. Another rule to follow when dealing with complicated material: Put only one idea to a sentence. And any time you can, find people who can help you tell the story, as Johnston did here with the Klaassens, a family with 13 children.

Funny, They Don't Look Like Fat Cats

By DAVID CAY JOHNSTON

Three decades ago, Congress, embarrassed by the disclosure that 155 wealthy Americans had paid no Federal income taxes, enacted legislation aimed at preventing the very rich from shielding their wealth in tax shelters.

Today, that legislation, creating the alternative minimum tax, is instead snaring a rapidly growing number of middle-class taxpayers, forcing them to pay additional tax or to lose some of their tax breaks.

Of the more than two million taxpayers who will be subject this year to the alternative minimum tax, or A.M.T., about half have incomes of $30,000 to $100,000. Some are single parents with jobs; some are people making as little as $527 a week. Over all, the number of people affected by the tax is expected to grow 26 percent a year for the next decade.

But many of the wealthy will not be among them. Even with the A.M.T., the number of taxpayers making more than $200,000 who pay no taxes has risen to more than 2,000 each year.

How a 1969 law aimed at the tax-shy rich became a growing burden on moderate earners illustrates how tax policy in Washington can be a hall of mirrors.

While some Republican Congressmen favor eliminating the tax, other lawmakers say such a move would be an expensive tax break for the wealthy—or at least would be perceived that way, and thus would be politically unpalatable. And any overhaul of the system would need to compensate for the $6.6 billion that individuals now pay under the A.M.T. This year, such payments will account for almost 1 percent of all individual income tax revenue.

"This is a classic case of both Congress and the Administration agreeing that the tax doesn't make much sense, but not being able to

Published: January 10, 1999.

agree on doing anything about it," said C. Eugene Steuerle, an economist with the Urban Institute, a nonprofit research organization in
Washington.

Mr. Steuerle was a Treasury Department tax official in 1986,
when an overhaul of the tax code set the stage for drawing the middle
class into the A.M.T.

In eliminating most tax shelters for the wealthy, Congress
decided to treat exemptions for children and deductions for medical
expenses just like special credits for investors in oil wells, if they cut
too deeply into a household's taxable income.

Congress decided that once these "tax preferences" exceeded
certain amounts—$40,000 for a married couple, for example—people
would be moved out of the regular income tax and into the alternative minimum tax. At the time, the threshold was high enough to
affect virtually no one but the rich. But it has since been raised only
once—by 12.5 percent, to $45,000 for a married couple—while the
cost of living has risen 43 percent. And so the limits have sneaked up
on growing numbers of taxpayers of more modest means.

"Everyone knew back then that it had problems that had to be
fixed," Mr. Steuerle recalled. "They just said, 'next year.'"

But "next year" has never come—and it is unlikely to arrive in
1999, either. While tax policy experts have known for years that the
middle class would be drawn into the A.M.T., few taxpayers have been
clamoring for change.

Among those few, however, are David and Margaret Klaassen
of Marquette, Kan. Mr. Klaassen, a lawyer who lives in and works
out of a farmhouse, made $89,751.07 in 1997 and paid $5,989 in Federal income taxes. Four weeks ago, the Internal Revenue Service sent
the Klaassens a notice demanding $3,761 more under the alternative
minimum tax, including a penalty because the I.R.S. said the Klaassens
knew they owed the A.M.T.

Mr. Klaassen acknowledges that he knew the I.R.S. would assert
that he was subject to the A.M.T., but he says the law was not meant
to apply to his family. "I've never invested in a tax shelter," he said.
"I don't even have municipal bonds."

The Klaassens do, however, have 13 children and their attendant
medical expenses—including the costs of caring for their second son,
Aaron, 17, who has battled leukemia for years. It was those exemptions and deductions that subjected them to the A.M.T.

"What kind of policy taxes you for spending money to save
your child's life?" Mr. Klaassen asked.

The tax affects taxpayers in three ways. Some, like the Klaassens,
pay the tax at either a 26 percent or a 28 percent rate because they have
more than $45,000 in exemptions and deductions. Others do not pay
the A.M.T. itself, but they cannot take the full tax breaks they would
have received under the regular income tax system without running up

against limits set by the A.M.T. The A.M.T. can also convert tax-exempt income from certain bonds and from exercising incentive stock options into taxable income.

It may be useful to think of the alternative minimum tax as a parallel universe to the regular income tax system, similar in some ways but more complex and with its own classifications of deductions, its own rates and its own paperwork. The idea was that taxpayers who had escaped the regular tax universe by piling on credits and deductions would enter this new universe to pay their fair share. (Likewise, there is a corporate A.M.T. that parallels the corporate income tax.)

At first, the burden of the A.M.T. fell mainly on the shoulders of business owners and investors, said Robert S. McIntyre, executive director of Citizens for Tax Justice, a nonprofit group in Washington that says the tax system favors the rich. Based on I.R.S. data, Mr. McIntyre said he found that 37 percent of A.M.T. revenue in 1990 was a result of business owners using losses from previous years to reduce their regular income taxes; an additional 18 percent was because of big deductions for state and local taxes.

But that has begun to shift, largely as a result of the 1986 changes, which eliminated most tax shelters and lowered tax rates.

When President Reagan and Congress were overhauling the tax code, they could not make the projected revenues under the new rules equal those under the old system. Huge, and growing, budget deficits made it politically essential for the official estimates to show that after tax reform, the same amount of money would flow to Washington.

One solution, said Mr. Steuerle, the former Treasury official, was to count personal and dependent exemptions and some medical expenses as preferences to be reduced or ignored under the A.M.T, just as special credits for petroleum investments and other tax shelters are.

Mortgage interest and charitable gifts were not counted as preferences, according to tax policy experts who worked on the legislation, because they generated more money than was needed.

But the A.M.T. has not stayed "revenue neutral," in Washington parlance.

The regular income tax was indexed for inflation in 1984, so that taxpayers would not get pushed into higher tax brackets simply because their income kept pace with the cost of living.

The A.M.T. limits, however, have not been indexed. The total allowable exemptions before the tax kicks in have been fixed since 1993 at $45,000 for a married couple filing jointly. For unmarried people, the total amount is now $33,750, and for married people filing separately, it is $22,500.

If the limit had been indexed since 1986, when the A.M.T. was overhauled, it would be about $57,000 for married couples filing jointly—and most middle-income households would still be exempt.

Mr. Steuerle said he warned at the time that including "normal, routine deductions and exemptions that everyone takes" in the list of preferences would eventually turn the A.M.T. into a tax on the middle class.

That appears to be exactly what has happened.

For example, a married person who makes just $527 a week and files her tax return separately can be subject to the tax, said David S. Hulse, an assistant professor of accounting at the University of Kentucky.

And the Taxpayer Relief Act of 1997, which allows a $500-a-child tax credit as well as education credits, may make even more middle-class families subject to the A.M.T. by reducing the value of those credits.

Two Treasury Department economists recently calculated that largely because of the new credits, the number of households making $30,000 to $50,000 who must pay the alternative minimum tax will more than triple in the coming decade. The economists, Robert Rebelein and Jerry Tempalski, also calculated that for households making $15,000 to $30,000 annually, A.M.T. payments will grow 25-fold, to $1.2 billion, by 2008.

Last year, many more people would have been subject to the A.M.T. if Congress had not made a last-minute fix pushed by Representative Richard E. Neal, Democrat of Massachusetts, that— for 1998 only—exempted the new child and education credits. The move came after I.R.S. officials told Congress that the credits added enormous complexity to calculating tax liability. Figuring out how much the A.M.T. would reduce the credits was beyond the capacity of most taxpayers and even many paid tax preparers, the I.R.S. officials said.

Even if Congress makes a permanent fix to the problems created by the child and education credits, it will put only a minor drag on the spread of the A.M.T. as long as the tax is not indexed for inflation. The two Treasury economists calculated that revenues from the tax would climb to $25 billion in 2008 without a fix, or to $21.9 billion with one.

In 1999, if there is no exemption for the credits, a single parent who does not itemize deductions but who makes $50,000 and takes a credit for the costs of caring for two children while he works, will be subject to the A.M.T, estimated Jeffrey Pretsfelder, an editor at RIA Group, a publisher of tax information for professionals.

If the tax laws are not changed, 8.8 million taxpayers will have to pay the A.M.T. a decade from now, the Congressional Joint Committee on Taxation estimated last month. Add in the taxpayers who will not receive the full value of their deductions because they run up against the limits set by the A.M.T., and the total grows to 11.6 million taxpayers—92 percent of whom have incomes of less than $200,000, the two Treasury economists estimated.

While many lawmakers and Treasury officials have criticized the impact of the tax on middle-class taxpayers, there are few signs of change, as Republicans and the Administration talk past each other.

Representative Bill Archer, the Texas Republican who as the chairman of the House Ways and Means Committee is the chief tax writer, said the A.M.T. should be eliminated in the next budget.

"Unfortunately, the A.M.T. tax can penalize large families, which is part of the reason why Republicans for years have tried to eliminate it or at least reduce it," Mr. Archer said. "Unfortunately, President Clinton blocked our efforts each time."

Lawrence H. Summers, the Deputy Treasury Secretary, said the Administration was "very concerned that the A.M.T. has a growing impact on middle-class families, including by diluting the child credit, education credits and other crucial tax benefits, and we hope to address this issue in the President's budget.

"Subject to budget constraints, we look forward to working with Congress on this important issue," he continued.

That revenue concerns have thwarted exempting the middle class runs counter to the reason Congress initially imposed the tax.

"You need an A.M.T. because people who make a lot of money should pay some income taxes," said Mr. McIntyre, of Citizens for Tax Justice. "If you believe, like Mr. Archer and a lot of Republicans do, that the more you make the less in taxes you should pay, then of course you are against the A.M.T. But somehow I don't think most people see it that way."

The Klaassens, meanwhile, are challenging the A.M.T. in Federal Court. The United States Court of Appeals for the 10th Circuit is scheduled to hear arguments in March on their claim that the tax infringes their religious freedom. The Klaassens, who are Presbyterians, say they believe children "are a blessing from God, and so we do not practice birth control," Mr. Klaassen said.

When Mr. Klaassen wrote to an I.R.S. official complaining that a $1,085 bill for the A.M.T. for 1994 resulted from the size of his family, he got back a curt letter saying that his "analysis of the alternative minimum tax's effect on large families was interesting but inappropriate" and advising him that it was medical deductions, not family size, that subjected him to the A.M.T.

Under the regular tax system, medical expenses above 7.5 percent of adjusted gross income—the last line on the front page of Form 1040—are deductible. Under the A.M.T., the threshold is raised to 10 percent.

Still doubting the I.R.S.'s math, Mr. Klaassen decided to test what would have happened had he filed the same tax return, changing only the number of children he claimed as dependents. He found that if he had seven or fewer children, the A.M.T. would not have applied in 1994.

But the eighth child set off the A.M.T., at a cost of $223. Having nine children raised the bill to $717. And 10 children, the number he had in 1994, increased that sum to $1,085—the amount the I.R.S. said was due.

"We love this country and we believe in paying taxes," Mr. Klaassen said. "But we cannot believe that Congress ever intended to apply this tax to our family solely because of how many children we choose to have. And I have shown that we are subject to the A.M.T. solely because we have chosen not to limit the size of our family."

The I.R.S., in papers opposing the Klaassens, noted that tax deductions are not a right but a matter of "legislative grace."

Mr. Klaassen turned to the Federal courts after losing in Tax Court. The opinion by Tax Court Judge Robert N. Armen Jr. was summed up this way by Tax Notes, a magazine that critiques tax policy: "Congress intended the alternative minimum tax to affect large families when it made personal exemptions a preference item."

Several tax experts said that Mr. Klaassen had little chance of success in the courts because the statute treating children as tax preferences was clear. They also said that nothing in the A.M.T. laws was specifically aimed at his religious beliefs.

Meanwhile, for people who make $200,000 or more, the A.M.T. will be less of a burden this year because of the Taxpayer Relief Act of 1997, which included a provision lowering the maximum tax rate on capital gains for both the regular tax and the A.M.T. to 20 percent.

Mr. Rebelein and Mr. Tempalski, the Treasury Department economists, calculated recently that people making more than $200,000 would pay a total of 4 percent less in A.M.T. for 1998 because of the 1997 law. By 2008, their savings will be 9 percent, largely as a result of lower capital gains rates and changed accounting rules for business owners.

"This law was passed to catch people who use tax shelters to avoid their obligations," Mr. Klaassen said. "But instead of catching them it hits people like me. This is just nuts."

Selection 6.4

Everyone has heard stories of how a particular city got a company to relocate jobs in exchange for tax breaks. Sometimes companies threaten to leave town unless they get fat payouts and special incentives. Timothy Egan looks at this story from another angle—what happens when a company gets the tax breaks and then leaves town. This story has a voice that comes from the outraged quotes the writer has collected. Here's a sample: "'We ought to sue them,' said Timothy Keyser, a Putnam County lawyer. . . . 'They sold the county a bill of goods.'" In too many stories, quotes simply state facts or restate the writer's points. Instead, quotes should add life and humanity to a story—and certainly a story like this one, about anger and broken hearts, can't settle for dull quotes. When you type quotation marks, you're telling readers: Here comes something unique. Don't ever add a quote just because you happen to have one in your notebook or on tape.

Towns That Handed Out Tax Breaks Cry Foul When Jobs Leave Anyway

By TIMOTHY EGAN

People in this big-shouldered town, birthplace of the poet Carl Sandburg, say Maytag broke their hearts. After a decade of tax breaks and union concessions to keep the company in a place that has been making refrigerators for more than 50 years, Maytag closed its factory last month, terminating 1,600 jobs.

Maytag may be done with Galesburg, but Galesburg is not done with Maytag.

District Attorney Paul L. Mangieri wants to sue Maytag to recoup what he says were excess tax breaks in a broad package of incentives to keep the company here. Much of the money, he said, came from a purse that would have gone to schools in this economically fragile community.

"We gave Maytag these incentives, and they accepted them," said Mr. Mangieri, a Navy veteran who grew up in a small town not far from here in western Illinois. "We did it based on faith and trust. If we don't do anything now, it sends a message that we lack the resolve to treat the rich and privileged the same as everybody else."

Maytag says it honored its agreement and took just the breaks to which it was entitled.

There are echoes of Mr. Mangieri's argument in Putnam County, Fla., which gave $4.5 million in cash and tax breaks to attract a call center owned by Sykes Enterprises, only to have it pull up stakes this month after less than five years in Palatka.

"We ought to sue them," said Timothy Keyser, a Putnam County lawyer who opposed the tax breaks from the start. "They sold the county a bill of goods."

Galesburg and Putnam are losers in the increasingly cutthroat game of using tax breaks to keep or attract jobs. Across the country, communities are competing with one another to offer the most lucrative incentives to lure good payrolls, from the giant assembly jobs at Boeing to small centers for processing credit cards, despite some studies that question the effectiveness of such tactics.

Most communities that lose business afterward lick their wounds and walk away, as Putnam County plans to do. But in Galesburg, some people have decided to take a stand, and it has split

Published: October 20, 2004.

this community, showing the challenges of fighting back against a corporation.

After initially cheering their prosecutor for trying to regain some of the money used to keep Maytag, some people say they are afraid that they may scare off future employers. They question whether suing to reclaim tax breaks will hurt the community even more, adding that they have to pay companies to compete and that it is the cost of doing business in a vulnerable town.

"Maytag's leaving town has devastated our community," said Jeff Klinck, a car dealer and the former chairman of the economic development office here. "But I don't think any good comes from revenge. We want to move forward, not move back."

The final decision on whether to sue will be made by November, Mr. Mangieri said. Galesburg, site of a ferocious debate between Abraham Lincoln and Stephen Douglas in 1858, has a fighting spirit. Residents say the current civic gut check may determine whether the town becomes another casualty of the force that has devastated communities throughout much of Middle America.

Next door in Iowa, officials are keeping one eye on the fight while trying to determine whether they should try to recoup up to $25 million in public money given to business partnerships that have not lived up to their agreements to increase employment.

In New York, State Comptroller Alan G. Hevesi said in an audit this year that a program that gives millions of dollars in tax breaks to businesses that promise to create work ended up rewarding some businesses that lost jobs. Other state officials disputed those findings.

"We're all in the same boat: we're hungry for business and we need the tax and job base," said Nancy S. Harris, a Putnam County commissioner. "But in the future, I think we have to do better background checks and tie tax breaks to length of stay and number of jobs."

Executives at Maytag and Sykes said they had lived up to their agreements in accepting the tax breaks. In return for cash and reduced taxes, the companies created payrolls that more than made up for the inducements from local governments, they said.

"We did not in any way break an agreement," Lynne Dragomier, a spokeswoman for Maytag at its headquarters in Newton, Iowa, said. "We believe we have paid our fair share of taxes in Galesburg."

The legal question in Galesburg centers on whether Maytag received excess property-tax breaks. Under Mr. Mangieri's interpretation of the original deal, Maytag was entitled to $1 million in reduced property taxes. That amount grew to $2.1 million without protest from the county because the company was staying, county officials said.

Though the dollar amount is relatively small, the company and Galesburg residents cite a larger principle.

Over the years, Maytag benefited from state and local tax abatements, as well as money raised when people agreed to increase the

sales tax. According to Mr. Mangieri, Galesburg raised $2.8 million
in sales tax revenue to retrofit the refrigerator plant here, the State of
Illinois came through with $5.8 million in aid, and Maytag was given
10 years of property tax abatements. Those breaks ended in 1999 and
were not to exceed $1 million, Mr. Mangieri said.

Ms. Dragomier said Maytag, which is moving most of the work
from Galesburg to a new plant in Mexico, had always been honest in
its dealings with Galesburg, population 33,000.

"It's very difficult to close a plant like this, and we understand
the pain it causes," she said.

The company has 11 manufacturing plants in the United States,
Ms. Dragomier said, and prides itself on its American workforce. But,
she said, it is under "competitive pressure" to make some refrigerators
at cheaper locations.

At a Labor Day rally here, union leaders decried tax breaks for
companies that do not agree to keep their jobs in the United States.
They backed a proposal for "patriot corporations" that some lawmakers are circulating. Under that program, a company would receive a
tax advantage if it kept production and a high percentage of sales in
the United States.

"Maytag betrayed us; everybody knows that," said Dave Bevard,
a leader of the International Association of Machinists and Aerospace
Workers local here. "What our district attorney wants to do is not a
vindictive act. It's an issue of fairness."

In Florida, Putnam County spent more money to lure Sykes,
which operates call centers that provide customer service for other
companies, than on any other economic development project, county
officials said. In addition to the cash, Sykes was given a five-year break
from local property taxes. The company opened its center in 2000.

In barely four years, the payroll more than made up for the public cash, said Andrea Burnett, a spokeswoman for the company, which
is based in Tampa.

"Yes, they gave us $4.5 million, but in return they got a $120
million payroll," Ms. Burnett said. "That's a good return on their
investment."

The company is closing some of its American call centers while
adding jobs to cheaper overseas centers, company executives have said.

Smaller businesses say there is also a fundamental issue of fairness. Why not give a tax break to the reliable little company that holds
a piece of Main Street real estate and never threatens to leave town?

"We let the other taxpayers down if we don't go after Maytag,"
said Robin Davis, the county treasurer here in Galesburg, who favors
a lawsuit to recover taxes from Maytag. "My sense is if people don't
want to work here and pay taxes, we don't want them."

There are six taxing entities that gave incentives to Maytag,
and several have decided not to pursue the company, arguing that it

sends the wrong message at a time the town is desperate to attract new jobs.

"When I first heard Paul Mangieri talk about suing Maytag, I cheered," Mr. Klinck, the car dealer, said. "But on further reflection, I thought this would negate our message."

Galesburg never tied its tax breaks and cash grants to a long-term stability, but the State of Illinois has since written certain requirements into its laws on enterprise zones.

The city has passed a bond issue to build a logistical center that it hopes will attract railroad jobs.

In Putnam County, Mr. Keyser was so incensed at Sykes's receiving cash and tax breaks that he sent a mock bill to county officials asking for a tax break of $25,000 for the one new employee he hired at his law firm.

"It's universal blackmail out there," Mr. Keyser said, "with corporations all playing the same game."

A Conversation with . . . David Cay Johnston

AUTHOR, LECTURER AND COLUMNIST

© The New York Times

David Cay Johnston was the principal tax reporter for The New York Times for 13 years. He left the paper in 2008 but continues to contribute as a freelancer, and now works as an independent author, lecturer and columnist. Johnston is the author of three books, including "Free Lunch: How the Wealthiest Americans Enrich Themselves at Government Expense and Stick You with the Bill." Johnston received the 2001 Pulitzer Prize for Beat Reporting for exposing loopholes and inequities in the U.S. tax code. He was a finalist twice, in 2003 and 2000.

Johnston previously worked as an investigative reporter at The Philadelphia Inquirer from 1988 to 1995, and before that the Los Angeles Times, Detroit Free Press and San Jose Mercury News. Johnston also is a Distinguished Visiting Lecturer at Syracuse University College of Law and recently was elected to the board of Investigative Reporters and Editors. The following is an edited transcript of a telephone interview.

What was your beat at The New York Times?
I covered taxes. The idea was to do them a different way. Historically, taxes were covered as follows: Here's what the politicians say, here is a bit of advice on how to save a few dollars on your tax return and here is the occasional

scandal which is presented by the government. My plan was to ignore all this and examine how the system works after the laws are passed.

Why wasn't the coverage of taxes better?

The assumption has always been that taxes are boring. When I got hired at The Times, a whole bunch of people got a hold of me and they said, "God, they should have hired you years ago." They would then ask, "What are you going to do?" I would then tell them, and you could hear the life go out of them. I would say, "No, no, you don't understand. This is a great opportunity. It is a badly covered subject."

Another problem is almost all journalism is what I call "he said" journalism. You are not questioning fundamentally what is going on, and everybody accepts that. Very little journalism is about independently saying what is going on here. And taxes involve a whole host of concepts that are not intuitive and difficult to understand. I understand them now, but I didn't understand them in the beginning.

So what was your plan when you joined The Times?

The idea was to bring to the subject of taxes the techniques of investigative reporting and do a running investigation. Nobody was doing this at the time. I just started writing stories about how the system was working. It was all enterprise—a lot of it was derived from these massive statistical reports the IRS puts out. We wanted to look at "how does the system actually work after the laws are passed"—ignore what the politicians say. All sorts of people told me, "You can't do that; it is impossible to do."

As I got deeper into it, I began to realize that all the rhetoric about the rich being taxed too much was nonsense. The system was actually a massive subsidy system for the people at the top, and numerous stories I wrote at The Times showed that the tax system was one of the key factors in the growing inequality of income and wealth. When I started finding this stuff in the data and I would call various experts because it was not what I had expected to find and they would say, "Yeah, that's correct," I would say, "Wait a minute, that is not what the whole country's political rhetoric is built around." So I quickly learned there was the massive disconnect between the popular cultural belief and the reality.

How did you go about finding stories?

Any large government bureaucracy produces an enormous amount of paperwork. I mined that paperwork. There are these statistical reports. There are things called revenue rulings. There are private letter rulings. The first two years, I was learning this stuff. My first tax shelter exposé? It reads like mud. That's because I was just learning the stuff. But I began making some headway, and it was noticed by tax lawyers.

I was able to get a lot of what I used from the IRS, court filings and the Securities and Exchange Commission. For example, for the stories I did about inequality in income, the IRS never issued a report saying incomes are growing unequal. I had to sit down with these statistical tables and analyze the data. You had to first figure out how to do it, what is fair and what is the relationship of this to that. I created thousands of spreadsheets over the years.

If someone wanted to follow in your footsteps, could they do it?
Yes. First learn the basic principles of property, law, economics and statistics. And then ignore the official version of events. What seems interesting? You need to develop your own judgment. The biggest problem I have always had with news is how much of it is the official version of events. It's: "Here's what the president said. Here is what the president's official critics said." I am in the unofficial criticism business.

Do you have a formal training in business law or taxes?
I dropped out of high school. I got my diploma from an adult high school. I went to seven different colleges. I had six years of college credit, but I do not have a degree because I skipped the undergraduate general requirements. I was bored. I took almost all upper-division and graduate courses.

Should students get a formal education before tackling life as a business reporter?
Oh, yeah, but I wouldn't get it in journalism. I would get it in business and statistics. What I tell students is get a minor in journalism. Go study statistics, history and chemistry—things that will give you a broad, deep base. Unfortunately, the whole idea of liberal arts education has been abandoned. People should have a broad understanding of the world. But students are told they don't need "frills" like music and art. Then we wonder why people don't see obvious things in their society around them. Well, they haven't been exposed to them. I have found students at top colleges who never read or hardly read a novel in high school. They were just shown movies or had to read short stories. My God, how are you supposed to learn how to think in a coordinated sort of narrative fashion?

How do you make a subject like taxes interesting?
Anything can be boring. I read stories all the time that are boring. To write about taxes I had to understand the fundamental theory. The problem is most journalists really don't deeply know what they are writing about.

You have to find the story. I knew the alternative minimum tax was hitting more families every year, but it wasn't until I found a family with 13 children and got them to give me all their tax returns, and put them all into Turbo Tax, that I was able to show that only because of the number of children they had, they had to pay this extra tax. And the more children they had, the more taxes they paid. Well, I got that story. The headline was "Funny, they don't look like fat cats." I knew about that story for a long time—but there were no people I could use to help tell the story. There are lots of stories I know about—but I don't have the case or the people to tell the story and make it resonate with people. You keep looking and you go on to other things. You need a story. Human beings learn through stories.

MAKING**CONNECTIONS** 🤝

1

Discuss why governments collect taxes.

Name three types of taxes governments collect. Discuss whom you would contact to find out about tax collections at the city, county and state government level.

2

3

Companies often seek tax breaks for relocating to a new city or state. Discuss the problems this poses for local government when taxes are abated.

4

Government tax cuts have traditionally favored what income group? Offer examples of three stories you might write that are related to tax cuts.

5

Why does the government cut taxes? Discuss the relationship between tax cuts, government deficits and economic growth.

BUSINESS CONCEPTS REVIEW

Alternative minimum tax (AMT)	Federal tax enacted in 1969 aimed at high-income households that weren't paying taxes. Because Congress failed to index the AMT for inflation, many taxpayers who aren't earning high incomes are being hit with the AMT.
Effective tax rate	The actual rate paid after including all forms, deductions and other types of taxation.
Flat tax	A tax system with a constant, fixed tax rate. The U.S. income tax is currently a progressive system, meaning individuals who earn more pay more.
Income tax	Tax on earned income levied against both individuals and corporations.
Internal Revenue Service	U.S. government agency responsible for tax collection and enforcement.
Marginal tax rate	Extra taxes paid on an additional dollar of income.
Property tax	Tax the owner must pay on the value of real estate, including land, buildings and improvements.
Sales tax	Tax collected on consumption, usually at the point of purchase, such as in a retail store.
Supply-side economics	Popularized by economist Arthur Laffer, who argued that cutting taxes actually raises tax revenue and spurs high-income individuals to make capital investments.
Value-added tax	Consumption tax based on the valued added to a product at each stage of its manufacture or distribution.

CHAPTER 7

wall street

HOW MUCH MONEY A BUSINESS EARNS is a measure of its success. Some companies, like McDonald's and Microsoft, are so big that they earn billions. They dominate their markets. But don't get fooled by size; big numbers can also be deceiving. Maybe the company's growth is slowing—or even if it earned a boatload in the most recent quarter, maybe a one-time gain is boosting profits.

Starting with this chapter, we move from making sense of the economy to focusing on businesses and the people who run them. We will spend the final four chapters looking at businesses and how they are managed, raise money, work with shareholders on Wall Street and conduct mergers and takeovers. A major section in each chapter is devoted to annotating specific stories with comments, so you can learn how to use numbers when writing about company earnings, mergers, takeovers and stock sales.

If you're like the average number-phobic journalist, you're probably tempted to skip all this and move on. Well, before you do, remember this: Companies are in business to make money. If they don't make money, they don't survive. And if you don't understand how a company makes its money, how can you ever write intelligently about it? Rest assured that understanding Wall Street and how it works doesn't require a degree in accounting.

But before we get to Wall Street, first you need to understand a few simple terms, like the difference between revenue and earnings. Revenue is what a company produces by selling its products or services. Earnings are what's left over after the firm pays its employees, taxes and other expenses.

Think of financial statements as how businesses keep score; they are either on the way up or the way down. It is much like the hitter who bats 400 one season and then can't top 200 the following year, or the team that vaults from last place to first. Writing about company earnings can sometimes seem a lot like sports writing—it tells readers who is winning and who is losing. Earnings give us the size of the win or loss.

Then there's a place called Wall Street, home to some of the world's biggest financial markets. Wall Street is where companies raise money by borrowing or investing. Financial statements are a company's scorecard. Just about everybody pays attention to that scorecard before making decisions: Banks want to know about a company's profitability before they make a loan, to ensure they'll be paid back. Vendors want to know that a company is going to stay in business before they ship it merchandise. And Wall Street investors closely watch a company's earnings before deciding whether to buy its stock.

Earnings also drive actions on Wall Street. That's why there are two anno-tated Wall Street stories in this chapter. One looks at Apple's earnings, serving as a model for how to write a comparable story when a company releases its quarterly financial report. The second outlines credit card processor Visa Inc.'s initial public offering of shares. Both stories offer details about what elements are needed, how to draw comparisons between numbers and how to assemble your information on deadline.

Two other stories about General Electric offer insight into companies and how their reported earnings are monitored by Wall Street. If a company does poorly, its stock price suffers. There is enormous pressure on firms to meet earnings expectations, which is why they sometimes play games with their financial statements. Floyd Norris discusses what happens to firms that fudge their numbers.

The only way to master writing about companies and their finances is to jump in and do it. If you still have questions after reading this chapter, that's healthy and expected. Good journalists always have questions. You'll learn more with each story you read and each one you write.

 STORY**SCAN**

Selection 7.1

Writing an earnings story is a critical skill that every business reporter needs to master. Earnings stories don't need to be complicated. Quickly summarize what happened: Did earnings rise or fall? What was the reason—and what is included or excluded in the earnings figures you're using? (See Gretchen Morgenson's story later in this chapter for a discussion of different types of earnings.) It's important to draw comparisons to earlier periods, but remember that the most recent information always comes first. When making comparisons, calculate the percentage change between two figures. Never make readers work to figure out what you're saying; if you do, they may stop reading.

Apple Earnings Up, but Stock Falls on Outlook
By LAURA M. HOLSON

Apple beat Wall Street expectations with its earnings report Tuesday, but its shares fell more than 11 percent in after-hours trading as investors fretted over its prospects.

The story starts with the impact of the earnings release, but it could just as easily start with how much Apple earned in the first quarter.

Published: January 23, 2008.

Apple earned $1.58 billion, or $1.76 for each diluted share, in the first quarter of fiscal 2008, compared with $1 billion, or $1.14 a share, in the period a year earlier. Revenue was $9.6 billion, up from $7.1 billion.

But while Apple executives paraded those as record-setting figures, investors focused on projections for the next quarter, which were lower than what analysts had expected. Apple said it expected revenue of about $6.8 billion for the second quarter, or diluted earnings of 94 cents a share. Wall Street was forecasting profit of $1.09 a share on revenue of $7 billion.

Peter Oppenheimer, Apple's chief financial officer, gave two reasons for the lower forecast: a decline in software sales and the normal slowdown in business after Christmas.

When asked whether the lumbering economy could be a factor in Apple's earnings outlook, Mr. Oppenheimer said: "We'll leave the economic forecasting to others." Instead, he said, "our focus is on managing our business."

A slowdown in the economy is likely to hurt technology companies like Apple, which are dependent on consumers shelling out hundreds of dollars for their products. Just last week, Sprint Nextel announced that it was losing customers more quickly than expected, raising fears that spending on cellphones and other devices was slowing across the industry. Intel was also cautious about its financial outlook last week, in part because of concerns about a recession.

A. M. Sacconaghi Jr., a senior analyst at Bernstein Research, said one reason for concern about Apple was that domestic sales of the iPod were less robust than the company had expected.

Indeed, Mr. Oppenheimer of Apple said that sales of the iPod in the United States were little changed in the quarter, although iPod sales abroad were quite strong. (Over all, Apple saw a 5 percent increase in iPod sales in the first quarter compared with the period a year earlier.)

What is worrisome, Mr. Sacconaghi said, is whether the flat domestic iPod sales are a harbinger of things to come for other Apple products.

"That's the big question," he said. "If they feel it here, could they feel it in other products and other parts of the world?"

Apple shares fell $5.72, or 3.5 percent, to close at $155.64. They were down more than $17 in after-hours trading.

The iPhone remained a bright spot for the company. Apple sold 2.3 million in the quarter, according to Mr. Oppenheimer, and is on track to sell 10 million in 2008, as projected.

Apple shipped 2.3 million Macintosh computers, and revenue from Macs grew 47 percent from the year-ago quarter.

Mr. Sacconaghi said sales of Mac computers could start showing lower year-over-year growth. IPod sales could suffer, he said, because the company has been slow to update its cheaper iPod models, and holiday sales of MP3 players at the retailer Best Buy were down.

At the Macworld Expo last week, Steven P. Jobs, Apple's chief executive, made several announcements about new products or expanded services, including a new ultra-light computer called the MacBook Air that, while elegant, has limited memory. Mr. Jobs also announced a deal with all of Hollywood's major studios to allow digital movie rentals through the iTunes Store.

A good, conversational quote adds plain-English perspective on the numbers.

Stories often list what happened after the U.S. markets closed. This can also be the last paragraph of the story.

Investors are always interested in what the view is for the coming quarters and how it compares to past performance.

Possible slowdown ahead? This statement offers important details about future sales.

The markets are always looking to the future. So should you in your reporting.

Selection 7.2

When writing an earnings story, reporters often turn to Wall Street analysts for explanation and perspective. These individuals are trained in financial analysis and often do a great job of offering insights into a company's operations. But analysts are sometimes pushing an agenda, namely to promote the stocks they follow. Most investment banks make their money by selling securities (stocks and bonds), not by offering free research. In other cases, analysts suffer from a herd mentality, and their forecasts can be wrong. This story is offered as a cautionary tale. Talk to analysts, but don't immediately take what they say as gospel.

Why Analysts Keep Telling Investors to Buy

By JACK HEALY and MICHAEL M. GRYNBAUM

Even now, with the recession deepening and markets on edge, Wall Street analysts say it is a good time to buy.

Still.

At the top of the market, they urged investors to buy or hold onto stocks about 95 percent of the time. When stocks stumbled, they stayed optimistic. Even in November, when credit froze, the economy stalled and financial markets tumbled to their lowest levels in a decade, analysts as a group rarely said sell.

And last month, as the Dow and Standard & Poor's 500-stock index suffered their worst January ever, analysts put a sell rating on a mere 5.9 percent of stocks, according to Bloomberg data. Many companies have taken such a beating in the downturn, analysts argue, that their shares are bound to bounce back.

Maybe. But after so many bad calls on so many companies, why should investors believe them this time?

When Internet stocks imploded in 2000 and 2001, Wall Street analysts were widely scorned for fanning a frenzy that had inflated dot-com shares to unsustainable heights. But this time around, credit rating agencies, mortgage companies and Wall Street bankers have shouldered much of the blame for the Crash of 2008, and few have publicly questioned the analysts who urged investors to buy all the way down.

"Analysts completely missed the boat again with the subprime and credit crises," said Jacob Zamansky, a securities lawyer who represents investors. "They should've given some early warning signs to investors to bail out, or at least lighten up their portfolios. That warning never came."

Instead, many recommendations urged investors to hold on to their shares, or double down, as the bloodletting worsened.

On Oct. 8, as Congress and the Treasury Department frantically tried to calm the plummeting markets, a Citigroup analyst upgraded Bank of America to buy. Since then, Bank of America shares have fallen 77 percent.

That same month, Jeffrey Harte, a top-rated analyst at Sandler O'Neill and Partners, also lifted Bank of America to buy, from hold, and a month later, he gave Citigroup the same upgrade, according to Bloomberg data.

"Our ratings are based on 12-month price targets," Mr. Harte said. "Given the nature of economic cycles and, really, the focus of the new administration, I did expect and still do expect that the sector will improve considerably over the long term."

Published: February 8, 2009.

With every wrenching decline, stocks seemed to be only better and better bargains to the most bullish market watchers, and their
buy ratings seemed to reflect a hope that the market would soon turn a
corner.

One analyst at Davenport & Company called the aluminum
maker Alcoa a strong buy on March 24, Bloomberg data shows, when
its stock was a buoyant $35 a share and commodities prices were ris-
ing. He then affirmed the rating 13 times as metals prices plunged,
manufacturing dried up and Alcoa shares fell more than 70 percent.

"You can look back and say you were wrong as you go back and
try to do a post-mortem on things," said John Rogers, director
of research at the market research firm D. A. Davidson & Company.
"I don't think there's ever 100 percent accurate predictive expertise.
I wish there was."

In July, Mr. Rogers put a buy rating on Chicago Bridge and Iron,
an engineering and construction company whose stock fell sharply
during the first half of 2008. The rebound Mr. Rogers hoped for never
came: the stock plunged 65 percent more.

Mr. Rogers said he did not expect oil prices, then hovering near
$145 a barrel, to dwindle to $40. He did not expect Chicago Bridge
and Iron to hit snags on British natural gas developments. And he did
not expect such a broad economic downturn.

"If I had a rewind button and I could have done it, I would have
downgraded on the day it peaked," he said. "I was wrong on that, and
I think any analyst would have to acknowledge that."

In their defense, analysts point out that most regulators, economists, journalists and investors failed to foresee this financial catas-
trophe. And the worsening economy did prompt a cut in their buy
recommendations.

Investors, for their part, may have simply been following the lesson that had been beaten into them time and again during the bull years
of the last decade: buy cheap because the market will always go up.

"The market went up, up, up and up. You were rewarded for
saying, 'Don't worry, be happy,' " said William A. Fleckenstein, president of Fleckenstein Capital, a money management firm in Issaquah,
Wash. "Each time the market went down was a new opportunity to
buy the stock even cheaper."

When the storms of last year hit, few investors realized that this
pattern would suddenly vanish, with disastrous results. "They didn't
understand the world they were operating in every year was a false
reference point," Mr. Fleckenstein said.

Still, the optimistic adage holds: the greater the fall, the greater
the upside. Just give it some more time.

"Any analyst with a buy rating looks bad in a bear market," said
Anthony Polini, an analyst at Raymond James who rates banks. "This
group is dramatically oversold. It's down 75 percent. If you don't have

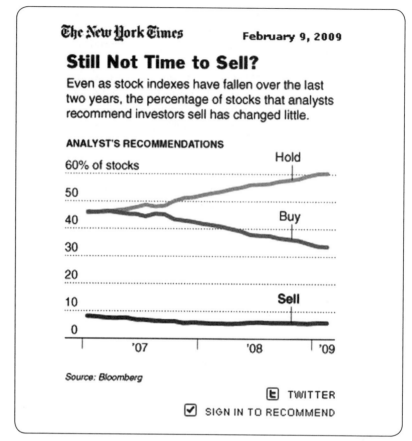

The New York Times

The New York Times   February 9, 2009

Still Not Time to Sell?

Even as stock indexes have fallen over the last two years, the percentage of stocks that analysts recommend investors sell has changed little.

ANALYST'S RECOMMENDATIONS

Source: Bloomberg

some strong buy ratings at this point, you're doing a disservice to your customers."

Mr. Polini, who has a strong buy rating on Bank of America, said it was a mistake to cut long-term outlooks for companies just because their stock price fell.

The actual investment recommendations coming from a sales desk can tell a different story from analysts' publicly released research. To gauge what clients are actually hearing from their investment managers, the investment-tracking firm First Coverage collects buy and sell recommendations from about 1,000 analysts that serve independent and midsize firms.

At the end of January, 34.5 percent of the recommendations seen by First Coverage were for a sell or short call. That was up from 24 percent in December 2007. At the height of the market crash, in October and November, the proportion of sell calls reached about 45 percent.

In all of 2008, sells never outweighed the buys.

Why, even amid cascading losses, could not the majority of analysts simply slash a company's rating to sell and tell investors to cut their losses?

"It doesn't matter if you're in a bear market, a bull market, a flat market, you're going to get 95 percent of the research coming out telling you to buy," said Randy Cass, chief executive of First Coverage. "It's just the way it's always been."

Although reforms after the dot-com bubble sought to make analysis more independent by separating it from investment banking, the broader culture on Wall Street still favors bulls.

Some attribute the surplus of optimism to a widespread expectation that stocks—like home prices—will always increase in value over time. After all, the S.&P. 500 has posted annual returns of more than 9 percent during the last 80 years. Analysts did not want to hit the sell button just as the markets bottomed out.

Selection 7.3

General Electric (GE) was a Wall Street darling during the 1990s. Under Chief Executive Officer Jack Welch, GE consistently delivered what Wall Street expected—higher earnings. Everyone marveled at how Welch and GE could do it quarter after quarter. The following two stories provide perspective on the pressure Wall Street investors put on companies to meet earnings targets. Each quarter, companies offer guidance as to what they will earn for the coming quarter. Analysts take this guidance and put together estimates. Investors use these estimates to make decisions on whether to buy that company's stock. Here's the rub: If a company fails to meet the expected earnings per share target and disappoints Wall Street, its stock price suffers. Some stocks get punished for missing targets by even a couple pennies per share.

G.E.'s Shortfall Calls Credibility Into Question

By NELSON D. SCHWARTZ and CLAUDIA H. DEUTSCH

For seven lean years, Wall Street has given General Electric and its chief executive, Jeffrey R. Immelt, the benefit of the doubt.

Even as shares of this quintessential blue chip languished, analysts and investors acknowledged the challenge of running a company that sells everything from jet engines to Hollywood blockbusters to light bulbs and patiently waited for Mr. Immelt's restructuring efforts to pay off.

Now, in the wake of a surprise earnings shortfall last week, Wall Street's patience has run out as the stock has plunged to its lowest level

Published: April 17, 2008.

in four years. While Mr. Immelt's job seems secure for now, stock analysts who have long supported both him and the company's sprawling
structure now say a rethinking is in order.

"There is no doubt that this is a historic event," said Steve Tusa,
an analyst with JPMorgan Chase. "The company has to convince
investors that something is going to change."

Once-isolated calls for at least a partial breakup of the conglomerate have become a chorus, with NBC Universal, appliances and GE
Money, the consumer finance unit, emerging as prime candidates for
a sale or spinoff. Unloading these divisions would return billions to
shareholders, advocates say, while allowing G.E. to focus on its booming infrastructure business, which sells big-iron items like locomotives, jet engines and power turbines.

"There's a point in time when you say this is a big old monster,
and parts could be better off on their own," said Scott Lawson, a portfolio manager at Westwood Capital Management, which owns G.E.
shares. "A breakup is looking more viable."

Shares of G.E. closed at $32.23 on Wednesday, down from about
$37 a week ago, and off sharply from where they were before Mr.
Immelt took over on Sept. 7, 2001.

For Mr. Immelt, the problem now is not just the earnings disappointment—the consensus estimate for the first quarter was 51 cents
and G.E. reported 44 cents—but a looming credibility gap. On March
13, he assured investors the company was on track to meet its profit
targets. And in December, he told analysts that G.E.'s goal of earnings
growth of at least 10 percent in 2008 was "in the bag."

To make matters worse, under Mr. Immelt and his predecessor,
John F. Welch Jr., G.E. was the kind of business that did not surprise
investors and delivered what it had promised, no matter how severe
the economic headwinds.

"I've been covering the company since 1996, and I've never seen
a miss this big," said Nicole Parent of Credit Suisse, who had rated
G.E. as her top pick but downgraded it to neutral after the earnings
report. "You have to ask what is the driving force behind the miss?
Is the company too big to manage?"

When the news broke shortly after 6 A.M. last Friday, Mr. Tusa
said: "I was on the train, and I almost fell out of my seat. It was a
shock—people thought it was a misprint."

The company blamed much of the shortfall on the widespread
credit crisis, especially the rapid deterioration in conditions over the
last two weeks of the quarter after Bear Stearns's near-collapse in
mid-March. Though G.E.'s huge finance business was its weakest per-
former, other segments like appliances and health care also fell short of
expectations.

Until nearly the last minute, G.E. thought it could pull the
quarter out. It knew health care was lagging behind, GE Money was
suffering, sales of appliances were weak, and advertising on local NBC

stations had slipped. But G.E. managers were confident that real estate sales and other financial transactions would make up for unexpected shortfalls elsewhere.

Then came the Bear Stearns implosion, and credit markets, already tight, locked up. "We had risks, but we had opportunities and plans that we thought would have enabled us to meet our guidance," said Keith S. Sherin, G.E.'s chief financial officer. "The risks came to be realized, but the opportunities didn't materialize."

Even defenders of Mr. Immelt admit that the juxtaposition of the rosy predictions and the ensuing shortfall have shaken the reputation of G.E., which is the sixth-largest American company by revenue as well as a barometer of the broader economy.

"What happened is he got caught and created a credibility issue," said Mr. Welch, who ran the company for 20 years before handing the reins over to Mr. Immelt in 2001. "He had all kinds of credibility a week ago, and he will get it back by delivering, but it will take some time."

The clock is ticking, though. "He can't have any more surprises if he wants to get his credibility back," said Noel M. Tichy, a professor at the University of Michigan Business School who once ran G.E.'s management school at Crotonville, N.Y. "This is Strike 1. If there's a Strike 3, it could take him out."

Until recently, Mr. Immelt had largely drawn accolades from Wall Street, both for his easygoing style and his effort to burnish G.E.'s image with investments in environmentally friendly technology like wind energy. Mr. Welch, on the other hand, was something of a lightning rod, earning the nickname Neutron Jack when he cut thousands of jobs in the 1980s, as well as the fear of any lieutenant who let him down.

This is Mr. Immelt's first major brush with investor anger, and indeed, in an interview, he said he understood Wall Street's ire and that he needs to restore credibility. "I'm not making excuses for the quarter," he said. "It wasn't what we expect from ourselves or what people expect from us. And we will see what we can do better on forecasting and communicating. But you don't rebuild credibility by talking about it. The execution of the balance of 2008 will be strong."

Mr. Immelt remains adamant that it would be foolish to break up G.E.

"I'm not going to panic over one bad quarter and do something that is not in the strategic best interest of the company," he said. "If I didn't think that a big portfolio move was right before the first quarter, I don't think it is now."

Analysts have talked for years about spinning off divisions like NBC Universal, questioning the entertainment giant's synergies with G.E.'s more traditional industrial and financial businesses. But institutional investors are now joining in the call for big structural changes.

Robert Spremulli, an analyst at TIAA-CREF, which owns G.E. shares, praised Mr. Immelt's move into green businesses, but he wants G.E. to be "more aggressive about getting rid of appliances and lighting, and getting out of GE Money." Big retailers like Wal-Mart have driven prices down so low that the margins on consumer goods are no longer attractive, he said.

Mr. Spremulli thinks G.E. should still have branded appliances in the market, but would be better off simply letting another company manufacture under the G.E. name. "G.E. should just get out of the consumer business," he said.

Even investors who like the portfolio as it is now are anticipating a shake-up within G.E.'s executive suite. "I believe there will be discussions of accountability behind closed doors at G.E., and I believe someone's head will roll," said Richard D. Steinberg, the president of Steinberg Global Asset Management, another institutional shareholder.

Although investors were reluctant to name names, many seemed particularly irked with management at G.E. Healthcare, the business run by Joseph M. Hogan. "If anyone loses their job, it should be in Healthcare," said Daniel J. Rosenblatt, an analyst at Marble Harbor Investment Counsel, which holds G.E. shares. In response, a spokesman for G.E. pointed out that the health care business has averaged double-digits earnings growth over the past five years.

Despite their very different styles, Mr. Welch was quick to praise his successor as "a hell of a manager."

And while Mr. Immelt has been apologizing for the shortfall, Mr. Welch was as quick as ever to defend the conglomerate he helped build, while firing back at critics. He noted that with financial giants like Lehman Brothers, Merrill Lynch and Citigroup writing off billions, G.E. is projected to earn over $20 billion in 2008.

Indeed, despite the turmoil in the financial sector, G.E is still likely to grow this year, Mr. Welch says. "This shows the strength of the G.E. model," he insisted. "This is a massive overreaction and it will pass."

Selection 7.4

If earnings are key to measuring a company's performance, what happens when a company cooks its books? Floyd Norris explains the behind-the-scenes maneuvering that goes on when a company is being investigated by the Securities and Exchange Commission (SEC). What Norris offers here is a context for the events surrounding the investigation into GE's reported earnings. He explains the significance of what has transpired and does it in such a way that you can't stop reading. Notice how Norris sets up the story, grabbing the reader with the statement that "GE was the shining star." We quickly learn that the company is in trouble with the SEC. How could this happen? After all, this is GE—the bluest of blue chips. We want to know what happened. Next comes a priceless anecdote told by a corporate manager who quit GE and became a priest. The anecdote allows Norris to narrate the story. Accounting can be complicated, but Norris never makes the subject feel that way.

High & Low Finance
Inside G.E., a Little Bit of Enron

By FLOYD NORRIS

A decade ago, General Electric was the shining star of American business. Its longtime chief executive, Jack Welch, was named manager of the century by Fortune Magazine, and its stock seemed always to go up.

It ran a bewildering array of businesses but somehow always managed to make the expected profits. That record was viewed as proof of superior management, and the battle to succeed Mr. Welch in 2001 was watched all over the business universe. When a winner emerged, the losers quickly were hired to run other major companies.

G.E. is different now. The stock has fallen and the aura has dissipated.

This week General Electric agreed to pay $50 million to settle a suit filed by the Securities and Exchange Commission that said the company fiddled with its books repeatedly early in this decade. In at least one case, that allowed it to preserve its reputation for making the numbers. Some of the details are eerily reminiscent of Enron.

As is customary in such settlements, G.E. neither admitted nor denied the charges. But it sounded contrite. "The errors at issue fell short of our standards, and we have implemented numerous remedial actions and internal control enhancements to prevent such errors from recurring," said a company statement.

Another view of G.E.'s accounting standards emerged a few years ago in a book written by a man who worked there for six years in the early 1980s, before concluding the corporate life was not for him and entering a seminary. James Martin may be the only Jesuit priest with a degree from the Wharton School of the University of Pennsylvania.

"The primary task of my first job was to issue very long, monthly statistical reports," he wrote in his book, "In Good Company: The Fast Track From the Corporate World to Poverty, Chastity and Obedience." "The first month," he recalled, "I informed one executive that our results were coming in low" because of losses in overseas operations.

"So what?" replied the executive. "Just reverse a few journal entries." Corporate headquarters, he explained, would come down hard on them if they missed the numbers.

Another boss told him he was "taking those accounting courses way too seriously."

The S.E.C. complaint makes it sound as if those days came back, assuming they ever left. It tells of corporate accountants discovering misstatements and secret side deals, and of more senior

Published: August 6, 2009.

executives telling them to sign off on the books anyway. It outlines four separate violations, two of which it says descended to the level of fraud.

It is notable how this investigation came to be. Post-Enron, the commission used its authority to look at G.E.'s books to figure out whether there were violations in the area of so-called hedge accounting, which determines whether companies can avoid reporting profits and losses from a variety of derivative securities.

The commission evidently found three violations, two in hedge accounting and the other in an Enronesque scheme to inflate profits with fake sales.

"It was like peeling an onion," said David P. Bergers, the director of the Boston office of the S.E.C., as one accounting issue led to another.

The fourth violation appears to have been reported by G.E. All have been fixed in restatements.

While it may seem odd to view the government as an underdog, it was. G.E. says it spent $200 million on outside lawyers and accountants in dealing with the investigation. By contrast, the S.E.C.'s entire annual enforcement budget, spread over thousands of inquiries and investigations, was less than $300 million when this investigation began in 2005.

You can be sure that G.E. spent a lot of time arguing that the amounts involved, only a few hundred million per violation, were not really material to a company its size.

There may be more to come. The S.E.C. said that its investigation of G.E. was over, but it did not say that about any of the accounting officials at the company, or any of the people at KPMG, G.E.'s longtime auditor.

KPMG's role is interesting. The complaint indicates that unnamed accounting officials at G.E. failed to provide important information to KPMG, but G.E. says that information was later given to the auditors.

The S.E.C. filing says that on one of the hedge accounting issues, the KPMG auditors consulted the accounting firm's national office. But when push came to shove, and the question was whether to approve accounting that the S.E.C. now says was clearly wrong, the local auditors signed off without telling the national office what was going on. Could it be that the local auditor feared the national office experts would have backbone, and force him to anger a very important client?

A KPMG spokesman declined to discuss any aspect of the case.

This all took place in January 2003, days before G.E. was to announce its annual profits for 2002, Jeff Immelt's first full year as chief executive. Had G.E. not fudged the accounting, it would have missed its profit forecast by $200 million. Not since 1994 had G.E. failed to make the numbers.

You may recall something similar happened at Arthur Andersen when it was auditing Enron. In that case, the local auditors chose to ignore the national office.

It is easy to have some sympathy for G.E. on the hedge accounting issues. The rules are devilishly complicated, and the accounting penalties for a small deviation can seem excessive. For good reason, the rules are being rewritten.

But that sympathy vanishes when considering the accounting alchemy that G.E. used to make its numbers at the end of 2003. In a move reminiscent of Enron's Nigerian barges deal, it "sold" some railroad locomotives to banks, with side letters and verbal promises to assure the banks they could not lose money. That enabled G.E. to book profits early and make the numbers.

The banks, facing S.E.C. actions for doing similar deals with Enron, asked G.E. to reassure them that KPMG knew about the side deals and concurred with the accounting. The banks had reason to be worried, given that G.E. executives had asked them not to refer to the side deals in documents seen by auditors.

At G.E., a spokeswoman, Anne Eisele, told me that it was wrong to think these violations were "indicative of some larger problem in G.E.'s overall culture, its finance function or compliance practices. G.E. is committed to the highest standards of accounting and good corporate governance. We are confident in our controls and culture, which have been made even stronger through the process that we've just completed."

It is interesting to compare the G.E. and S.E.C. versions of the locomotive deal. In a company filing in 2007, G.E. said "several individuals in our rail business and in our capital markets group engaged in intentional misconduct that misled those responsible for accounting oversight." It added that the accounting oversight team failed to adequately review the transactions.

The S.E.C.'s complaint makes it sound as if the matter was thoroughly aired inside G.E. in 2002, when it was first used, and again in 2003. The corporate audit staff challenged the accounting in 2002, but was overruled by a "senior accountant," the S.E.C. said.

G.E. added that the amounts involved were so small that they were not material, "less than 0.2 percent" of the company's total revenue or profits each year. The S.E.C. says the fudges caused quarterly profits of the G.E. Transportation Systems business to be overstated by as much as 40 percent.

All those numbers are accurate. Tricks to take profits in the wrong quarter, as in this case, are not likely to change annual earnings very much, particularly for the conglomerate. I doubt anyone at G.E. thought at the time it would have been immaterial if the company missed its profit forecasts.

I called Father Martin, now an editor at America magazine, a Jesuit publication, and asked him to read the S.E.C. complaint and call me back. He did.

"Little of this is surprising," he said.

"I was sometimes asked to squirrel away 'excess earnings' in fake accounts with made-up names, to be used when earnings were down in later months," he said. One such account was called "Plug."

Ms. Eisele, the G.E. spokeswoman, declined to comment on Father Martin's book.

Much has changed at G.E. since Father Martin was hired. The long paper spreadsheets that he used have been replaced by computers. Some of the financial instruments involved in G.E.'s hedge accounting violations had not been invented.

But some things, it appears, never change.

Selection 7.5

This is a more technical accounting story. It examines one aspect of writing about companies and the earnings they report. What is the quality of the earnings being reported? Net income is what companies earn after they have paid all their taxes and expenses. But another form of earnings is called operating earnings. Simply put, operating earnings measure what the company earned from its operations, but they exclude write-downs and restructuring charges incurred because of bad decisions. As writer Gretchen Morgenson explains, there is a growing gap between earnings from operations and the reported bottom line. She recommends paying close attention to what is included in the reported figures. Companies naturally try to make their numbers look as good as possible—even if that means shading the truth or sometimes ignoring it altogether.

What? They Never Heard of WorldCom?

By GRETCHEN MORGENSON

What a week.

Bernard J. Ebbers, founder of WorldCom, got to add felon to his already colorful curriculum vitae. Maurice R. Greenberg, dictator in chief at American International Group, the global insurance giant, was toppled after almost 40 years at his post. The Federal Reserve told Citigroup it could not make any major acquisitions until it cleaned up its compliance act. And General Motors laid a big, scary earnings egg.

Isn't it nice to know these incidents are anomalies and that most American companies are chugging along, reporting good solid earnings?

Published: March 20, 2005.

Sure would be. But contrary to popular belief, the quality of corporate earnings is on the slide again and, as a result, Richard Bernstein, chief United States strategist at Merrill Lynch, is advising investors to tread carefully.

"There is an impression that the quality of earnings has improved dramatically," he said. "That is true relative to the worst levels of post-bubble reporting, but relative to history, the absolute quality of earnings is quite poor."

And getting poorer.

Mr. Bernstein reaches this depressing conclusion by analyzing the difference between the earnings that Standard & Poor's 500 companies have reported under generally accepted accounting principles and operating earnings, the figures companies typically trumpet because they do not include write-offs and other unusual items.

The difference between the two figures, Mr. Bernstein says, is the G.A.A.P. gap.

And it is widening. In the most recent period—the fourth quarter of 2004—the gap was 13.7 percent. In other words, operating earnings were on average 13.7 percent higher than reported earnings. While that figure is well down from the 40 percent gap reached in 2002, it is much higher than the long-term, pre-bubble average of 6.7 percent.

The result: while stock valuations may not be so high as they were before the bubble burst, the quality of earnings appears to be worse.

Of course, none of this might matter if investors bought stocks based on G.A.A.P. earnings. But too many buy shares based on what companies report in their press releases and on their quarterly conference calls, which are often heavily skewed to earnings before the bad stuff.

"The fact is, stocks trade on press releases, on what the headline number is," Mr. Bernstein said. "And on the conference calls, companies talk about whatever numbers they want to talk about. Investors should still be very skeptical of the quality of earnings."

Mr. Bernstein said that he thought the recent downturn in earnings quality began, not surprisingly, a couple of quarters ago, when the profit surge started to subside. "If times are good, companies are not under pressure to keep their growth profile up," he said. "In tough times, when you get a cyclical company that has been coined by the Street as a growth company, it feels pressure to keep up that profile." That's when the earnings games usually begin.

By focusing on operating earnings, rather than on more stringent reported figures, companies try to steer investors away from mistakes such as asset write-downs or restructuring charges. But these factors reflect bad choices by managers—such as overpriced acquisitions—and should definitely not be excluded from investors' analyses.

"The difference between operating and reported earnings is an indication of how well executives are managing the balance sheet of their company," Mr. Bernstein said. This is often lost on investors who pay little heed to the balance sheet.

The five companies with the widest gap between reported earnings and operating income currently, according to the Merrill Lynch analysis, are: Eastman Kodak; Georgia Pacific, a paper products company; Rowan Companies, an oil drilling concern; Ford Motor; and Clorox.

Mr. Bernstein said the vast majority of companies with the biggest gaps between reported earnings and operating income are of lesser-quality, those whose common stocks are ranked B or below by S.&P.; among the five with the widest gap, all are rated B or below except Clorox, which is rated A. So investors can often limit their exposure to earnings shenanigans by sticking with high-quality issues.

But such a strategy won't offer full protection. As Mr. Bernstein noted, 22 percent of the companies with the largest gaps between reported and operating earnings were rated B+ or better by S.&P.

Mr. Bernstein said he thought the earnings games would be curtailed sharply if the Securities and Exchange Commission required that all company communications with investors reflected figures computed in accordance with generally accepted accounting principles.

Then there would be no confusion among investors about what a particular company really earned in a quarter.

"The reason you have G.A.A.P. is so investors have consistent clear information," Mr. Bernstein said. "The U.S. has always prided itself on having the most transparent financial markets.

"But over the past 5 to 10 years, the U.S. market has become more opaque, and foreign markets have become more transparent. That has huge implications for the economy as a whole and for the cost of capital."

STORY**SCAN**

Selection 7.6

One of the biggest events in a company's history is when it decides to sell shares of its stock to the public. This is called an initial public offering, or IPO. Companies first must file a registration statement with the Securities and Exchange Commission explaining the terms of the offering and how the proceeds raised through the stock sale will be used. The SEC documents are voluminous and contain a great deal of detail about the company and its financial history. This story is a fairly typical advance piece written before an IPO. Nearly all the information here would come from the publicly available registration statement filed with the SEC. Identifying the kinds of information in this story on Visa will give you some ideas of what elements should be included in an IPO story.

Visa Plans $17 Billion Public Offer

By ERIC DASH

Undaunted by recent turbulence in the financial markets, Visa Inc., the nation's biggest credit card network, said Monday that it would forge ahead with what would be the largest initial public stock offering in United States history.

Visa plans to sell as much as $17.1 billion of stock in late March following in the footsteps of its smaller rival, MasterCard, which went public in May 2006.

Visa and MasterCard are prospering as Americans increasingly flex plastic, rather than use cash, to pay for just about everything. The companies have not been hurt by the credit squeeze, because they do not actually make credit card loans; they merely process transactions for banks that do.

If all goes as planned, Visa's offering would generate a windfall for thousands of its so-called member banks, which own the company. The largest gains would go to many of the nation's biggest banks, which have been stung by losses stemming from mortgage-linked investments.

"Visa will be able to tell its story, even in an uncertain market, because its story is a good one," said David Robertson, publisher of The Nilson Report, a payment industry newsletter. "If investors think MasterCard is a good story, Visa looks like the same thing on a bigger scale."

Visa plans to sell 406 million Class A shares for $37 to $42 a share, with just over half going to the public and the rest to Visa's member banks.

The first $3 billion will be placed into a special account to cover outstanding antitrust and unfair-pricing claims brought by merchants. Visa will use some of the new money to streamline its operations, expand in fast-growing emerging markets and invest in new technology like systems that enable people to make card payments via cellphone. But the bulk of the capital will end up in the banks' coffers, from repurchasing stock from them.

Published: February 26, 2008.

Good hard news lede. Story points out how unusual it is for Visa to sell stock at a time when the IPO pipeline has been dry. This simple fact makes the story more interesting.

First, readers always want to know the size of the offering—number of shares and the dollar amount. Next, the offering needs a benchmark: How big compared to what?

Explain the company's business—how does it make money?

Who is getting the proceeds from the sale, and who could reap big profits from the first day of trading?

First, more details: Is there more than one class of stock? How many shares are being sold, and at what price?

Midpoint price, because we don't know the actual price yet. You should still break down who gets what in terms of dollars.

Visa's member banks can use the extra cash. If Visa's shares are valued at a midpoint price of $39.50, JPMorgan Chase, the company's largest shareholder, would receive an estimated $1.1 billion for its stake. Bank of America would get about $545 million; National City would get about $380 million; and Citigroup, U.S. Bancorp and Wells Fargo can each expect around $240 million or more.

"The credit crunch is pretty cyclical; the prospects for Visa are very strong long-term," said Marc Abbey, the managing partner of First Annapolis, a consulting firm that works with many banks and payments companies. "I am sure it is convenient for them to have extraordinary gains at the same time they have extraordinary losses."

Put the offering in perspective. Visa is going public—MasterCard soared when it went public.

Since going public nearly two years ago, MasterCard shares have soared 408 percent, closing at $198.45 on Monday. It now has a market value of $26 billion.

MasterCard's successful I.P.O. prompted Visa to move forward with its own plans to go public. Since October 2006, Visa has reorganized its sprawling management structure, bringing together all of its global operations with the exception of those in Europe.

Insiders who will benefit.

It has also hired Joseph W. Saunders, the former head of the Providian Financial Corporation, as its new chairman and chief executive, giving him a pay package worth $11.1 million in cash for 2007. Upon completion of the I.P.O., he is expected to receive an additional $11.5 million in stock and options, according to Equilar, a compensation research firm.

This paragraph gives us an idea of the size of Visa's market share. Investors are always looking for this type of information.

Visa transactions accounted for roughly 66 percent of all credit and debit card purchases in the United States in 2006, compared with about 26 percent for MasterCard, according to The Nilson Report data.

Growth in card transactions, the foundation of the companies' businesses, has historically held up well, even when the economy and consumer spending slows.

The New York Times   February 26, 2008

Visa I.P.O. Could Be Largest Ever

Visa's initial public offering could reap $17.1 billion, in what would become the largest ever for a U.S. company.

10 LARGEST U.S. OFFERINGS

YEAR	COMPANY	VALUE, IN BILLIONS	
2008	**Visa**	**$17.1**	
2000	AT&T Wireless	10.6	
2001	Kraft Foods	8.7	
1999	United Parcel Service	5.5	
2002	CIT Group	4.6	
1998	Conoco	4.4	
2007	Blackstone Group	4.1	
2002	Travelers Property Casualty	3.9	
1999	Goldman Sachs Group	3.7	
2001	Agere Systems	3.6	

Source: IPO Scoop.com

THE NEW YORK TIMES
The New York Times
TWITTER
SIGN IN TO RECOMMEND

The New York Times

A Conversation with . . . **Floyd Norris**

CHIEF FINANCIAL CORRESPONDENT

© The New York Times

Floyd Norris, the chief financial correspondent of The New York Times, writes a weekly column that appears on Fridays and the "Off-the-Charts" feature on Saturdays. He has been the chief financial correspondent since September 1999, after spending more than a year as a member of the editorial board of The Times. He joined the paper in October 1988 as a financial columnist. Before joining The Times, Norris had been with *Barron's National Business and Financial Weekly* since December 1982, where he began as a staff writer and subsequently was promoted to stock market editor. He is the recipient of three lifetime achievement awards in business journalism from different organizations: the Financial Writers Association of New York, the Society of American Business Editors and Writers, and the UCLA Anderson School of Management, which honored him with the Gerald Loeb Award for Distinguished Business and Financial Journalism. The following is an edited transcript of a telephone interview.

How long have you been at The New York Times?
I have been here a little over 20 years.

What's your beat?
I don't have one. My current title is chief financial correspondent. When I was originally hired, it was to write the stock market column. My columns gradually grew from that. When you look at the markets, there is not a whole lot that you can't fit under that subject heading.

Do you have a formal business education?
I have an education, but not a background. I became a business writer after doing other things, including covering politics and working for a senator. In 1979 I went to work for the Associated Press. After doing that for three years and being frustrated by a lack of information, I got what was then known as the Bagehot Fellowship at Columbia University. I stayed on at Columbia for two more semesters and finished my MBA. I discovered that I absolutely love accounting, and that has been a focus of my journalism ever since.

Should journalists get a business education?
I think it is extremely helpful in knowing what you are writing about. The problem with that idea, of course, is the financial arithmetic. I blew what was my life savings on that final year of business school. The fellowship paid the first year. But the final two semesters I had to pay tuition, and that wiped out what savings I had. When I was about to graduate from business school, I refused to interview with companies because I was deathly afraid that someone would offer me more money than what I could earn in journalism and I would take it. I did not want to leave journalism because I felt if I had, I would have spent the rest of my life wondering if I could be successful in journalism. Clearly, that education has been a great help to me. Without what I learned at Columbia, I would not have been able to do much of what I have done. I don't have a college degree, but I have a master's. I don't like to publicize that—it is only because my college days were a little messed up.

So how did you get an MBA without a bachelor's degree?
The Bagehot program had no educational requirements, so that meant that I was able to take the first semester of the MBA and then apply for the MBA.

At Columbia, it turns out they required a bachelors' degree or equivalent preparation.

You actually like numbers? Most journalists avoid them.
That is a cliché. That was never true of me. I have always enjoyed numbers greatly. I love accounting. Accounting allows people to play games. And over the years, I have seen people who have played outrageous games with their accounting, which is always great fun to write about.

What's your goal as a reporter?
I am just trying to find something that I find is interesting, and therefore that I think others will find as interesting. Being a journalist is great fun. You get to ask questions and satisfy your curiosity. You get to keep learning stuff through your entire career.

How do you find your stories?
I talk to some people. But if you look at my columns you will find that I quote fewer people than the vast majority of other financial journalists. I do this because years ago I concluded that I wanted to become my own expert. There obviously is a place for journalism where Expert A says the world is made of cream cheese and Expert B says it isn't. But I would much rather figure it out and understand it.

It is difficult in some areas to find experts who are objective. In the case of financial statements, the only people who pay attention to a company's financial statements are a company and people who either are long or short in the stock. There's nothing wrong with such people. I just find it much better to do your own work if you can.

What's one of the more challenging topics you have covered?
This whole financial crisis has been challenging. It has been embarrassing to find that I am suddenly learning about a lot of stuff that I should have known about to begin with—such as understanding CDOs [collateralized debt obligations], the whole mortgage-backed securities structure. So many people didn't understand them.

Do you ever go to a professional if you don't understand something?
I do that sometimes when I am really perplexed. I might go to an accounting expert to help me understand accounting rules or analysts who I hope understand companies.

What tips do you have for beginners?
They should understand accounting. Accounting for better or worse is the language of business. It is certainly possible to be a foreign correspondent who does not speak the local language, but obviously it is a lot easier if you

do. If you are trying to cover France without speaking French, you can't watch the local TV, you can't interview men on the street, there is a lot you can't do.

You need to be able to admit up front that you don't know something. Our offices used to be a lot more cramped than they are now. We could hear each other's conversations. And some of the people here were amazed by my conversations. I would just say to someone, "I don't understand this; explain it to me." Or, "I know I should understand this, but I don't." People just think I am being disingenuous by saying that, but I am not. I figure I should understand all this stuff, but I am embarrassed that I don't. So I ask questions. It is better to have one guy go home and tell his spouse, "I just talked to an idiot from The Times today" than it is to be wrong and have a whole lot of people conclude that you don't know what you are talking about.

MAKING**CONNECTIONS** 🤝

1

Explain how you would use earnings to tell a story about a company's progress. Why is it important that you include this information in business stories?

What are some reasons companies fudge their accounting statements? What problems do these present for you as a reporter when you must rely on published financial statements?

2

3

Reporters often have to write stories about a company offering stock to the public in an initial public offering. Discuss why it is important that this event be covered and who beyond potential investors might be interested in reading such a story.

4

Who are securities analysts? Why should you be cautious in using the information they offer about a company?

5

BUSINESS CONCEPTS REVIEW

Balance sheet	Financial statement that details a firm's financial condition on a given date.
Bond	Debt obligation or certificate of indebtedness issued by a government or company. Investors buy the bond allowing the issuer to use their money for a specified time period. The issuer is usually required to pay interest at specific intervals to the bondholder.
Book value	The cost of an asset, less depreciation, as carried on a company's books. It often has no relation to market value.
Common stock	Share of ownership in a corporation providing the owner with a vote for each share held. Owners are usually entitled to receive dividends on their holdings.
Earnings per share	Measures how much profit a company earned for each share of stock outstanding. It is calculated by dividing net income by the company's average outstanding shares.
Fully diluted earnings per share	Earnings per share measure that takes into account how many shares of common stock would be outstanding if all convertible securities were immediately converted into shares of common stock.
Generally Accepted Accounting Principles (GAAP)	A widely accepted set of rules and practices outlining how to accurately report financial information.
Income statement	Financial statement outlining a firm's revenue and expenses.
Initial public offering	Occurs when a company offers shares of stock to the public for the first time.
Net income	Sum left after all expenses have been deducted, synonymous with net earnings. If expenses exceed revenue, the result will be a net loss.

BUSINESS CONCEPTS REVIEW (continued)

Operating earnings	Sales minus the expenses associated with generating sales. Also known as operating profit.
Revenue	Sales generated by providing customers goods and services.
Securities analyst	An individual who performs investment research examining the value of stocks, bonds and other securities.
Securities and Exchange Commission	Federal agency established by the Securities Exchange Act of 1934 to uphold federal laws governing the issuance, registration, sale and trading of securities.
Standard & Poor's 500	An index of 500 large capitalization stocks that are actively traded.

mergers

WHAT IS A MERGER? It is simply a combination of two companies. But nothing about that combination is ever simple. Mergers involve protracted negotiations, complicated financial statements and stacks of documents with tiny print. Legions of attorneys, bankers and executives hold lots of meetings behind closed doors. Afterward, the parties emerge with bags under their eyes and wrinkles in their pinstriped suits. They have reached a deal.

The chief executives hold a press conference and gush about the future and the importance of the merger. Sometimes the two CEOs hug and get emotional. The atmosphere is one of celebration.

Beyond all the fanfare, mergers do have benefits. Companies get entry to new markets and access to new products and technology that they couldn't develop on their own. Mergers can provide growth and new jobs for the communities where the combined companies operate. And mergers are part of the natural evolution of companies that operate under a capitalist system. Profit-seeking firms either grow or they die.

But mergers can have huge downsides for communities and ordinary workers. Top executives parachute out with big payouts, leaving the company behind to struggle with big debt loads and overlap between product lines and divisions. The result? Big job cuts and lots of lost tax revenue for local government.

Covering business mergers is like learning a new language. And for better or worse, mergers are a part of business.

So what is a merger? It is a combination of two or more firms that have different strengths. The companies decide that the best growth strategy necessitates combining operations with another company. The word *merger* is really a business euphemism for an *acquisition,* since only one company survives. Technically, the terms mean two different things for accounting and tax purposes, but the words *merger* and *acquisition* are often used interchangeably by journalists.[1]

If one company declines to be acquired and the company continues to pursue it, the deal is then called a *hostile takeover.* Then there are *leveraged buyouts,* a term for an acquisition of a company with borrowed money. Often the assets of the company being acquired are used as collateral to ensure the debt will be repaid.

When you're new to the business beat, all this terminology can be confusing. Don't worry. This chapter will help you make sense of some of this business-speak. You don't need to be an investment banker or an analyst to write about mergers. What you do need is an understanding of some key terminology and a dogged persistence to run the story down.

One term you are likely to hear is *merger of equals.* First, forget any notion about two businesses being equal. They almost never are; if they were, they wouldn't be merging. One company has something the other company wants. That's why someone else has offered to buy it. Andrew Ross Sorkin discusses this later in the chapter when he pulls apart the XM-Sirius satellite radio deal.

Why do some mergers work while others fizzle? The question can best be answered by looking at individual companies like Citigroup and AOL–Time Warner. During the 1990s, Citigroup's architects went on a buying binge, assembling a collection of insurance, investment banking and financial service companies serving 200 million customers in 140 countries. As this volume went to press, Citigroup was considering breaking itself up. Both the Citigroup and AOL–Time Warner deals discussed in this chapter are textbook examples of what can go wrong with mergers.

Regardless of how any deal turns out, covering mergers is action-packed. Big-dollar deals make a splash and attract a lot of attention. There's the suspense of what is going to happen next. You are on the frontlines covering big news, chasing down a story before the competition can report it. It can be exhilarating, not to mention a lot of fun.

Covering big stories is why people become business reporters. And covering mergers is just one place where the thrills begin.

👀 STORY**SCAN**

Selection 8.1

Every merger story has certain elements—purchase price, financing, breakup fees, asset sales and new executives. Most mergers are acquisitions—one company is buying another. For accounting purposes it may be called a merger, but only one company is going to survive upon the deal's completion. As you will notice in the following story about Pfizer buying Wyeth, the terms acquisition and merger are used interchangeably. Be specific and accurate in your terminology, but don't confuse your readers with accounting jargon. This story offers ideas on how to structure a merger story and what items are the most important to include.

In Tight Market, $68 Billion Deal Is Reported for Pfizer and Wyeth

By ANDREW ROSS SORKIN and DUFF WILSON

The board of Pfizer, the world's largest drug maker, agreed on Sunday night to acquire a rival, Wyeth, for $68 billion, according to people involved in the negotiations.

How big is the merger in dollars? Compare to other recent mergers.

The deal would not only create a pharmaceutical behemoth but would be a rarity in the current financial tumult: a big acquisition that is not a desperate merger of two banks orchestrated by the government.

Implications of merger on employees, customers and the markets.

It would also be the first big merger backed by Wall Street in months. While credit has been notoriously tight of late, five banks have agreed to lend Pfizer $22.5 billion to pay for the deal. Pfizer, which has roughly $26 billion in cash, would finance the deal through the loans, some of its cash and stock.

Terms of the deal. How will the parties finance the deal: Cash? Stock? Debt?

If the transaction is completed as planned, it would be the biggest merger since AT&T and BellSouth combined in a $70 billion deal in March 2006, according to the research firm Capital IQ.

Details on size here. But this could easily have been put in the lede or the second graf.

The deal is expected to be announced Monday, the people involved in the negotiations said.

Always note timing. In this case, the story is being written in advance of the announcement.

The merger almost came unhinged at the 11th hour. While the boards of both companies agreed to the broad outlines of the deal and its price before the weekend, these people said, one issue was still a sticking point: whether Pfizer would be allowed to back out of the deal if the economy worsened or Wyeth's prospects faded.

What chance is there the deal could still fall through?

In better times, deals often falter on matters of strategy or price. But in this case, because of the ailing economy, Pfizer has agreed to pay a staggering breakup fee, $4.5 billion, if it does not complete the deal under certain circumstances—if, for example, its credit rating drops and it can no longer finance the deal. That is almost twice the typical breakup fee for a deal of this size.

Watch for hefty breakup fees if the deal falls apart.

Published: January 26, 2009.

If the acquisition is completed, it may demonstrate that Wall Street is willing to lend again, at least to the nation's top companies with the best credit ratings.

"If banks need to send a message that they're loaning, they want to be loaning to this quality of company," said Catherine Arnold, an analyst at Credit Suisse.

Pfizer's bid is being financed by four banks that received federal bailout money: Goldman Sachs, JPMorgan Chase, Citigroup and Bank of America, the people involved in the deal said. Such banks have been criticized for not doing more lending since they received the government aid.

Barclays, which acquired Lehman Brothers out of bankruptcy in the fall, is also providing financing, these people said.

Pay close attention to whether the acquiring company is getting a bargain or is overpaying.

Pfizer appears to be taking advantage of the bad market for credit to buy Wyeth at a lower price than it might fetch if competing bids were to emerge, which analysts do not expect.

"They have a unique opportunity now because not everybody can get that capital," said Barbara Ryan, an analyst at Deutsche Bank.

Because the combined company is expected to generate more than $20 billion in cash a year, Ms. Ryan said, "even when they borrow money, they will still have plenty of revenue."

You always want to list the deal in per share terms and in total dollars.

Under the terms of the deal, Pfizer would pay $50.19 a share for the company—$33 a share in cash and 0.985 Pfizer shares worth $17.19 a share based on Pfizer's closing price on Friday. That is roughly a 29 percent premium over the share price before word of the deal leaked on Friday.

Wyeth's management team would depart, the people involved in the negotiations said. Pfizer is also planning to cut its quarterly dividend in half to 16 cents, these people said, in an effort to maintain its credit rating.

Impact of any announcement on the stocks of the two companies.

After news reports disclosed the talks on Friday, investors applauded the possibility of a deal. Shares of Wyeth rose $4.91, or 12.6 percent, to close at $43.74. Pfizer climbed 24 cents, or 1.4 percent, to close at $17.45.

Pfizer expects to save $4 billion annually by combining with Wyeth; those savings will be phased in over three years.

Pfizer's chief executive, Jeffrey B. Kindler, first approached Wyeth last spring with a phone call, people involved in the talks said. The negotiations heated up in the summer but appeared to collapse when the banking system went into a tailspin in September and October.

Since then, there were several brief moments when it appeared the deal would move ahead, but then the talks would fall apart once again, usually over financing, these people said. It was apparently only within the last week or so that the financing commitment came together.

For Mr. Kindler, a lawyer who came to Pfizer from McDonald's, the deal may be a job-saver. His and the company's most pressing challenge has been the impending expiration of patent rights to the cho-lesterol-lowering drug Lipitor—which accounted for a quarter of the company's 2007 revenue of $48 billion and remains the best-selling drug in the world. The patent ends in 2011.

Still, even with the Wyeth deal, much would remain undone for Pfizer as it faces product, patent and pipeline problems for other drugs as well.

"It's not just Lipitor," Ms. Arnold wrote last year in a report to investors. Pfizer faces a run of 14 patent expirations through 2014, which would add up to lost revenue of about $35 billion as those drugs give way to cheap generics, according to Ms. Arnold. Pfizer's patent problem is not unique among the big drug makers. Merck, Bristol Myers Squibb and Eli Lilly are all facing their own patent losses in the next five years. "Everybody's staring at the same challenges down the road," Ms. Ryan said.

She said that Mr. Kindler, who became chief executive in July 2006, had probably not been in a position to make a play for a company like Wyeth until after he had cut costs, revamped Pfizer's core business and accepted the reality that the research pipeline was not producing blockbusters. "Hope springs eternal from the research pipeline," Ms. Ryan said.

Cost savings is one reason always given for mergers. You should ask: Are these savings achievable?

As part of the deal with Wyeth, both companies will have to repatriate tens of billions of dollars back into the United States, which could have a high tax cost. Pfizer reported $25.3 billion in revenue, 52.2 percent of its total, from overseas operations in 2007, according to securities filings.

If foreign profits were repatriated to the United States, Pfizer would have to pay the difference between the tax paid in the foreign country, as low as 5 percent in Ireland, for example, and the 35 percent tax rate in the United States.

Ms. Arnold said some tax penalties might be expected, but could be reduced by doing some of the buying and selling overseas.

"The experts that we've spoken to have very definitely said you can use offshore cash to buy offshore assets, and Pfizer and Wyeth both have very significant offshore subsidiaries that they place cash in," Ms. Arnold said. For example, she said, "Pfizer Ireland can use its cash to buy Wyeth Ireland or Wyeth Singapore."

Wyeth, with sales of about $23 billion for the 12 months that ended Sept. 30, has about $2.7 billion in cash and liquid assets, according to David S. Moskowitz, an analyst at Caris & Company, an investment bank.

Pfizer was advised by Goldman, JPMorgan and Barclays; Wyeth was advised by Morgan Stanley and Evercore Partners.

Erik Gordon, a professor at the Ross School of Business at the University of Michigan who follows biomedical industries, said Pfizer and Wyeth were a great fit that made the deal creditworthy.

First, because Pfizer has so much cash, the deal does not have to be highly leveraged with debt, Mr. Gordon said. Second, the two companies have enough overlap that they can achieve considerable saving through consolidating duplicate operations and cutting costs. And finally, parts of a combined operation could be spun off to raise money.

Mr. Gordon pointed to the animal health businesses of both companies—which, considered together, accounted for $2.8 billion in revenue and about $600 million in profit in the first nine months of 2008.

Readers always want details on where cost savings will come from.

What is the makeup of the two companies—in terms of revenue and profits?

"They could sell that business for billions of dollars to either pay down the debt or service the debt," he said. In addition, he said Pfizer could resell Wyeth's consumer products business. He added: "This deal is the rare thing. This'll be the only money investment bankers make in a while."

Selection 8.2

Mergers are one of those breaking news events that every reporter has to cover. The deals are complex, forcing reporters to rely heavily on the parties closest to the deal for details—company executives and securities analysts. This sometimes results in a lopsided story since the parties assembling the deal have vested interests at stake. Each side stands to make a boatload of money if the deal goes through. This story on Citigroup is the first of several stories in this chapter examining an underreported side of a merger: what happens months or years later after the merger closes. Citigroup was heralded as a great deal for shareholders and customers. Yet, in the longer term, the deal ended up being a disaster. Pay close attention to the reasons Eric Dash offers as to why this deal was a bad idea from the start. Dash's reporting may be hindsight, but it could be helpful in your own reporting.

A Stormy Decade for Citi Since Travelers Merger
By ERIC DASH

Ten years ago this Sunday, on April 6, 1998, Sanford I. Weill rewrote the rules of Wall Street.

That day, at 7:41 in the morning, Mr. Weill unveiled the mega-merger that created Citigroup, the biggest financial services company the world had ever seen. The deal—as daring and brazen as the man himself—tore up a crucial chapter of the legal canon that had guided American banking since the Depression.

The rest is history—but not the history that Citigroup hoped for. A decade later, Mr. Weill's watershed deal is regarded by some as one of the worst mergers of all time.

Today, the behemoth formed by the union of Citicorp and Travelers seems to lumber from one crisis to another. Bloated costs, outmoded technology and political infighting have hobbled the giant company, which employs 374,000 people in more than 100 countries.

Published: April 3, 2008.

Even within Citigroup, many have rejected Mr. Weill's grand vision of a globe-spanning financial supermarket, an agglomeration of investment and commercial banking, insurance and fund management that could prosper in both good times and bad. The company has even abandoned its famous Weill-era Travelers logo, the red umbrella, in favor of an emblematic red arc.

The stock market has rendered the harshest judgment of all. Shares of Citigroup closed at $24.02 on Wednesday, nearly $10 lower than they were on that hopeful April day a decade ago. Citi, once the country's most valuable financial company, has fallen to third place, behind Bank of America and JPMorgan Chase.

"I cannot think of one positive thing that developed as a result of these two companies," said Richard X. Bove, a financial services analyst at Punk Ziegel. "The miracle of Citigroup is that it still is in the position it is in, given the massive mismanagement."

Vikram S. Pandit, the new chief executive of Citigroup, is struggling to steer the titanic company through the most turbulent period in its decade long history. Just over 100 days into the job, he must reckon with the legacy of Mr. Weill, who retired as Citigroup's chairman in 2006, and his own immediate predecessor as chief executive, Charles O. Prince III.

Mr. Pandit, like Mr. Prince before him, is shying away from Mr. Weill's strategy of providing one-stop shopping for financial services. Instead, he is focusing on businesses and markets that generate higher investment returns.

To help, Mr. Pandit has brought in several outsiders, as well as old confidants from his time at Morgan Stanley, to strengthen Citigroup's management. His decision to go outside is a crushing blow to Citigroup executives, who have long prided themselves on grooming the best and brightest in the industry. Recent hires include new heads of investment banking, alternative investments and consumer banking, as well as a new risk chief.

This week, Mr. Pandit announced the bank's 10th major management shake-up since 2002 and its latest reorganization, moves that underscore Citigroup's failure to integrate and invest in its operations over the last decade. Executives caution that the road ahead will be rough. For example, it may take at least five years before the company's technology systems catch up to those of its main rivals.

Don Callahan, the chief administrative officer of Citigroup, said the company's original model has evolved over time. "Vikram Pandit is now taking the bold steps essential to ensure proper execution across all businesses and geographies, for the benefit of our clients, employees and shareholders," he said in a statement.

Mr. Pandit must move quickly. Citigroup is being battered by the troubles in the credit markets. So far, the company has taken more than $20 billion in write-offs, and in recent months has raised billions of dollars from foreign investors. Wall Street analysts expect Citigroup to disclose billions of dollars of new losses when it reports earnings this month.

Whatever happens at Citigroup, the aftershocks of the 1998 Citicorp-Travelers merger are still reverberating through the financial system. The deal paved the way for the repeal of the Glass-Steagall Act of 1933, the law that separated investment banks, which underwrite securities, and commercial banks, which accept deposits and make loans.

The end of Glass-Steagall ushered in an era of consolidation and integration within the financial services industry, with mixed results. Mergers between Wall Street and Main Street banks helped American institutions compete with foreign rivals. But the deals also fostered some of the financial innovations that many say contributed to the subprime mortgage crisis. The Bush administration's plan to remodel the system regulating the financial industry has rekindled the debate over the government's role in the markets.

In a brief interview last month after JPMorgan's bid to buy Bear Stearns, the troubled investment bank, Mr. Weill said Citigroup, as a diversified company, could weather the storm better than old-fashioned Wall Street banks. Citigroup's ability to raise capital "says a heck of a lot about the diversified model," he said.

But even Mr. Weill seemed to back away from his once-vaunted notion of the financial supermarket.

Citigroup has "got to determine what are the core assets and what are the assets that are going to get the returns they want," Mr. Weill said. "They have got to get their costs in line, and they have got to get their management together."

Whatever the case, Mr. Weill's appetite for profits, rather than an orthodox belief in the diversified banking model, always drove his deal-making. The "financial supermarket" was part of the Wall Street sales pitch. Over the years, Mr. Weill built his empire by making big acquisitions and then wringing out costs. He pressed his business heads to maximize profits every quarter to finance his next deal.

But Mr. Weill, reluctant to sacrifice those earnings, failed to connect Citi's sprawling operations. Instead, Citigroup stuck businesses together but ran them independently.

"It was like they were painting the house without making sure the plumbing was strong as it needed to be," said one longtime Citi follower who was not authorized to speak by his company. "After a while, that catches up."

Under Mr. Weill, each part of Citigroup was run like a separate fief, leaving the company without a single, cohesive culture. Even now, some Citigroup bankers recount the glory days of Citicorp, while old hands on its bond trading desk answer their phones "Salomon Brothers!"

Mr. Weill also struggled to retain his best managers. He and John S. Reed, the head of Citicorp, clashed from the start. Many of Mr. Weill's lieutenants eventually left. Among them was James Dimon, Mr. Weill's operational whiz and one-time heir apparent, who now runs JPMorgan.

Mr. Weill finally chose Mr. Prince, his chief lawyer, to run the company and extricate Citigroup from several regulatory messes. In the late 1990s and early part of this decade, Citigroup bankers were at the center of some of the biggest corporate scandals of the time, including the collapse of Enron and WorldCom and the investigations into Wall Street research tainted by conflict of interest.

But with little operating experience, Mr. Prince was ill equipped for the top job. He cut jobs and sold several businesses, but he was eventually forced out last fall after Citigroup ran up steep losses on complex mortgage investments.

The question now is whether Mr. Pandit can make a leaner Citigroup work. He recently announced plans to give more authority to four regional heads to try to speed decision-making, and to centralize areas like legal affairs, technology and risk management.

Guy Moszkowski, a longtime financial services analyst, said the idea behind Citigroup—that one company could do it all—was sound.

"I do actually think the premise is one that makes sense," Mr. Moszkowski said. "The problem Citi has had is in executing it. It has been deeply flawed and much more difficult than they imagined."

Selection 8.3

Company executives drool over synergy. What does it mean? Combining two or more parts produces something better. At least that's the theory. The word has kept its mystical power despite the fact that synergy king Harold Geneen, who created International Telephone and Telegraph during the 1960s by putting hundreds of unrelated businesses together, later acknowledged that the concept was flawed. Thirty years later, "synergy" was again sold as justification for the AOL–Time Warner merger. The deal flopped. As Rob Walker notes, any utterance of synergy or its close cousin "convergence" should evoke skepticism. Reporters should ask this question: Is putting these companies together better, or is it just something the business executives cooked up to sell the deal and get rich?

Creating Synergy Out of Thin Air

By ROB WALKER

If there's any silver lining to the storm clouds now hovering over the merged AOL Time Warner, it's that it will probably be a long time before we hear anybody boasting about "synergy" again.

Synergy is a word that practically demands to be rendered in quotes. As often as it has been used, its actual meaning is invariably hard to pin down. That's just as true now that the concept has become sort of a vague albatross rather than the magical creature it was supposed to be. Plenty of onlookers today say that most of the pieces of AOL Time Warner are perfectly sound and actually worth more than investors are willing to pay for them as a merged whole; the problem, apparently, is the very fact that they're linked.

This seems like a shocking turnabout. Back in January 2000, when the merger was announced, it was met with barely concealed— and sometimes baldly stated—anticipatory glee. "The deal has potential synergies that make some observers drool," reported The Wall Street Journal. At the time, what synergy apparently meant was that the gathering of many media properties and distribution platforms was, by definition, a source of awesome power. With CNN, Time Inc. magazines like Sports Illustrated and People, and Looney Tunes characters all "linked" to AOL's millions of subscribers, well, something wonderful was bound to result.

There are many reasons that nothing wonderful at all has resulted so far. But a few stand out, and at their core is what seems like a failure to understand what synergy was really supposed to be—apart from a surprisingly durable buzzword.

There is, for starters, a gap between the theory of far-flung businesses working in seamless concert and the reality of protecting corporate turf. Reports have detailed the intense lack of interest among various divisional chiefs at AOL Time Warner in consolidating ad-selling operations and cutting sweeping marketing deals across multiple units; apparently, some of those units felt they could get a better price on their own. When this sort of behavior hurts the bottom line, the relevant managers are pilloried for "protecting their fiefdoms." But when it helps (as it can), they're hailed for "thinking like entrepreneurs." The difference is generally a matter of hindsight, but either way, it's the opposite of synergy.

It's at least possible that this problem can be overcome, or a middle ground reached, but there's another problem: depending on what form it takes, synergy can give regulators pause. Let's say your favorite restaurant merges with another one. You like all the new menu items, but if you can get the house salad you've enjoyed for years only by ordering a three-course meal you don't want—well, you might think synergy is just another word for pushing consumers around. Government approval of the AOL Time Warner merger took a year, during which the companies' honchos stressed that the various divisions were "different in character" and "will not be dominating any one segment." That sounds rather at odds with synergy, but just to make sure, regulators made Time Warner promise to open its cable lines to AOL's competitors.

This hints at a third take on the meaning of synergy, which carries the biggest problem of all. Synergy is almost always thought of in a top-down way: Mix and match the corporate properties (compiling a bigger menu, in a sense) and consumers will fall in line. But if you're an AOL subscriber, are you really more likely to subscribe to Sports Illustrated? Or buy more Bugs Bunny paraphernalia? (One of the corporate fantasies that's always tossed out is that some day we'll be able to watch "Sabrina, the Teenage Witch," admire something Sabrina is wearing, and in a few clicks buy the same outfit. Does anybody want to do this? Wouldn't it be humiliating to show up at a cocktail party and have someone say, "Oh, I saw that sweater on the WB last week"?)

One of the more puzzling conundrums of synergy can be found in what one might call the money-to-stuff ratio. Basically, consumers want more stuff for less money; companies want to sell more stuff, but for more money. Synergy makes a vague promise to consumers that it will deliver the first scenario, and to investors that it will deliver the second.

The underlying problem certainly isn't that people are resistant to learning, and embracing, new ways of consuming music, movies, books or other digital content.

The obvious example—to the great chagrin of record label executives everywhere—is in the realm of music. Millions of music fans are enthralled with the benefits of new synergies between their computers and their stereos. Particularly for those who are ambivalent about intellectual property rights, it's proved to be a spectacular means of pumping up their money-to-stuff ratio. Unfortunately for record companies, artists and even the various newfangled start-ups that hoped to exploit this turn of events, pretty much nobody has figured out how to make a dime off of it In fact, this form of synergy has been actively resisted.

Maybe we haven't heard the last of synergy or its close cousin, "convergence." But if it ever returns, let's hope that it does so in a form that has some tangible meaning—preferably one that's grounded in something consumers actually want.

Selection 8.4

Are mergers good or bad? Gretchen Morgenson looks to academic researchers who have studied the subject to get some answers. Their conclusion: Mergers are often consummated for the wrong reasons. Yet mergers are sold to investors and the public as something that enhances shareholder value and will result in growth, new jobs and prosperity. Reporters record what the various cheerleaders tout about the proposed deal, barely scratching the surface. Investors often buy the same arguments. But years later the merged company is broken up into pieces. The executives who put the deal together are gone, many employees have been laid off and an otherwise great company has been wrecked. This long piece from The New York Times Sunday Magazine gives reporters some perspective on the issues surrounding mergers so they can tackle the subject intelligently.

What Are Mergers Good For?
By GRETCHEN MORGENSON

The Dark Side of the Deal
To most investors, mergers are the stock market's equivalent of catnip. Takeover bids typically provide a nice boost to investors' portfolios and confirm their stock-picking smarts. And to hear the executives orchestrating them tell it, they always produce greater profits at the combined company down the road. Business publications and newspapers, including The Times, celebrate the deals with breathless tales of how they came together, complete with photographs of smiling executives shaking hands in front of a crowd.

This year, with the stock market moving sideways, buyouts and the gains they generate are prized all the more. There have been a lot of them, too. This year, according to Thomson Financial, the first quarter's combinations were valued at $308.2 billion, up 17 percent from the value of deals announced in the same period in 2004. If this activity continues, 2005 will be the fourth-largest year in deal size.

And yet, for all the profit and promise that mergers seem to hold, the truth about companies combining their operations is a darker one. Academic research suggests that few mergers add up to significantly more prosperous or successful companies and also that acquisitions during buyout booms, like the one we are in now, are more likely to fail than those made in other periods. And when one company acquires another using its own stock as currency, as commonly happens today, shareholders' stakes in the acquiring firm typically decline.

Published: June 5, 2005. Full text available at: www.nytimes.com/2005/06/05/magazine/05MERGERS .html

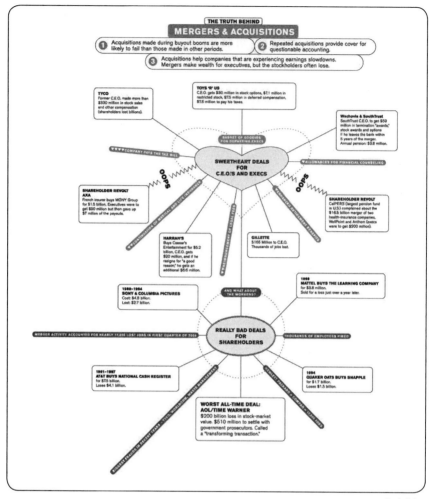

Paula Scher

Mergers are sweetheart deals for top executives who receive big payouts, but they can be really bad deals for shareholders.

What's worse, there is a disturbing trend among some of the most aggressive corporate acquirers to use deals to mask deteriorating financial results at their companies and to reap outsize executive pay. The complexity of folding companies into one another makes it more difficult, whether by accident or by design, for investors to fathom what's really going on. Because mergers require the extensive use of estimates on matters like job cuts and asset write-offs, for example, deals represent an opportunity for management to throw everyday expenses into the merger cost bucket and make operating results look better than they actually are. It's probably no coincidence that some of the biggest frauds in recent years have involved serial deal makers like Tyco International, Waste Management and WorldCom. (Long before a jury found him guilty of securities fraud in federal court in March, Bernard J. Ebbers, the chief executive of WorldCom, entertained himself and his friends aboard his 118-foot yacht called the Aquasition.)

Perhaps the biggest downside to mergers, however, is their human toll. Deals that combine companies are becoming a bigger factor behind large-scale layoffs across the nation.

Some Bad Unions of the Recent Past

Robert F. Bruner, professor of business administration at the Darden School of Business at the University of Virginia, has compiled a list of colossal merger failures in a new book, "Deals From Hell." High up on his roster is the Sony–Columbia Pictures merger in 1989, which cost $4.8 billion initially but ultimately resulted in a $2.7 billion write-off in 1994. Also on the list is the 1991 deal in which AT&T bought National Cash Register for $7.5 billion. Five years later, AT&T spun off NCR for $3.4 billion, for a loss of $4.1 billion. Another entry is the December 1994 purchase of Snapple Beverage by Quaker Oats for $1.7 billion, a deal that eventually produced a $1.5 billion loss. In late 1998 Mattel acquired the Learning Company, an educational software firm, for $3.8 billion in stock. Just over a year later, Mattel sold it for a loss.

But the champion of all failed mergers, even years later, remains the AOL–Time Warner combination, announced in January 2000 just as the technology stock bubble was about to burst. Time Warner's chief executive, Jerry Levin, called the deal a "transforming transaction"—an accurate assessment, as it would turn out, if not precisely in the way he hoped. The deal resulted in a $200 billion loss in stock-market value and a $54 billion write-down in the worth of the combined company's assets.

What's more, in merging with AOL, Time Warner inherited accounting irregularities that attracted the attention of the Justice Department and the Securities and Exchange Commission. In December, the company agreed to pay $510 million to settle with the S.E.C. (neither admitting nor denying wrongdoing) and also to enter into a deferred-prosecution agreement with the Justice Department. Prosecutors said they would put off bringing criminal securities-fraud charges against the America Online unit as long as Time Warner adopted measures to correct past problems and engaged an independent monitor to oversee AOL's financial operations for two years.

"The AOL/Time Warner transaction dwarfs other deals from hell in almost all respects," Bruner writes. "It leads the field in meltdown in value. The executive firings and resignations, the civil litigation, criminal investigation and the erasure of AOL from the corporation's name reveal a remarkable wipeout of the vision of the deal's architects."

What Does It Profit a C.E.O.?

Given all the forces that seem to be lined up in opposition to mergers, it may be a bit surprising that the deals keep on coming. But there are people for whom they make perfect sense: the executives and the Wall Street bankers behind them. There are several reasons for this—for example, acquisitions enable companies to show earnings growth that rising stock prices, and therefore investors, require—but the most compelling case for mergers may simply be the immense wealth that they generate.

Executives began reaping big rewards from deals during the 1980's, when so-called golden parachutes were introduced. (Today those payouts look positively quaint.) Back then, shareholders viewed large payouts to managers at a company subject to takeover as a way to induce entrenched executives to consider a change in control there. Those inducements then became embedded in every executive's employment contract, growing to the gargantuan levels of today.

The actual numbers associated with some of the bigger deals can be staggering. James Kilts, the chief executive of Gillette Company, stands to make $165 million from merging that venerable Boston company with the Cincinnati-based Procter & Gamble. That payout was so large that Joseph F. Turley, the company's former president, and Joseph E. Mullaney, a former vice chairman of Gillette's board, deplored the merger in an open letter to Gillette's directors. "Thousands of Gillette's employees will soon receive pink slips," they wrote. "Their 'leader' will receive $170 million."

While the Gillette pay stands out, it is by no means a singular occurrence. In April, Toys "R" Us disclosed that 21 current and former officers and directors could receive more than $170 million for selling the toy retailer to an investment group that includes Kohlberg Kravis Roberts & Company and Bain Capital, two buyout firms, and Vornado Realty Trust, a real-estate investment trust. The $6.6 billion deal will result in a $63 million payout to John H. Eyler Jr., the toy retailer's chairman and chief executive officer who has been with the company since 2000. That includes some $30 million in stock options, $7.1 million in restricted stock, an $11 million cash severance if he leaves after the deal closes, $7 million in deferred compensation and $7.5 million to pay taxes generated by the payout.

Last year, AXA, the French insurer, bid $1.5 billion for the MONY Group, a United States financial services company. In that deal, top MONY executives were set to receive $90 million in severance and other payments, but enraged MONY shareholders threatened to vote against the merger. Only then did the executives agree to forego about $7 million.

"Shareholders have to ask sometimes, Was this executive team motivated to do this deal only because they knew this pot of gold was waiting for them at the end of the rainbow?" Pat McGurn, special counsel at Institutional Shareholder Services, an investor advisory firm in Rockville, Md., says. "In some cases, it does border on what could be considered corporate waste."

Unfortunately, shareholders find out how much of a merger's costs will wind up in the pockets of one or both company's executives only after the deals are announced. And because uncovering the payouts requires digging through complex corporate filings, some shareholders never learn about them at all. Michael S. Kesner, principal in charge of the executive compensation practice at Deloitte Consulting, says it is not uncommon for payouts to management to reach 8 percent of a merger's total cost.

How to Justify a Merger: It's All About the Growth—Really

"I speak with senior executives in the course of my research," Robert Bruner, the Darden business school professor, told me. "They all tell stories about how they are charged with maintaining earnings growth. They can only get 5 to 6 percent growth organically, yet the C.E.O. has set a target that is much more ambitious, and they must make up the difference by acquisitions." Bruner is critical of this process, which he calls financial cosmetics. "It invites the creation of growth for appearance rather than growth that creates wealth for investors and society," he says.

Indeed, shareholders who own stock in companies that make a lot of acquisitions—serial acquirers—should consider whether the deals are being cooked up by executives concerned about a slowdown in growth inside their operations. (Of course, shareholders who expect rising stock prices are not without guilt themselves. As James A. Fanto, a professor at Brooklyn Law School, wrote in a study of mergers he conducted in 2000, "It is not too strong an expression to say that investors have become addicted to these transactions.")

"The only thing people get paid for these days is growth, not running a company well," Jack Ciesielski, editor of The Analyst's Accounting Observer in Baltimore, says. "The cult of growth will always encourage companies to buy other companies to paper over the valleys in their earnings patterns."

Perhaps the best—or worst—examples of acquisitions performed for earnings expediency were those made by Tyco International, a conglomerate, during the years it was run by L. Dennis Kozlowski. Founded in 1960 as a technology company, Tyco soon became a manufacturer of industrial products. By the late 1990's, however, it had begun promising investors that it would produce reliable earnings growth in excess of 20 percent a year. Kozlowski, who became chief executive in 1992, wanted to pattern his company after General Electric, which had produced remarkably steady earnings gains for years. Today Tyco has operations in fire and security services, health-care products and electronic components.

In 2002, Kozlowski and an associate were accused of stock fraud and of looting the company of $600 million (a figure later reduced to $150 million). After an earlier mistrial, he is currently on trial for the second time in New York State Supreme Court in Manhattan.

Whether or not Kozlowski is found guilty of fraud—at the time this article went to press, the trial was winding down—his acquisition record certainly turned out to be flawed. Since he left Tyco, the company has registered $9 billion in losses and impaired assets.

Kozlowski, however, received more than $330 million in stock sales and other compensation in his last three years running Tyco. A good bit of his compensation was based on achieving certain financial results. Tyco cleared most, if not all, of these hurdles, at least in part because of its many acquisitions. For example, in 2001, according to Tyco's regulatory filings, Kozlowski received a cash bonus of $4 million, based on the company's 39 percent increase in net income, before nonrecurring items, and on its 31.3 percent increase in operating cash flow. That year, the company made more than 10 acquisitions that contributed to both net income and cash flow.

The Bigger the Company, the More the C.E.O. Gets (Never Mind How the Company's Doing)

An academic study from 2000 examined the relationship between chief-executive compensation and mergers in the banking world. Richard T. Bliss, a professor at Babson College in Massachusetts, and Richard J. Rosen, then a professor at the Kelley School of Business at Indiana University, studied bank mergers that occurred from 1986 to 1995. They found that these deals had a positive effect on the size of executive compensation and that even when an acquiring bank's stock declined following a merger, the compensation paid to the chiefs running the institutions grew significantly enough to offset any losses to their stockholdings.

"The net result is that even mergers which reduce shareholder value can be in a manager's private interest," Bliss and Rosen concluded.

Their study found that more than three-quarters of the mergers in the sample led to a 10 percent or greater boost in executive compensation. The median change in compensation following a merger, the study showed, was an increase of between 20 and 30 percent of a chief executive's premerger pay.

* * *

👀 STORY**SCAN**

Selection 8.5

Sometimes negotiations behind mergers make little sense, as represented in this story about the XM and Sirius merger. Once the deal is struck, a press release is issued, a press conference is called and the chief executives trot out and start saying things like this deal will be a "merger of equals." What does that actually mean? In this case, one company is paying a premium for the other even though the target company is an "equal." As Andrew Ross Sorkin points out in this column, there is so much more to mergers than just the price and financing, namely politics and egos. Sorkin does a great job of pointing out the contradicting statements being offered in support of the merger.

DealBook
When Unequals Try to Merge as Equals
BY ANDREW ROSS SORKIN

Here's a tip about deal-making: When companies start talking about a "merger of equals," someone is usually getting the better deal. It is especially true in the proposed merger of XM Satellite Radio and Sirius Satellite Radio.

It is being billed as a merger of equals, with each company getting exactly half of the new entity.

Loaded, overused term.

But here's the unequal part: The stock market thinks that Sirius is worth almost $1 billion more than XM. To get the numbers to work, Sirius offered to pay a handsome 22 percent premium to shareholders of XM. (The premium is actually almost a whopping 30 percent if you account for the run-up in XM's shares the Friday before the deal was announced, as word began to leak.)

Translation: stock market capitalization of Sirius, which is number of shares outstanding multiplied by the current price.

So why did Mel Karmazin, the chief executive of Sirius, dress up the deal as if both companies were on the same footing?

I called Mr. Karmazin soon after the deal was announced to ask just that.

Investors bid up the shares upon announcement or prior to an announcement.

Published: February 25, 2007.

This is a killer quote.

"If you give me a lie detector test," he said, "I'll tell you that I believe we're worth more than them."

Premium to the company's market value.

In most mergers of equals these days, the buyer—and there is always a buyer—pays little or no premium. Both companies simply participate in a stock swap on the assumption that the shares will rise because of the cost savings and "synergies"—to bring back a dirty word from the 1990s.

Here is that word again: synergy.

The enormous premium for XM appears, at first glance, very curious.

The merger will create a monopoly. Sirius is paying a premium for XM. Yet, there are no other buyers. So why pay a premium?

It's not as if there was another buyer for XM that Sirius needed to outbid.

Sirius and XM had always been natural partners—assuming that regulators are willing to let them combine.

Things become clearer, though, when you look beyond the numbers and consider the psychology behind the deal. Because of the possibility that Washington could block the transaction, Mr. Karmazin said that nobody wants to look like the loser if things go bad. "You want to make sure if it doesn't happen, no harm, no foul," he said.

Interesting analogy— will these companies stay together if the merger is approved? Or get a divorce at some point?

Of course, others have been down this road before. Remember Daimler-Benz's takeover of Chrysler? Several years after the deal, Daimler's chief executive, Jürgen E. Schrempp, explained that they called it a merger of equals "for psychological reasons." (As it happens, Daimler is now considering selling off Chrysler.)

If Mr. Karmazin was willing to pay a premium, why didn't he just buy the company outright?

All the questions in my head apparently went through Mr. Karmazin's head, too.

When he first approached XM's chairman, Gary M. Parsons, he was prepared either to buy the company at a premium or pursue a no-premium "merger of equals."

A sale was no-go. "They said they were not for sale," Mr. Karmazin explained.

So, Mr. Karmazin then pushed for a no-premium merger. This was perhaps an even harder sell because Mr. Parsons said he believed that XM was worth more than Sirius, even though neither the stock market nor Mr. Karmazin agreed with him.

Mr. Karmazin said: "I told them that all of their reasons were bogus."

Mr. Parsons argued that his company had more subscribers and more revenue, but that its investors, mostly institutions like Axa and Legg Mason, didn't value the company highly enough. Empirically, Mr. Parsons' argument is right, despite the wisdom of crowds: "It never made any sense analytically that XM was worth less than Sirius," said Craig E. Moffett, an analyst at Sanford C. Bernstein. "If anything, I was surprised that the premium was as small as it was."

Shares of Sirius, meanwhile, which just a year and a half ago were worth less than XM's, had leaped, partly on the back of high-profile deals like the one it signed with Howard Stern.

Those deals attracted thousands of retail investors, not considered the smart money, like moths to a flame into Sirius stock.

And then Mr. Parsons played his ace: If Mr. Karmazin wanted to create the enormous savings they both projected would result from a deal—worth more than $5 billion, more than the value of either company—they needed each other. And Mr. Parsons would not play unless his shareholders could capture half of those savings.

As Mr. Karmazin explained, if the deal had been done simply, with no premium, Sirius would own about 55 percent of the company and XM would own about 45 percent. If they had tried to split the cost savings 50–50—which Mr. Karmazin conceded was "the only fair thing to do," Sirius would own a little more than 52 percent of the company and XM would own a bit more than 47 percent.

Company is valued by subscribers and ability to produce revenue.

Always good to have outside sources backing up point(s) you are trying to make.

Questions you would want to ask the dealmaker: How did the company arrive at the figures it is paying Howard Stern, and how much is Sirius losing because of this deal?

Great analogy.

Based on percentage of common stock outstanding.

So why didn't it stop there? Well, Mr. Parsons is a pushy negotiator. And Mr. Karmazin said he was willing to give in.

"I can't do the deal without them," he said. "I thought it was more important for our shareholders that we do the deal."

Here are those alleged savings again. You need to ask how the company arrived at these figures.

Even by giving the 22 percent premium, Sirius stands to save billions of dollars a year if the deal goes through.

In a statement, XM, which has hosts like Bob Dylan and Oprah Winfrey, said, "Each company believed the value of coming together was more important than one party or the other having a majority of the new combined company."

Still, it seems as if Mr. Karmazin may be paying a premium to do the deal now so that it can be rushed through the regulatory maze while the Bush administration is still in power. Many partners in mergers of equals wait around—often for years—until their stocks align.

Mr. Karmazin disputes that view, contending that he wants a deal as soon as possible so that the savings can start. His view is that there "is no regulatory window."

In fact, he believes that the longer the companies, both now money losers, wait to merge, the better their chances would be in Washington. That's because new technologies will continue to emerge that may prove to be competitive with satellite radio.

Deals are often expressed in both per share and total dollar amount.

Strong walk off.

But if anyone is a master of timing, it's Mr. Karmazin. He took Infinity Broadcasting public for $17.50 a share; four years later, he sold it to CBS for $170 a share. Now his willingness to make this deal at such a curious price may be an acknowledgment of the fairy dust in Sirius stock.

Tim Sloan/Agence France-Presse

Mel Karmazin, foreground, chief of Sirius Satellite Radio, pushed for the merger with XM Satellite Radio on the grounds that the combination would offer benefits to consumers.

MAKING**CONNECTIONS** 🤝

1

List five elements that should be in every merger story.

Both Citigroup and AOL–Time Warner are offered as examples of mergers that were ill-fated from the start. Review the readings in this chapter and offer several reasons why these mergers didn't work.

2

3

Discuss why the various stakeholders involved in a merger (outside shareholders, chief executives, employees, etc.) don't view such transactions with a more critical eye.

4

How could reporters do a better job of reporting on mergers? Use the stories in this chapter to help formulate your response.

5

After reading the story about the XM-Sirius merger, do you feel this was a good deal for the shareholders of the two companies? Explain your answer.

6

BUSINESS CONCEPTS REVIEW

Acquisition
Transaction in which a company buys and takes control of another company, also known as a takeover or a buyout.

Breakup fee
Fee paid to the purchaser in a takeover deal should a seller fail to meet the conditions of the transaction or walk away from the agreement.

Conglomerate
A group of unrelated businesses owned by a parent company for the purpose of maximizing profits. Each business is run independently of the central company, and is viewed as a distinct operation and profit center.

Derivative
Financial contract whose value is derived from an underlying asset such as real estate, stocks, bonds, commodities, residential mortgages or even interest rates. Derivatives are often used to hedge risk, but they can also be used to speculate.

BUSINESS CONCEPTS REVIEW (continued)

Investment bank	Financial institution that acts as an agent for companies and individuals wishing to raise money and trade securities (stocks, bonds). Investment banks also act as financial advisers to companies engaged in mergers and acquisitions.
Junk bond	A bond rated BB or below because of its high risk of default. Used when other forms of financing are not available. Investors demand an interest rate of 3 to 4 percentage points higher than blue chip corporate bonds to cover the increased risk.
Leveraged buyout (LBO)	Takeover of a company's assets through the use of borrowed money and the target company's assets as collateral. Strategy relies on borrowing money to acquire all the outstanding shares, taking the company private. LBOs often result in considerable debt load and risk to the owners and creditors.
Market capitalization	The number of shares of stock outstanding multiplied by the current market price.
Merger	Transaction where two companies' assets and liabilities are absorbed. The surviving firm retains its identity.
Prospectus	Written document issued for investors describing a new securities offering and the proposed business plan by the company.
Proxy fight	A group of shareholders join forces to take a major action such as pushing out management or selling the company.
Security	A stock, bond, debt instrument or derivative contract that carries value and can be sold or traded for something of value.
Synergy	Philosophy holds that the sum of two companies' parts will improve economic performance, lead to efficiencies and benefit shareholders. In reality, the benefits of synergy are often overstated.
Underwriter	Investment bank that assumes the risk of purchasing securities from a government or company for resale to the public.

writing profiles

● FEW WRITING ASSIGNMENTS are more challenging than a company profile. Though a business profile is not a personality profile, all good company profiles do contain an element of personality. You need a main theme and a main character or protagonist who is attempting to overcome some obstacle or who has achieved some milestone worth writing about. The protagonist could be a chief executive, an entrepreneur, an employee or an outsider who is trying to buy the company. But in every case, that person needs to be *doing* something worth your audience's attention.

"I like the human drama—the crimes of it, the victories of it, the triumphs," says Times business columnist Joe Nocera. "I just think there are lots of storytelling opportunities in business if you think of it as human drama, as I think of it, as opposed to balance sheets and income statements." The success of any profile starts with the reporting. If you collect garbage, your story will be garbage. And before you can do your reporting, you need to do some basic research about the company. You need to understand the particular business and the industry in which it operates, as well as something about the background of the person you plan to interview.

Knowing what questions to ask is only half the battle. You also need to be able to understand what the person you interview is talking about. This is why you do research. You should never waste people's valuable time asking questions whose answers you could easily have found online, in the library or in documents. Save your interview time for the good stuff, the information you can't find or would never obtain without a personal interview.

The focus here is the protagonist and the company he or she runs. You are exploring how the central figure's aspirations and ideals mesh with reality. As you interview family, friends, co-workers, customers and present and former employees, the personal details will slowly unfold. You want to collect observations, anecdotes and as many details as possible before you do your final interview with the chief executive or whoever is the story's central figure. Some of this information will be for background, and sources won't want it attributed to them. In other cases, they will be happy to go on the record and spill the beans. You will find little nuggets in these interviews. Cooperative sources will point you to other tidbits of information in public documents.

Readers crave personal details. They want to know what makes an individual tick, particularly if it is someone with considerable power and influence, someone they've heard about in the news and been wondering about. You may be one of the few people who have gotten to interview this person. Still, you can't expect the chief executive to drop everything and spin a unique, entertaining yarn that you can then just copy down into your notebook. Most of what prominent business people have to say is scripted. They've been coached by public relations handlers, and federal regulations limit how and when financial information can be disclosed.

A CEO of a company whose stock is publicly traded can be sued for saying the wrong thing. A simple slip of the tongue could result in the stock market punishing the company's stock price. So the stories you hear, at least at first, are likely to be the same stories the executive has told many times before. This makes it even more imperative that you study the company and know what direction you want to take before you show up on the CEO's doorstep. This doesn't mean that you discount the chief executive's words. But you can't get someone to reveal unique insights unless they respect you and take you seriously. You have to earn that respect during the interview.

The more you know about the company and the person, the more asking around you've done before the interview, the smoother the interview will go. You'll also have a better chance of asking a question or making a comment that nudges your interviewee toward something he or she has never said before.

Sometimes that moment you have been waiting for comes when you least expect it. For example, after finishing a long day of interviews with a CEO you find yourself discussing his love of fly fishing and how he'd like to have more time to pursue his hobby. The CEO looks at you and says, "I am thinking about retiring. I have had offers to sell the company and quite frankly I don't know what to do. Not even my wife knows about this. She'd kill me if she knew I was even considering this."

You can't believe what you are hearing. But you have just been handed a killer opening for your story, one that will set the markets abuzz and could earn you a journalism prize. Be ready for when great nuggets like this fall in your lap.

It is these unpredictable moments that make interviewing people so exciting. You never know what they are going to tell you. People you interview will confess to having had affairs, stealing money or being abandoned by their parents and growing up in an orphanage. Some of the best material comes from one-on-one personal interviews, and it often comes after you have closed your notebook.

The stories in this chapter will show you how the masters play the game. Among other things, you'll get an up-close look at computer tycoon Michael Dell, Starbucks founder Howard Schultz and foul-mouthed airline CEO Michael O'Leary, whose concept of customer service is telling disgruntled Ryanair passengers to get lost. In all three stories, The Times writers capture the essence of the CEOs and how they shape the companies they direct. That's what is so much fun about business reporting—you get to travel, meet interesting people and get them to tell you things they might tell no one else.

 STORY**SCAN**

Selection 9.1

This story of Michael Dell returning to fix his namesake, Dell Inc., is a classic business profile. Business profiles always have central figures who are doing something. In this case, the action revolves around helping Dell Inc. get back on its feet. Business profiles are not personality profiles, although they often contain personal and biographical information. Notice how Steve Lohr writes this story with Dell as the central figure, but Dell clearly is not the main source of the information. This is fairly commonplace in corporate profiles. Why? It usually comes down to politics and timing. Sometimes the chief executive won't sit for an interview. Or he or she agrees to be interviewed and says very little that is useful. Good reporters anticipate this by doing their reporting prior to the big interview. They build the story from the outside, figuring out the story, its framework and what needs to be collected. When interviewing a CEO, hope for the best and plan for the worst—in case he or she doesn't tell you anything you can use.

Erich Schlegel for The New York Times

"Some of our competitors jumped over us in a Darwinian way," Michael S. Dell says. "Now it's our turn." He recently returned as C.E.O.

Can Michael Dell Refocus His Namesake?

By STEVE LOHR

Round Rock, Tex.—On a recent afternoon at his company's headquarters here, Michael S. Dell is seated in a spacious conference room named Dobie Hall—in honor of the University of Texas dormitory where, in 1984, he started the computer giant that bears his name.

Simple anecdote establishes Michael Dell as the protagonist.

He boasts that Dell Inc. has just reported quarterly profits that exceeded Wall Street projections. It's an encouraging sign, he says, that the company—buffeted by high-profile production problems and accounting shenanigans—is finally regaining momentum.

Over the last few years, Dell, once the gold standard among PC makers, has simply overlooked major growth trends in personal computing. It missed significant shifts in notebook computer sales and the consumer market as a whole, lagged competitors in international sales, and lost the profit edge that it enjoyed from its superior procurement-and-supply network. Hewlett-Packard, having overcome its own woes, passed Dell last year as the largest seller of PCs worldwide.

Nut graf: why someone should read this story. Offers perspective and background.

Dell's ills also extend beyond the nuts-and-bolts of making and marketing PCs. After a yearlong internal investigation, Dell conceded last month that some managers had falsified quarterly results to meet sales targets from 2003 to 2006. The company expects to reduce earnings over those years by $50 million to $150 million, tiny sums compared with the billions of dollars in profits it earned during that same period. (Dell posted annual sales of about $57 billion last year.) Yet the accounting disclosures suggest a corporate culture in which at least some senior managers felt under such pressure that they doctored the numbers; the disclosures have prompted a Securities and Exchange Commission investigation.

Challenges. Bolsters nut graf. Offers scope and larger picture.

Notice how numbers are used here to help make the case to the reader.

Published: September 9, 2007. Full text available at: www.nytimes.com/2007/09/09/technology/09dell .html

Reasoning: Explains how the company got into this mess. Note how the reasoning comes from the story's central figure or protagonist.

This story assumes the reader knows Dell's history to stardom. That's probably a safe assumption for New York Times readers, but not always a good one to make.

Here the writer is letting the reader know the culture at Dell Inc. is closely tied to its founder, Michael Dell.

Dell background. Educates readers who are unfamiliar with Michael Dell about his legacy and the competitive landscape.

Move—there is a change, a cultural shift occurring. Michael Dell, the protagonist, is going to lead the charge. He did it once before—why can't he bring Dell Inc. back?

Enter with countermove. Like a "move," this is a very important element to any story. Dell

"The company was too focused on the short term, and the balance of priorities was way too leaning toward things that deliver short-term results—that was the major root cause," explains Mr. Dell, dressed for the Texas summer in a short-sleeved polo shirt and jeans.

The recent setbacks would be humbling for any company, but especially so for Dell, a smooth-running machine for years and a model of the efficiencies that the shrewd use of technology and customer information can produce. Dell was widely admired beyond the technology industry, and it was cited in business-school studies alongside companies like Wal-Mart Stores.

Successful entrepreneurs, of course, are hardwired by inclination and necessity to look beyond immediate hurdles for opportunities, and Mr. Dell is no exception. He says he is not leading a simple turnaround, but rather a long-term campaign to transform a company known for a cultlike adherence to a certain way of doing business.

As the company surged to the lead in the PC industry, the "Dell model" relied on direct sales over the Internet and by telephone rather than through retail stores, cutting prices to gain market share, focusing on computer hardware rather than services, leaning heavily on the American market and avoiding acquisitions. But since Mr. Dell reclaimed the role of chief executive in late January, he has changed all that.

At internal meetings, he repeatedly emphasizes that the Dell model "is not a religion," according to staff members. Moreover, Mr. Dell—who once ran a company famous for its laserlike devotion to next week rather than next year—no longer champions short-term goals and fixes. "We're moving the needle in terms of getting focused on the right long-term issues," he says.

But re-engineering the Dell model will be a daunting challenge. "Dell continued to do the same old thing, when it was no longer working," observes David B. Yoffie, a professor at the

Harvard Business School. "This is going to be about changing the way they do business at many levels."

"Dell can do it," Mr. Yoffie adds, "but it's going to take a lot more innovation on more fronts than the company has shown in the past."

Last year was, to borrow a term, the annus horribilis for Dell. Its problems kept building throughout 2006: sluggish growth, disappointing financial results, complaints about customer service, even a high-profile safety recall of notebook computer batteries. Not all of these were the company's fault. For example, Sony made the batteries that could overheat and catch fire, causing other companies like Apple to also issue recalls.

But there was no disputing that Dell had stalled. Wall Street, as well as Dell's own board, had become impatient with the company's management. So a change came quickly early this year, at the end of January. Dell's outside directors voted unanimously that the company needed a single leader instead of having a chairman (Mr. Dell) and a separate chief executive (Kevin B. Rollins, who had been C.E.O. since 2004).

* * *

So, on Jan. 31, Mr. Dell became chief executive—again—and Mr. Rollins, a former Bain consultant who joined Dell in 1996, was out. Mr. Dell describes Mr. Rollins as a "great business partner and friend." Other executives at Dell also point to Mr. Rollins's contributions over the years, as the operating field general beside Mr. Dell during the years of torrid growth. But Mr. Rollins, they say, was seen as the foremost practitioner, and advocate, of the old Dell model, even when pushing the same buttons no longer worked.

Still, Dell executives are quick to say that Mr. Dell's return as chief executive has nothing to do with any sharp differences between him and his predecessor. Rather, it was due to the depth of Dell's troubles and the need for someone to assume control and forcefully take the company on a different path.

says he is going to do this—but will it actually work? Moves and countermoves provide tension. They also help the writer narrate the story and hold the reader's attention.

Move—of course he can do it!

Countermove—Dell has a steep climb back to the top. Here the writer tells you what is involved.

History—always helps provide context for the reader, explaining the most recent developments.

History—Dell built the company and stepped aside. Now, Dell needs help. Enter Michael Dell as Mr. Fix It.

"It's not all about Michael versus someone else before," says Paul D. Bell, a senior vice president. "Michael was here. He was chairman. But it was up to Michael to take the first-mover role in driving change and he did it."

Mr. Dell began shaking things up immediately. He has recruited senior executives to lead the company's marketing, consumer products, operations and services business. He is also paring layers of middle management as part of a plan to trim Dell's payroll by 10 percent, or roughly 8,800 workers.

Changes in strategy are always worth noting.

In recent months, the company has stepped beyond selling over the Internet and by telephone—the famous Dell direct model. It has forged retail agreements to sell computers at Wal-Mart stores in the United States, at Carphone Warehouse outlets in Europe and at Bic Camera stores in Japan. More retail deals are in the works.

Rethinking the retail business was a matter of necessity. A lot has changed, Mr. Dell notes, since the company tried and abruptly exited retail sales in 1994. The shift in the consumer computer market and toward notebooks, which customers want to touch before buying, is part of it. So is Dell's need to do better in markets abroad, where people are less comfortable buying computers by phone or over the Internet. "We're going after those new customers with retail partners," Mr. Dell says.

He also moved quickly on another front. Whereas the Dell of old shunned acquisitions, the company is now willing to go shopping. It has made three deals in the last two months—business and consumer software companies—and there will

Again, a shift in strategy—Dell is making acquisitions.

be more, Mr. Dell says. But he says that they will be limited to purchases of smaller companies and start-ups, with 50 to 500 employees, to add technology and expertise that promise to "turbocharge growth" in businesses earmarked for investment and rapid expansion, like services, consumer offerings, international sales and building data centers tailored for big Web companies.

The consumer market looms large for Mr. Dell. Consumers were traditionally an afterthought at Dell, which garners more than 80 percent of its sales from corporate customers. Home computer users generally had to settle for business computers that were tweaked a bit for the masses and were little more than bland, generic boxes.

Future—always good to give the reader a look ahead.

But in recent years, consumers became picky. Where users once focused on price, processing speed and storage capacity, they now looked for stylish, well-designed machines as well—a trend common throughout the entire consumer electronics business, but one that was lost on Dell.

Countermoves—challenges, obstacles.

"On the consumer side, we're drastically changing what we're doing," Mr. Dell says. "We're only touching the surface of the opportunity now."

Ronald G. Garriques, who joined Dell from Motorola in February, is guiding the change in Dell's consumer strategy. Selling machines with more flair in retail stores is part of the plan, said Mr. Garriques, president of the global consumer group, a new position at Dell. But he suggests that Dell will take a hybrid approach, offering hardware options, extra features and services through its Dell.com site on machines that it also sells in stores.

Move/future—possible solutions, strategies. Writer is giving the reader a look forward toward what is likely to happen at Dell. The rest of the story focuses on possible solutions to Dell's problems. This gives the reader a reason to keep reading.

Dell's direct online relationship with customers, Mr. Garriques says, can help it develop services that link PCs, software and cellphones. To illustrate Dell's thinking, he describes as a possibility a service that would allow parents to use Web maps and cellphone signals to track family members on the screen of a Dell PC in the kitchen. "With Dell's direct-to-consumer model," he says, "we can bring that as a solution to families."

Move—introduce Dell's strategy to dig itself out of its hole. Answer: Sell more services.

Such offerings, he says, don't have to generate big profits on their own. "Great services sell a lot of devices that use those services," says Mr. Garriques, noting how Apple's iTunes music service has fed iPod sales.

Move—solutions/ strategies beyond PCs.

Dell also hopes to offer services on hardware beyond PCs. Last month, the company agreed to buy Zing Systems, a Silicon Valley start-up that makes software for hand-held devices that manage and exchange entertainment wirelessly, without the need for a PC. Zing's founder is Tim Bucher, a former product designer at Apple.

Countermove—dull products. What is the company doing about this?

Stale design remains an issue, and something the company has to continue to address if it wants to lift consumer sales. It recently recruited designers from around the world and more than doubled the size of its design group, to 80, in the last year. Dell designers now speak of product "love" and "lust," observes Ken Musgrave, the director of industrial design—a far cry from just a few years ago, when design always took a back seat to competitive pricing.

Move—again, here is another strategy aimed at solving Dell's problems.

In June, Dell introduced notebook computers in eight colors. And color, Mr. Musgrave says, is merely the "first level of personalization" for Dell. He showed off prototype notebook shells in different materials and designs, noting that Dell's build-to-order system gives it the freedom to make highly stylized and personalized machines in limited runs of just dozens to a few hundred. "There are a lot of different design levers to pull for the future," he says.

* * *

Selection 9.2

Dell is hardly alone when it comes to revolving-door chief executives. Starbucks founder Howard Schultz is trying to get the coffee king's mojo back. It turns out that Schultz has been running around complaining about how Starbucks has become commoditized. But wait a minute—wasn't it Schultz who built Starbucks into a giant chain with more than 13,000 stores? Joe Nocera points this out with devastating effects. He casts Schultz as his central figure, asking if he has a split personality: "Is it possible that there are actually two Howard Schultzes lurking around Starbucks headquarters in Seattle?" This column is a powerful 1,800-word profile that quickly gets the reader to the point by highlighting the inconsistencies in Schultz's message.

Talking Business
Give Me a Double Shot of Starbucks Nostalgia
By JOE NOCERA

Is it possible that there are actually two Howard Schultzes lurking around Starbucks headquarters in Seattle? I think it is.

The first Howard Schultz is the man who has coffee in his veins. He's the one who bought what was then the tiny Starbucks company in 1987 and turned it into one of the dominant brands of the age. Starbucks coffee was a step above other coffee, and it also offered a "coffee experience" that made customers willing to pay $4 for something that used to cost them 60 cents.

Starbucks was a place where people could hang out, read the paper, and make friends with the "baristas" behind the counter; Mr. Schultz used to call it the "third place," a respite from both the workplace and the home front. Starbucks had its own language and culture. Its part-time staff got stock options and health insurance. It didn't exploit its coffee growers. It had a huge social responsibility program. And Mr. Schultz, who is chairman of Starbucks, took deep pride in all the things that made Starbucks special.

Last week, this Mr. Schultz was on vivid display when an internal memo he wrote to his top executives was leaked to Starbucksgossip .com. The memo is a cri de coeur from Mr. Schultz, a lament for what has been lost as Starbucks has grown from 6 stores in 1987 to more than 13,000 stores today. He pointed, for instance, to the company's decision some years ago to install automatic espresso machines, which, he wrote, "solved a major problem in terms of speed and service," but also made buying a cup of Starbucks coffee a more antiseptic experience.

He complained about the loss of aroma because the baristas no longer scooped fresh coffee beans from bins and ground them in front of customers. He said that streamlining the company's store designs had caused them to lose "the soul of the past and reflect a chain of stores vs. the warm feeling of a neighborhood store." He said that the Starbucks experience was becoming commoditized, and he urged the executive team to "go back to the core."

The memo was widely lauded as an example of an entrepreneur who understood the importance of recapturing what made his business special before it was too late. "While I wouldn't argue that the Starbucks brand is in its death knell, I would argue that the efficiencies and economies of scale have introduced a virus in need of serious care," wrote Mike Neiss on the Web site of the Tom Peters Company.

Published: March 3, 2007.

"And it looks like Howard Schultz just might be the healer they need."

Warren Bennis, the leadership guru who has served as an informal mentor to Mr. Schultz, said, "This is something every successful chief executive should do every once in a while."

But then there's the other Howard Schultz, the one who signed off on the very compromises he complained about in the memo, precisely because they would help the company grow faster. This second Howard Schultz can talk Wall Street's language: he goes on the quarterly conference calls and spits out data about same-store sales, return on investment, and, most of all, growth. Though it has lagged recently, his company's stock price has risen 5,000 percent since it went public in 1992, in large part because Mr. Schultz has been so fanatical about growth. It closed yesterday at $29.88.

"Starbucks is the fastest-growing retail story of all time," said John Glass, an analyst with CIBC. "It has grown faster than McDonald's ever did."

This second Howard Schultz shows no signs of slowing down anytime soon. "I want to say this as loud as I possibly can," he told Maria Bartiromo on CNBC last November, after Starbucks released its quarterly earnings. "Three to five years, 20 percent revenue growth, 20 to 25 percent earnings per-share growth. And we're headed to 40,000 stores." Those are astounding goals for a company the size of Starbucks: no company in history has ever built 40,000 retail outlets. (McDonald's, by contrast, has 30,000 stores worldwide.) And 25 percent earnings growth is something only the most aggressive of growth companies shoot for.

The quandary Mr. Schultz faces, assuming there is only one of him, is that he wants two things that are incompatible. If he wants to recapture the soul of the old Starbucks, then he has to slow down the company's growth. But if he slows the growth, the stock will collapse. He has to choose. Truth is, though, Mr. Schultz has already chosen.

Once, maybe 10 years ago, Mr. Bennis asked Mr. Schultz why it was so important to him that Starbucks grow so rapidly. "He said something to the effect that if he didn't do it, Starbucks could be cannibalized by another chain that would wipe it out," Mr. Bennis told me.

As I discovered when I asked around, Mr. Schultz is an enormously competitive businessman; I wound up thinking that the idea of relentless growth is just as powerful a driving force for him as coffee itself. In the memo, he complained that Starbucks' competitors have become emboldened to go after Starbucks customers. "This must be eradicated," were the startling words he used.

But to give him his due, Mr. Schultz has always struggled with the problem of trying to stay true to the company's roots while growing aggressively. "Last October or November, he made comments very similar to the thoughts in the memo at a dinner with investors," Mr. Glass said. And according to Anne Saunders, Starbucks' senior vice president for global brand strategy, what he wrote in the memo was nothing Starbucks executives hadn't heard from him many times in the past. "Howard is often challenging us," she said.

"We have grown as a company because we have chosen to do business in a different kind of way," she continued. "If growth comes from doing things that are out of whack, then it is not the right kind of growth." Ms. Saunders went on to say that she, and the rest of the company's managers, believed that the company had grown in ways that remained compatible with its culture.

Maybe. But from where I'm sitting, it just looks as though whenever push has come to shove, the growth imperative has usually won out.

Take, for instance, food. "I remember when Starbucks went public," said Ron Paul of Technomic, a food retail consulting firm. "I went to one of the roadshow presentations. Howard said that they would never serve food. He thought it would dilute the experience." (A Starbucks spokeswoman said Mr. Schultz was pointing out that Starbucks was a coffee company, not a restaurant chain.)

But one of the most important metrics for Wall Street is same-store sales increases. If growth is being generated purely from the opening of new stores—and not from increased sales in stores that are already open—that's viewed as a bad sign. It means that once the company runs out of places to put stores, it will stop growing. For Starbucks, there was always going to be a limit to how much coffee it could sell in any one location, so to goose same-store sales, it began selling food. (Not very good food either, but that's a whole other story.) Most recently, it has begun selling hot breakfast sandwiches in a number of markets, yet another move it would never have made, say, five years ago. The same principle applies to music, to books and all the other things Starbucks now sells in its stores.

The food and brand consultants I spoke to were unanimous in their feeling that Starbucks had hurt itself by expanding so far beyond its coffee and coffeehouse roots—and that it needed to return to those roots. "He is right that Starbucks is losing its soul," said Harvey Hartman, who heads the Hartman Group in Bellevue, Wash. "They were built on the coffee experience, and by moving so far beyond that, they are jeopardizing everything else."

Robert Passikoff, president of the brand consultant Brand Keys, said that Starbucks had taken its eye off the brand. "In trying to migrate from a coffee brand to a lifestyle brand, there has been a certain brand dilution." He agreed that the "whole European coffeehouse experience" was no longer how people thought about Starbucks, to the company's detriment. Mr. Passikoff's firm just completed a survey of 20,000 people by phone and in person that showed that Dunkin'

Donuts now had higher customer loyalty than Starbucks. He also pointed out that Consumer Reports recently asserted that McDonald's coffee was superior to Starbucks's. Both Mr. Passikoff and Mr. Hartman felt that the memo made a great deal of sense.

The Wall Street folks I spoke to, though, saw the memo differently—as a kind of longing for a memory that will never return. "When you grow as big and as fast as they have, you have to make compromises," said Howard Penney, who covers the company for Prudential. "The complexity of the menu has changed dramatically since it first opened," he said. That complexity required automation and other techniques to keep waits for coffee from being too long. (As anyone who buys Starbucks coffee in New York knows, the company doesn't always succeed.)

Mr. Glass of CIBC said: "If it remained a coffee destination and nothing else, same-store sales would not increase. It's a public company. Their job is to make money for the shareholders by selling more stuff." Both Mr. Glass and Mr. Penney pointed out that Starbucks plans to open 2,400 stores this year. That's more than six new stores every day. Tell me how you're going to do that if the baristas start grinding coffee by hand again?

Of course, that's never going to happen, as Ms. Saunders of Starbucks quickly acknowledged when we spoke. "Our business has never been better," she said. "We are really doing well." But the company didn't want to ever rest on its laurels—and it didn't want to sacrifice what made it special just for the sake of growth, she said. "The question is always, how do you keep things in balance?"

For lovers of Starbucks, I suppose it's comforting to know that Mr. Schultz and his team sit around worrying about whether they are watering down the customer experience. But it would be even more comforting if they actually did something about it. Because someday, the growth will slow and the stock will slide—that's inevitable. And how will customers feel if, when that happens, their customer experience has been turned into a drive-through window, just like McDonald's.

Oops, I forgot. Starbucks has already started putting in drive-through windows.

Selection 9.3

Some uninitiated observers of business journalism may view this as a personality profile, but it is really a business profile written by focusing tightly on the chief executive. We learn about how large Ryanair is (850 routes), how much the airline made in profits during the past year ($149 million) and how many passengers it will carry this coming year (68 million). Ryanair's *cantankerous chief executive, Michael O'Leary, gives Sarah Lyall great material to work with here. The writer is able to blend the mundane details— like fares costing $56—in between great quotes. Few CEOs are this colorful and engaging. Count the number of times O'Leary says customers can "go away" if they don't like Ryanair's policies. The phrase appears so many times it can almost be used as a standard transition. By using this device, the writer cleverly frames an image of an executive who isn't afraid of confrontation.*

THE SATURDAY PROFILE
No Apologies From the Boss of a No-Frills Airline
By SARAH LYALL

LONDON—Michael O'Leary, chief executive of the European budget airline Ryanair, was discussing his new scheme to charge passengers to go to the bathroom.

Most passengers—the "discretionary toilet visitors," as he calls them—would eventually forgo in-flight bathroom use altogether, he predicted. Which is good, because he would also like to reduce the number of bathrooms per plane, to one.

What if the plane were stricken by some nasty, effluent illness, like food poisoning?

A snorting noise wafted over from the chair where Mr. O'Leary was sitting. "We don't serve enough food for everybody to get food poisoning," he said.

At 48, the quick-talking, blue-jean-wearing Mr. O'Leary is one of the most successful businessmen in Ireland, presiding over an airline that is, remarkably, flourishing in a brutal climate for airlines (and most other businesses). He is known for thick-skinned aggression, outrageous public statements and an implacable belief that short-haul airline passengers will endure nearly every imaginable indignity, as long as the tickets are cheap and the planes are on time.

"Soon he'll be charging us for oxygen and number of limbs," The Sun groused in a column in June, when he unveiled his latest proposal—getting people to carry their own bags to the plane.

Mr. O'Leary revels in his persona as national pugilist and provocateur, alternately charming and offending.

He once dressed as the pope to advertise Ryanair's new route from Dublin to Rome. He has declared that fat people should pay more for their seats, but that it would take too long to weigh them at the airport. And, at a news conference to discuss the possibility of starting trans-Atlantic flights, he suggested—to the consternation of the young woman gamely translating his remarks into German—that business-class customers would receive oral sex.

Published: July 31, 2009.

Mr. O'Leary may sometimes seem as if he is throwing out insane suggestions for their shock value. But in private, he is known as a tough negotiator whose canny timing and sharp elbows help him extract favorable deals, as when he put in a huge order for new planes when the market collapsed, after the Sept. 11 attacks.

His avowed enemies include unions (his workers are not unionized), politicians who impose airport taxes, environmentalists, bloggers who rant about poor service, travel agents, reporters who expect free seats, regulators who thwart his plans and airport owners like BAA, whom he once called "overcharging rapists."

There is method in all this, it seems.

Insulting, or, "slagging off," as they say here, "the BAA and the British government and the rest is all designed to send strong signals to everyone who deals with Ryanair that you're not going to get away with anything," said Joe Gill, director of equity research at Bloxham Stockbrokers in Dublin.

Ryanair flies more than 850 routes across Europe, often to obscure airports far away from big cities—"from nowhere to nowhere," in the scoffing words of Sir Stelios Haji-Ioannou, who runs the competing airline EasyJet. Ryanair's post-tax profit fell by 78 percent in the year that ended in March, but still amounted to $149 million. While most carriers are hemorrhaging passengers, Ryanair expects its passenger numbers to increase, to 68 million this year from 57 million in 2008.

The mystery is why so many people are willing to put up with an airline that, in the words of The Economist, "has become a byword for appalling customer service, misleading advertising claims and jeering rudeness towards anyone or anything that gets in its way."

"Nobody helps you—it's as simple as that," said Malcolm Ginsberg, editor in chief of the travel newsletter aerbt.co.uk, describing what happens to Ryanair passengers who need assistance at the airport.

That is not the point, Mr. O'Leary said in a recent interview. "Our customer service is unlike every other airline, which has this image of, 'We want to fall down at your feet and you can walk all over us and the customer is always right,' and all that nonsense."

By contrast, Mr. O'Leary continued, Ryanair promises four things: low fares, a good on-time record, few cancellations and few lost bags.

"But if you want anything more—go away! Will we put you in a hotel room if your flight was canceled?" Mr. O'Leary asked rhetorically. "No! Go away."

He was sitting in a cafe at the chamber of commerce here in London, drinking coffee. Soon, he would hold a news conference where, among other things, he would call Prime Minister Gordon Brown a "twit" and a "Scottish miser."

During the interview, he began riffing on the theme of when Ryanair grants refunds, which is never.

"Will we give you a refund on a nonrefundable ticket because your granny died unexpectedly?" he asked. "No! Go away. We're not interested in your sob stories! What part of 'no refund' do you not understand?"

Miss your flight because you had to wait too long at a Ryanair help desk? Too bad! Your luggage is slightly overweight? Throw away the excess, or wear it on the flight! Try to tote your duty-free purchases onto the plane in a shopping bag, when you already have a carry-on bag? Prepare to fork over $40 at the gate.

Ryanair's fares are only 40 euros, or $56, on average. Mr. O'Leary just announced that he would sell one million seats for 5 euros apiece this fall. The airline offsets this with money from deals with hotels, car-rental services, and other partners, along with fees for everything from airport check-in ($56) to online check-in ($7).

Mr. O'Leary runs a tight ship in his office, too. Post-it notes and highlighters are banned. Executives bring in their own pens. To illustrate his commitment to that principle, Mr. O'Leary produced two pens from his pocket, both stolen from hotel rooms.

He stays in budget hotels. He always flies Ryanair, startling fellow passengers by taking their tickets at the gate and by boarding the plane last, where he invariably gets a middle seat.

Mr. O'Leary does not sit in an executive lounge, has no BlackBerry and does not use e-mail because, he says, "I couldn't be bothered with all the crud and the crap and the rubbish that gets sent to you on e-mails."

He grew up outside Dublin and went to a Jesuit boarding school, where his nickname was Ducksie, on account of the way he walked.

"Was the education doled out with a good stiff slap?" he asked. "Yes. Did we suffer great emotional trauma? No."

He began working at Ryanair in 1988, became its deputy chief executive in 1994 and its chief executive in 1997. His personal fortune is estimated to be about $500 million.

"He's one of the few home-grown successes in corporate Ireland in the last 40 years whose success has been sustainable," Mr. Gill, the equity research director, said.

Mr. O'Leary lives on a farm outside of Dublin, raises cattle and racehorses, and rarely takes vacations. He irritated the Irish government by paying thousands of dollars for a taxi medallion for his Mercedes so that he could use the taxi lane, thereby circumventing traffic.

At home, Mr. O'Leary and his wife have three children age 4 and under. One of them was born this summer. There is no nanny. "That's why I'm traveling frequently and overnighting in London," he said, mostly joking.

Mr. O'Leary brushes off the criticism about customer service, pointing to Ryanair's record of responding to complaints within seven days. Most come from people demanding refunds, who are told to go away. Also, the aggrieved have to complain by fax or letter. If they use e-mail, no one will respond.

"People will say"—here Mr. O'Leary adopted a whiny voice— "'As the Founding Fathers wrote down in the American Constitution, we have the inalienable right to bear arms and send in our complaints by e-mail.'

"No, you bloody don't! So go away."

Selection 9.4

A corporate profile doesn't always have to focus on the chief executive. Sometimes the chief executive isn't available for an interview or the interview turns out to be a dud. What do you do? Julie Bosman offers an alternative approach. She cleverly decides to find another central figure to tell the story. In this case, that figure happens to be the Avon lady. Using this device, Bosman shows us how Avon is trying to change its image and become more relevant in the Internet age. This approach works because the Avon lady is closely associated with the Avon brand.

For the Avon Lady, a World Beyond Ringing Doorbells

By JULIE BOSMAN

Luz Stella Bongiovi has a job that many people would envy. After 12 years in the same business, she supervises more than 100 employees and logs about 50 hours a week, coming into work at 10 A.M. and often working at home. She has been sent on junkets to Hawaii, Las Vegas and Puerto Rico. Her earnings total nearly $170,000 a year.

Her job title: Avon lady.

The folks at Avon, however, would call her a sales representative, the updated term for the 468,000 people in the company's work force generating more than 95 percent of sales revenue. But to the public, "Avon lady" has stuck, ever since the company's sales representatives began ringing doorbells in 1886.

Ms. Bongiovi is an example of how to succeed the old-fashioned way: she started small, worked hard and took advantage of her natural business sense to build a living slowly by selling Avon to her extended

Published: May 1, 2006.

network of family, friends and acquaintances. But now, Avon is trying to force itself to step into the future—and bring the sales reps with it, turning its distinctly mid-20th-century sales model into a 21st-century version.

In fact, Avon will announce a new initiative this month to encourage more business to move to the Internet, said Thomas Kelly, Avon's senior vice president for direct selling in the United States. "We really are guns blazing with our excitement about the Internet," he said. "We're moving from just ordering online to supporting their efforts to sell online."

The company is teaching its sales reps to file customer orders online; before, reps would phone in their orders. Now, more than 80 percent use the Internet to do business. Avon is also encouraging its sales reps to set up individual pages on the company's Web site for customers to make online purchases. For instance, by typing in their ZIP code, customers will be directed to their sales rep's page.

But Avon is still holding on to the fundamental part of its business model—a sales force that is paid only by commissions, without salaries, health care or benefits. Signing up is simple: a potential rep pays a $10 fee, fills out a form and receives a starter kit. Then it's up to the newly minted representative to go out and garner sales. That person is also responsible for day-to-day operating expenses and promotions.

Ms. Bongiovi pays for print advertising from her own budget. For example, if a rep wants business cards printed with her name, she pays for them herself. Asked to define the employment status of sales reps, an Avon spokeswoman responded, "Self-employed."

On a recent morning, Ms. Bongiovi was sitting behind a desk in her office in Bushwick, which doubles as a retail space with a storefront on Myrtle Avenue, where she sells Avon products and performs occasional walk-in makeovers. Avon began for her as it had for many women—a side job for stay-at-home mothers who want to earn a little extra money. (The reps are predominantly female.) Ms. Bongiovi grew up in Colombia. Her father owned a supermarket, and she often watched him working in the store and fantasized about her own future.

"I used to dream, 'Oh, I want to have a business when I grow up,' " she said.

Marriage and three children intervened, but one day she signed up for Avon on a whim, getting her first order mostly from family and friends in her neighborhood.

"My first order was $500, and I thought, 'Hmm, this is good,' " said Ms. Bongiovi, who wore a neatly cut blazer, violet-framed eyeglasses and gleaming red nail polish.

Soon, she began recruiting other people to become sales representatives in her "downline," Avon's term for sales reps' own staff members whom they personally recruit and supervise.

Ms. Bongiovi's sales pitch to potential reps reflects her own life story. When she first started selling Avon, she had children at home and no income of her own. Now she owns a six-unit apartment building in Brooklyn and is going through a divorce, dividing up assets and income.

When talking to potential reps, she said, "I tell them: 'What about if your husband leaves you? What if you don't have a husband anymore?' I like to help them, I like to give them support. I teach them how to earn money with Avon."

It is a pitch that falls on welcome ears to Mr. Kelly, the Avon executive. It may be partly a company pitch with a feminist slant, but fundamentally, he said, the business will always be about serving the needs of women.

"Initially, what drove us to this place is that women would like a significantly greater earning opportunity," he said.

But the ability to earn money through Avon may be getting more difficult as the one-on-one sales model goes out of style. How many women today would buy cosmetics from a door-to-door seller? And in an era when many women buy makeup at superstores like Sephora or buy online, how does the Avon sales rep stand a chance?

Candace Corlett, a principal at WSL Strategic Retail, a marketing and retailing consulting company in New York, said the door-to-door model needs to evolve.

"It's just the selling situation that becomes tougher when people aren't home," Ms. Corlett said. "We have moved into an era where you don't necessarily wait for your Avon lady. You go on the Internet."

Donna C. Barson, the president of Barson Marketing in Manalapan, N.J., said that even though Avon is "a company that has a lot of marketing savvy," one part of the model has lost its luster.

"The Avon lady itself doesn't have the cachet it once did," Ms. Barson said.

Mary Lou Quinlan, the chief executive of Just Ask a Woman, a marketing company in New York, said she thought that many women were too busy to sit down and talk to sales representatives.

Still, "it's amazing how women will make the time for face-to-face, woman-to-woman events when they want to," she said. "You do tend to buy more when you're buying face to face with someone."

Mr. Kelly said that the individual sales representative was a retro image that Avon was not willing to let go of.

"I really feel an obligation, like we're a public institution," he said.

But 2005 was difficult for Avon, as Andrea Jung, the company's chairman and chief executive, has acknowledged. At a conference in February in Scottsdale, Ariz., Ms. Jung unveiled a multiyear restructuring plan that would cost the company nearly $500 million. The money is to be spent on increased advertising, enhanced support and programs for sales representatives, additional product research and development and market research. When the company reduced ad spending last year, the sales reps felt it, as did management. Mr. Kelly said the company's top line, or revenue, "is all related to the performance of our sales representatives." While sales representatives once had only one way to make money—by selling Avon personally—now the more ambitious reps can earn fees from the reps they recruit. Ms. Bongiovi said she earned $75,000 yearly just in fees generated from her downline.

Besides making itself more tech-proficient, Avon has also tried to shed its fusty image by taking on the college market. In 2003, the company introduced Mark, a cosmetics line aimed at teenagers and women in their 20's.

The plan was twofold: to introduce Avon to younger women who considered the brand grandmother territory; and, after these women were established customers, encouraging them to become sales reps themselves.

Gyda Arber, 26, an actress who lives in Manhattan, is one such woman. She became aware of Avon through a television commercial for Mark. While visiting avon.com, and buying more than $150 in Mark merchandise, she noticed an online ad on the site that offered 40 percent off a purchase, if you signed up to be an Avon sales representative. Ms. Arber signed up.

"Living in Manhattan, you don't run into a lot of Avon ladies," she said. But after she began pitching products to her friends and colleagues in local theater, she found herself with a part-time job.

"There have been periods where it's been 100 percent of my income," Ms. Arber said, citing the unpredictability of her acting work.

Ms. Arber also gives home parties once or twice a month, inviting friends and acquaintances.

It is a technique that has been borrowed by retailers much more fashionable than Avon. The Body Shop (recently acquired by L'Oréal) has a feature on its Web site, thebodyshop.com, allowing customers to host a "girls' nite out" to sell products to friends at home. The Body Shop has also begun a service encouraging customers to sign up as "independent consultants," a sales model like Avon's.

Other companies may be trying to mimic the personalized Avon technique. Makeup, after all, is a product that many women like to get professional advice on before they buy. The free makeovers offered at makeup counters in department stores often result in women walking away with a bagful of personally recommended cosmetics.

MAC, the cosmetics retailer, has a feature on its Web site, maccosmetics.com, called "e-mail an artist," where company-trained specialists handle questions online.

Getting advice from Avon sales representatives could be described as the one-on-one consultation that many women want, albeit from a friend or acquaintance who is considered more trustworthy than a stranger in a lab coat at a cosmetics counter.

In an industry often focused on buzz, the service that Avon offers is still about trust between sellers and consumers, said Andy Sernovitz, chief executive of Word of Mouth Marketing Association, a trade group in Chicago.

"Coming off a decade of all automated commerce, more and more companies are understanding the value of the personal touch," Mr. Sernovitz said. "The reason word of mouth exists, and the reason we exist, is very much tied to people's desire to connect to other people."

A Conversation with . . . **Joe Nocera**

TALKING BUSINESS COLUMNIST; STAFF WRITER,
THE NEW YORK TIMES MAGAZINE

© The New York Times

Joe Nocera writes the "Talking Business" column for The New York Times and is a staff writer for The New York Times Magazine. Before joining The Times in 2005, Mr. Nocera spent 10 years at Fortune magazine, where he held a variety of positions, including contributing writer, editor-at-large and executive editor. In the 1980s, he served as a contributing editor at Newsweek, as executive editor of New England Monthly and as senior editor at Texas Monthly. His most recent book is "Good Guys and Bad Guys: Behind the Scenes with the Saints and Scoundrels of American Business (and Everything in Between)" (Portfolio, 2008). He was a 2007 Pulitzer Prize finalist. The following is an edited transcript of a telephone interview.

What is your beat or area of coverage?
My beat is pretty undefined. I cover Wall Street, finance, food, pharma. Sometimes I write about those topics. But a lot of times I try to write about things we don't write about all that much in the business section—the plaintiff's bar, or individual companies that fall between the cracks. I am trying to give people a perspective of business they wouldn't otherwise get in The Times.

What attracted you to The New York Times after being at Fortune magazine?
It isn't that much different. I sort of write a magazine story in disguise every week. They give me a lot of space and I try to create the kind of context that magazine stories do, giving people a framework to think about a particular

issue. I try to get to the back story and the subplot a little more than you would in a news story. The writing is a little different, but I don't find that it has been a radical transformation from what I did vs. what I do now.

Who are you trying to reach with your columns/stories?
At Fortune you really were writing to business people. At The New York Times you are writing a lot to people who are not part of the business world. These people are hungry for information and ways to think about it. It does feel like a very different audience. I want to educate and illuminate, but I want to do it through the vehicle of a story. I like to find a story that can serve as a thematic example for a larger problem that I am trying to illuminate. Storytelling is a device I use to keep the reader interested, to engage the reader.

How did you develop your expertise as a business writer?
Well, I did it on the fly, to be honest. I moved to Texas in 1982 working for Texas Monthly, and I really didn't know anything about business. I had been a political writer. I was assigned to write a profile of a guy named T. Boone Pickens Jr., and I happened to write about him at the moment that he did his first big hostile takeover that put him on the map. He liked me and he invited me to come to the Waldorf and watch him try and take over Cities Service oil company [now Citgo]. It was a remarkable, fascinating, incredibly dramatic story. I was hooked on business after that. I couldn't get enough of it.

So what fascinates you about business reporting?
I like the human drama—the crimes of it, the victories of it, the triumphs of it, the innovation of it. I just think there are lots of storytelling opportunities in business if you think of it as human drama, as I think of it, as opposed to balance sheets and income statements. Somehow business captured my imagination in a way that politics never did.

So how did your Fortune and Texas Monthly experience help you?
At Texas Monthly I learned to tell a story. It was a great narrative institution in the 1980s and it still is. You got to write really long stories. You really had to hook the reader. It really taught me how to write a business narrative. Fortune gave me rigor. It taught me about the importance of numbers, a rigorous approach toward understanding profits, return on equity and how to cut through the B.S. I just felt like I came out of Fortune with a business education that was invaluable.

What sort of cookbook approach would you recommend to beginning writers?
I was afraid you were going to ask me that. I know what I am going to recommend is heresy, but I think journalists would be better off if they spent six months inside a company to see how it actually works. I believe you need to get to know people in business and listen to what they have to say and not necessarily assume that they are out to gouge you or screw you. Sometimes they are and sometimes they aren't. I have a lot of empathy for business people, and I don't mean that I am sympathetic. I express empathy as a way to get inside their heads and understand them—I don't think enough business journalists do that and I think it would be very, very helpful to business journalism.

So would you say there are a lot of misconceptions about business?

I think there are some. Businessmen are not inherently evil. A lot of the things that go on in business are driven by institutional imperatives. One of the things my column tries to do is say here is a situation that may look black and white, but it is actually gray.

How do you frame a story before doing the major interview?

I want to do enough research so I can ask questions based on knowledge and not be just a transcriber. But I also want it to feel like I am having a conversation. I am a columnist, so I am going to have a point of view. I will often go into an interview wanting the person that I am interviewing to buttress my point of view or to knock it down. I tend to go into an interview knowing what I want to get out of it.

What vehicles do you employ to put the subject at ease?

I don't really believe in interviewing anybody for more than two hours at a stretch because I think it is diminishing returns. I would rather quit the interview and come back a couple days later and pick it up. But how I put a person at ease is by trying to make the interview as conversational as possible. I don't believe in asking a series of pointed questions where the subject doesn't really know where you are coming from or where you are going. I don't do that. I often say "the reason I am asking this question is because of such and such." Sometimes I make a little speech. In a long interview, one of the best ways I know to keep people engaged is to ask about themselves. People like to talk about themselves.

What is the most challenging interview you have done?

Let me think, George Steinbrenner yelling at me, maybe? I did a story on [Apple CEO] Steve Jobs at one point. He is so controlling, there is always a high degree of difficulty. I had a situation a year ago where he called me up and called me a slime bucket. Then I wanted him to talk to me about his health issues on the record. He didn't want to do it. He would say if you want to hear what I have to say it is going to be off the record. That was very difficult. The hard part is where you know you are going to rough somebody up and you have to call them and ask them the tough questions. That is never fun. It never gets easier, but you have got to do it and you have got to give them their say.

What advice would you have for recent graduates?

I think business is going to continue to grow in importance. Look at the financial crisis. People have a much better understanding of the role of business in their lives and people are in the stock market in a way they didn't use to be—they are interested in individual companies. With the rise of business Web sites, there is a much greater need for business journalists than there ever was before. So actually I think it is a great career path. It is never going to make you rich. But you don't go into any form of journalism to get rich.

MAKING**CONNECTIONS**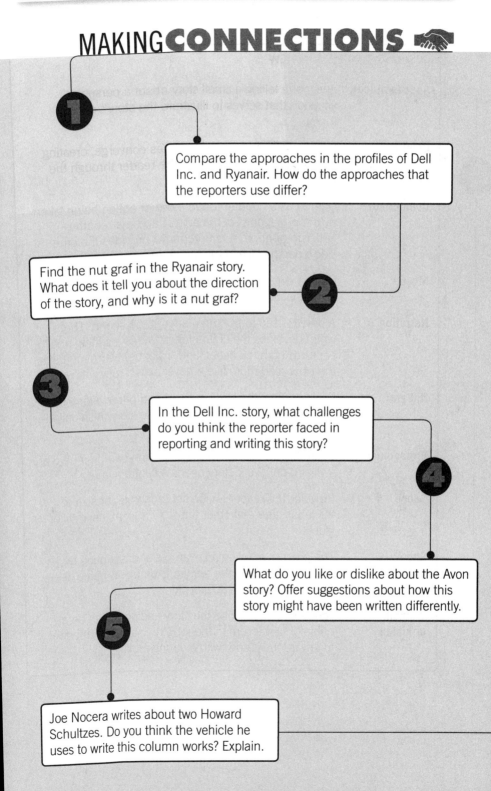

1 Compare the approaches in the profiles of Dell Inc. and Ryanair. How do the approaches that the reporters use differ?

2 Find the nut graf in the Ryanair story. What does it tell you about the direction of the story, and why is it a nut graf?

3 In the Dell Inc. story, what challenges do you think the reporter faced in reporting and writing this story?

4 What do you like or dislike about the Avon story? Offer suggestions about how this story might have been written differently.

5 Joe Nocera writes about two Howard Schultzes. Do you think the vehicle he uses to write this column works? Explain.

BUSINESS CONCEPTS REVI

Anecdotal lede   A vignette
situation
theme.

Conflict   Comes when
tension. Conflic
story.

Countermove   Offered as a counter to the move or action being taken
by the protagonist of the story. Can be a rebuttal,
criticism or gripe. A countermove provides the other
side's perspective to the argument.

Move   Occurs when the story's central figure or protagonist
takes the story in a direction.

Narration   A device used to put the reader at the scene. The
writer develops the character, provides a setting and
captures both the action and dialogue. Narration helps
the story read more like a novel than a news story.

Nut graf   Explains what the story is about and offers a larger
context of what is yet to come in the story. Also called
the focus graf.

Protagonist   Central figure of the story. The person can be a hero or
a villain, but every story needs a central figure.

Scope   Provides the reader an idea of proportion or size of
the landscape—whether the story is local, national or
global.

Show,
don't tell   The process of using an example or description to
illustrate a point to the reader. Example: A bottle of
Maalox sat on the CEO's desk.

Walkoff,
or kicker   Term used to describe the story ending. It can be a
quote or clever turn in the story. It is always important
to reward the reader with a strong ending.

CHAPTER 10

investigative reporting

● NO BOOK ON BUSINESS REPORTING would be complete without some mention of investigative reporting—the enterprise stories that dig deep under the surface, examining problems and exposing abuses.

Business plays an important role in society. Commerce creates jobs, leading to economic growth and prosperity. But business isn't immune to shenanigans—accountants cooking books, chief executives collecting multi-million-dollar bonuses while the government bails out their firms, con artists bilking investors and corporations bribing foreign government officials. Other, more nefarious characters sell drugs, embezzle funds and commit fraud or even murder to earn a profit.

This is where investigative reporters come in. They play a critical role in democracy, shedding light on problems and corrupt practices. By doing so, journalists can help protect the poor, the vulnerable and the downtrodden.

At its best, investigative reporting prompts changes. Maybe lawmakers will propose new legislation or regulation. Maybe shareholders will be spurred to push for a new chief executive. Or maybe citizens will pound on courtroom doors, demanding that current laws be enforced.

Reforms benefit everyone and lead to a better society. At least that is the theory. But despite their importance, investigative journalists are unfortunately in short supply lately. Some critics blame cost-cutting in the news industry, which has led to layoffs and less energy being channeled toward expensive investigations. That may partially explain why so much financial fraud went undetected until it boiled over during the Great Recession of 2007–2009.

Investigative reporting sounds exciting, and for people who love doing it, it is. But it can involve weeks, months or years of interviewing hundreds of sources, combing through documents and analyzing spreadsheets to get to the bottom of what is going on. The work can be tedious, the payoff uncertain. Targets of an investigation may threaten lawsuits and sometimes even bodily harm. Only an elite few get to work on an investigation full time. Most fit their investigative stories around basic beat coverage.

"I had to squeeze in investigative reporting projects amongst my daily reporting assignments. There is not a way to do that if you don't plan," says Diana B. Henriques, an investigative reporter at The New York Times. "After

I do enough fishing, I frame a thesis and ask myself what I need to learn to prove that thesis—or, as important, disprove or revise it." Henriques was a 2005 Pulitzer Prize finalist for her series detailing the financial exploitation of military personnel by financial service companies. The series prompted legislative reform and cash reimbursements for tens of thousands of service members. "There was an enormous outpouring of thanks from the families," says Henriques, who speaks at length about investigative reporting in this chapter.

Business stories have moved to the forefront of investigative reporting during the past decade, becoming a staple at the annual Pulitzer Prize ceremony. This shift is a sign that business writing has come to command a new respect in newsrooms.

The McWane Inc. story featured in this chapter is a good example. It examines the safety record of one of the world's largest makers of cast iron and sewer pipe. The reporters found a hellish place that was one of the most dangerous work sites in America, with workers suffering crushed limbs and lost lives. The McWane stories were part of a series on workplace safety that won the Pulitzer Prize for Public Service in 2004.

Four years later, Walt Bogdanich and Jake Hooker won the 2008 Pulitzer Prize for Investigative Reporting for their riveting series about suppliers who were poisoning people by adding the toxic industrial solvent diethylene glycol to drugs, cold medicine and toothpaste. The solvent made the goods less expensive and therefore easier to sell in the global marketplace—but, as the reporters discovered, ended up poisoning thousands of people around the world.

As you will see in this chapter, investigative business reporting plays an important role in our democracy. It also offers some of the most rewarding journalism around. Untold stories are everywhere; you don't have to work a big beat for a major media outlet to find one.

Happy hunting.

Selection 10.1

The beauty of this story is that it's presented in a stark, simple way that everyone can understand. In the United States today, we tend to think of dying at work as something from the bygone Industrial Age, when working conditions were far more hazardous. A story like this grabs attention because it shows how unexpected danger can lurk beneath the surface of something that seems mundane and ordinary. Workers in the United States take safety for granted. As for the reporting, incident reports related to the workers' deaths provided a foundation. From there, the reporters branched outward. Some of the reporters' best sources were people who worked at the plant. But what really makes the story is how the reporters capture the workplace culture at Tyler Pipe by reconstructing what it was like to work there.

At a Texas Foundry, an Indifference to Life

BY DAVID BARSTOW and LOWELL BERGMAN

TYLER, Tex.—It is said that only the desperate seek work at Tyler Pipe, a sprawling, rusting pipe foundry out on Route 69, just past the flea market. Behind a high metal fence lies a workplace that is part Dickens and part Darwin, a dim, dirty, hellishly hot place where men are regularly disfigured by amputations and burns, where turnover is so high that convicts are recruited from local prisons, where some workers urinate in their pants because their bosses refuse to let them step away from the manufacturing line for even a few moments.

Rolan Hoskin was from the ranks of the desperate. His life was a tailspin of unemployment, debt and divorce. A master electrician, 48 years old, he had retreated to a low-rent apartment on the outskirts of town and taken an entry-level maintenance job on the graveyard shift at Tyler Pipe.

He would come home covered in fine black soot, utterly drained and dreading the next shift. "I don't know if I'm going to last another week," his twin brother recalls him saying. The job scared him; he didn't know what he was doing. But the pay was decent, almost $10 an hour, and his electricity was close to being cut off. "He was just trying to make it," his daughter said.

On June 29, 2000, in his second month on the job, Mr. Hoskin descended into a deep pit under a huge molding machine and set to work on an aging, balky conveyor belt that carried sand. Federal rules require safety guards on conveyor belts to prevent workers from getting caught and crushed. They also require belts to be shut down when maintenance is done on them.

But this belt was not shut down, federal records show. Nor was it protected by metal safety guards. That very night, Mr. Hoskin had been trained to adjust the belt while it was still running. Less downtime that way, the men said. Now it was about 4 A.M., and Mr. Hoskin was alone in the cramped, dark pit. The din was deafening, the footing treacherous under heavy drifts of black sand.

He was found on his knees. His left arm had been crushed first, the skin torn off. His head had been pulled between belt and rollers. His skull had split. "If he fought that machine I know his last thought was me," said his daughter, April Hoskin-Silva, her dark eyes rimmed with tears.

It was not just a conveyor belt that claimed Mr. Hoskin's life that warm summer night. He also fell victim to a way of doing business that has produced vast profits and, as the plant's owners have

Published: January 8, 2003. Full text available at: www.nytimes.com/2003/01/08/national/08PIPE .html and the series "Dangerous Business" is available at: http://topics.nytimes.com/topics/news/ national/series/dangerousbusiness/index.html?scp=2&sq=Texas%20Foundry%20series&st=cse

McWane Inc. had been found guilty on 30 counts of safety and environmental crimes at its plant in Phillipsburg, N.J.

admitted in federal court, deliberate indifference to the safety of workers at Tyler Pipe.

Mr. Hoskin worked for McWane Inc., a privately held company based in Birmingham, Ala., that owns Tyler Pipe and is one of the world's largest manufacturers of cast-iron sewer and water pipe. It is also one of the most dangerous employers in America, according to a nine-month examination by The New York Times, the PBS television program "Frontline" and the Canadian Broadcasting Corporation.

Since 1995, at least 4,600 injuries have been recorded in McWane foundries, many hundreds of them serious ones, company documents show. Nine workers, including Mr. Hoskin, have been killed. McWane plants, which employ about 5,000 workers, have been cited for more than 400 federal health and safety violations, far more than their six major competitors combined.

No McWane executive would be interviewed on the record. But in a series of written responses, the company's president, G. Ruffner Page, acknowledged "serious mistakes" and expressed deep regret for Mr. Hoskin's death. "Our intensified focus on safety speaks to lessons learned," he wrote. At the same time, he sought to explain and strongly defend the company's business methods.

"Over the years, McWane has grown by the acquisition of troubled companies that had become uncompetitive," he wrote. "Through substantial investment in new plant and equipment and more disciplined management practices, McWane transformed these underperforming companies into efficient and viable operations." Disciplined management, he said, has allowed McWane to stave off foreign competitors who have no regard for safety.

In the last decade, many American corporations have embraced such a vision of capitalism—cutting costs, laying off workers and pressing those who remain to labor harder, longer and more efficiently. But top federal and state regulators say McWane has taken this idea to the extreme. Describing the company's business, they use the words "lawless" and "rogue."

The company's managers call it "the McWane way."

The story of Tyler Pipe, drawn from company and government documents and interviews with dozens of current and former workers and managers, is a case study in the application of the McWane way. It is the anatomy of a workplace where, federal officials and employees say, nearly everything—safety programs, environmental controls, even the smallest federally mandated precautions that might have kept Rolan Hoskin alive—has been subordinated to production, to the commandment to keep the pipe rolling off the line.

Federal safety inspectors tried to make a difference. They cited and fined and cajoled. But for years, records show, little changed.

"You put people at risk," a former senior plant manager at Tyler Pipe said. "We did every day."

Which is why even now the toughest of Tyler Pipe veterans remember the day McWane came to town as the day they were, as one of them put it, "kicked into hell."

Introducing 'the McWane Way'
Tyler, a city of 85,000 an hour and a half's drive east of Dallas, began as a stagecoach town, but it came of age around two precious commodities, East Texas crude and some of the finest roses on earth. Oil and roses still help define Tyler, or at least a certain conjured Tyler. The municipal rose garden alone has 38,000 bushes, and the old oil families still carry clout.

But by the early 90's, the shuttered storefronts down by the county courthouse explained why local leaders were so endlessly worried about the care and nurturing of Tyler's contemporary crown jewels—the Kelly-Springfield tire plant, two air-conditioner factories and Tyler Pipe.

These big manufacturers, they knew, represented something extremely valuable and increasingly rare: places where someone with a high school diploma and a strong back could make $15 an hour, where a Mexican immigrant with little English could firmly grasp the next rung.

The pipe foundry occupies several hundred acres northwest of downtown. Its smokestacks rise high above a north and south plant, each with its own cupola, a multistory furnace that melts tons of scrap metal to produce smoky white rivers of molten iron. The molten iron is poured into spinning cylinders to form pipes, into molds of packed black sand to make fittings.

The company would not let a reporter tour the plant. But employees describe simply stepping inside as an overwhelming experience. First is the heat, wave upon wave of it, sometimes in excess of 130 degrees. Then there is the noise—of pipe slamming into pipe, of pneumatic tools that grind and cut, of massive machines that shudder and shake, of honking forklifts and roaring exhaust systems. Dust and fumes choke the lungs and coat the lights, leaving the plant floor a spectral labyrinth of glowing pipes and blackened machinery.

In the early 90's, Tyler Pipe employed about 2,800 people and did about $200 million in business a year. It was modestly profitable, and the owners, the Tyler Corporation, were conventionally paternalistic. They distributed turkeys at Christmas and door prizes at the annual employee barbecue. Regulators said the plant, while far from perfect, made an effort to comply with safety and environmental rules.

In late 1995, the Tyler Corporation sold the foundry to McWane. In one stroke, McWane had bought one of its main rivals and acquired its largest plant.

Within weeks, senior executives flew in from Birmingham and set about executing a plan of stunning audacity: Over the next two years, they cut nearly two-thirds of the employees, yet insisted that production continue apace. They eliminated quality control inspectors and safety inspectors, pollution control personnel and relief workers, cleaning crews and maintenance workers.

"It got pretty bad," recalled Kevin Fowler, the human resources manager from 1996 to 1999. "If I walked into a department people would wonder if I was coming with their termination."

Alarmed by the layoffs, city leaders sought meetings with McWane executives. Their requests were rebuffed. "They just disassociated themselves from the city," Thomas G. Mullins, the chamber of commerce president, recalled.

To keep up production, McWane eliminated one of three shifts; instead of three shifts of eight hours, there were two 12-hour shifts. At the end of a shift, supervisors often marched through yelling, "Four more hours!" So employees worked 16-hour days, sometimes seven days a week.

Men who operated one machine were ordered to operate three. Breaks were allowed only if a relief worker was available, but McWane had reduced the number of relief workers and forbade supervisors to fill in for hourly workers. The policy hit hardest near iron-pouring stations, where workers had to drink plenty of fluids to withstand the heat. The humiliating result, six workers said in separate interviews, was that men were sometimes forced to urinate in their pants or risk heat exhaustion.

Even the most basic amenities did not survive. The barbecues and 401(k) plan were easy enough targets. But items like soap, medicated skin cream and hand towels were eliminated from the plant stockroom as unnecessary "luxuries," company records show. If they were available at all, they had to be specially ordered with approval from top managers.

Several workers said they were told by their bosses to bring their own toilet tissue. Near the cupola, managers rationed crushed ice for the workers' drinks, company records show. Out by the loading docks, they eliminated portable heaters used by forklift drivers to warm up in winter. "We do not provide comfort heat for individual employees," Dick Stoker, the works manager, explained in a memorandum.

Restrictions were placed on safety equipment. Protective aprons, safety boots and face shields were no longer stocked and readily available. Heavy, heat-resistant $17 gloves were replaced by $2 cloth ones. As a result, workers wrapped their hands in duct tape to protect from burns.

The union was helpless to resist, past and current leaders agree. Organized labor had never been a potent force at Tyler Pipe, and the layoffs devastated the union's membership. The contract barred strikes, permitted 16-hour days and let breaks be canceled.

"My hands was tied," said Bobby Hopson, former president of Local 1157 of the United Steelworkers of America.

Morale plummeted, but profits soared. Senior managers say they were told that Tyler Pipe earned more than $50 million in 1996— double the reported profits for the five-year period before McWane arrived.

Four years after the takeover, inspectors from the federal Occupational Safety and Health Administration spent several days taking the measure of the new regime. They found more than 150 safety hazards. They found poorly maintained equipment. They found a work force that was poorly trained, ill equipped, overworked.

"Throughout the plant, molten metal is seen spilling from the cupolas, bulls and ladles," their report said. "The forklift trucks transport the metal, and the ground behind the trucks often smokes with puddles of molten metal. Workers are covered with black residue from the foundry sand. Many work areas are dark, due to poor lighting and clouds of sand. Despite all the ignition and fuel sources, exit paths are not obvious. Many workers have scars or disfigurations which are noticeable from several feet away. Burns and amputations are frequent.

"This facility is located in a relatively small town where jobs are not plentiful. Throughout the plant, in supervisors' offices and on bulletin boards, next to production charts and union memos, is posted in big orange letters: REDUCE MAN HOURS PER TON."

*   *   *

Additional reporting by
James Sandler and Robin Stein.

Selection 10.2

We take it for granted that food and medicine should be free from contamination. But great stories often turn conventional wisdom on its head. Who would ever think that someone would deliberately put a prime ingredient from antifreeze into drugs, cough syrup and toothpaste? The fact that it is happening and people are dying is stunning. Notice how Walt Bogdanich and Jake Hooker lay out the problem first and then take the reader on a poison trail—tracing how the offensive ingredients made their way into the food and drug chain. First we learn about the developing world and then, much later, the United States. The reporters are in essence bringing the story home. This makes the risks real and gives the story greater impact. This isn't just a botched supply-chain problem affecting China or India; it is deliberate tampering! And the tampering is affecting people on a global scale. In other installments of this multipart investigation, Bogdanich and Hooker show how the solvent has gotten into toothpaste sold in U.S. prisons and hospitals. The reporters do a great job of breaking down a complex supply chain, explaining the risks and showing the harm the tampering has caused.

From China to Panama, a Trail of Poisoned Medicine

By WALT BOGDANICH and JAKE HOOKER

The kidneys fail first. Then the central nervous system begins to misfire. Paralysis spreads, making breathing difficult, then often impossible without assistance. In the end, most victims die.

Many of them are children, poisoned at the hands of their unsuspecting parents.

The syrupy poison, diethylene glycol, is an indispensable part of the modern world, an industrial solvent and prime ingredient in some antifreeze.

It is also a killer. And the deaths, if not intentional, are often no accident.

Over the years, the poison has been loaded into all varieties of medicine—cough syrup, fever medication, injectable drugs—a result of counterfeiters who profit by substituting the sweet-tasting solvent for a safe, more expensive syrup, usually glycerin, commonly used in drugs, food, toothpaste and other products.

Toxic syrup has figured in at least eight mass poisonings around the world in the past two decades. Researchers estimate that thousands have died. In many cases, the precise origin of the poison has

Published: May 6, 2007. Full text available at: www.nytimes.com/2007/05/06/world/06poison.html

A Toxic Pipeline: Coverage by Walt Bogdanich and Jake Hooker

Report an Error

☑ SIGN IN TO RECOMMEND
✉ E-MAIL

Stories in this Pulitzer Prize-winning series have examined how dangerous and poisonous pharmaceutical ingredients from China have flowed into the global market. Reporting on four continents, Walt Bogdanich and Jake Hooker traced the illicit ingredients through traders and middlemen that formed a supply chain stretching from small factories in rural China to consumers around the world. The stories detailed the devastating, sometime deadly, human cost of this toxic pipeline.

Articles in the Series

Heparin Find May Point to Chinese Counterfeiting
By WALT BOGDANICH; DAVID BARBOZA CONTRIBUTED REPORTING FROM SHANGHAI, and JAKE HOOKER FROM BEIJING
Chinese drug counterfeiting may be the cause of 19

Multimedia

▣ Video
Dubai Rx: Conduit for Fake Drugs
Massive free trade zones like those in Dubai are being used by counterfeiters to smuggle fake drugs from China to Europe and the United States.

▨ Interactive Graphic
A Poison's Path From China to Medication in Panama
How a toxic solvent made its way into medication in Panama.

Photos *Click on a photo to view related article*

The New York Times

Additional articles and multimedia in the Pulitzer Prize–winning series "A Toxic Pipeline" are available at: http://topics.nytimes.com/topics/news/international/series/toxicpipeline/index .html?scp=1&sq=A%20toxic%20pipeline&st=Search

never been determined. But records and interviews show that in three of the last four cases it was made in China, a major source of counterfeit drugs.

Panama is the most recent victim. Last year, government officials there unwittingly mixed diethylene glycol into 260,000 bottles of cold medicine—with devastating results. Families have reported 365 deaths from the poison, 100 of which have been confirmed so far. With the onset of the rainy season, investigators are racing to exhume as many potential victims as possible before bodies decompose even more.

Panama's death toll leads directly to Chinese companies that made and exported the poison as 99.5 percent pure glycerin.

Forty-six barrels of the toxic syrup arrived via a poison pipeline stretching halfway around the world. Through shipping records and interviews with government officials, The New York Times traced this pipeline from the Panamanian port of Colón, back through trading companies in Barcelona, Spain, and Beijing, to its beginning near the Yangtze Delta in a place local people call "chemical country."

The counterfeit glycerin passed through three trading companies on three continents, yet not one of them tested the syrup to confirm what was on the label. Along the way, a certificate falsely attesting to the purity of the shipment was repeatedly altered, eliminating the name of the manufacturer and previous owner. As a result, traders bought the syrup without knowing where it came from, or who made it. With this information, the traders might have discovered—as The Times did—that the manufacturer was not certified to make pharmaceutical ingredients.

An examination of the two poisoning cases last year—in Panama and earlier in China—shows how China's safety regulations have lagged behind its growing role as low-cost supplier to the world. It also demonstrates how a poorly policed chain of traders in country after country allows counterfeit medicine to contaminate the global market.

Last week, the United States Food and Drug Administration warned drug makers and suppliers in the United States "to be especially vigilant" in watching for diethylene glycol. The warning did not specifically mention China, and it said there was "no reason to believe" that glycerin in this country was tainted. Even so, the agency asked that all glycerin shipments be tested for diethylene glycol, and said it was "exploring how supplies of glycerin become contaminated."

China is already being accused by United States authorities of exporting wheat gluten containing an industrial chemical, melamine, that ended up in pet food and livestock feed. The F.D.A. recently banned imports of Chinese-made wheat gluten after it was linked to pet deaths in the United States.

Beyond Panama and China, toxic syrup has caused mass poisonings in Haiti, Bangladesh, Argentina, Nigeria and twice in India.

In Bangladesh, investigators found poison in seven brands of fever medication in 1992, but only after countless children died. A Massachusetts laboratory detected the contamination after Dr. Michael L. Bennish, a pediatrician who works in developing countries, smuggled samples of the tainted syrup out of the country in a suitcase. Dr. Bennish, who investigated the Bangladesh epidemic and helped write a 1995 article about it for BMJ, formerly known as the British Medical Journal, said that given the amount of medication distributed, deaths "must be in the thousands or tens of thousands."

"It's vastly underreported," Dr. Bennish said of diethylene glycol poisoning. Doctors might not suspect toxic medicine, particularly in poor countries with limited resources and a generally unhealthy population, he said, adding, "Most people who die don't come to a medical facility."

The makers of counterfeit glycerin, which superficially looks and acts like the real thing but generally costs considerably less, are rarely identified, much less prosecuted, given the difficulty of tracing shipments across borders. "This is really a global problem, and it needs to be handled in a global way," said Dr. Henk Bekedam, the World Health Organization's top representative in Beijing.

Seventy years ago, medicine laced with diethylene glycol killed more than 100 people in the United States, leading to the passage of the toughest drug regulations of that era and the creation of the modern Food and Drug Administration.

The F.D.A. has tried to help in poisoning cases around the world, but there is only so much it can do.

*   *   *

In China, the government is vowing to clean up its pharmaceutical industry, in part because of criticism over counterfeit drugs flooding the world markets. In December, two top drug regulators were arrested on charges of taking bribes to approve drugs. In addition, 440 counterfeiting operations were closed down last year, the World Health Organization said.

But when Chinese officials investigated the role of Chinese companies in the Panama deaths, they found that no laws had been broken, according to an official of the nation's drug enforcement agency. China's drug regulation is "a black hole," said one trader who has done business through CNSC Fortune Way, the Beijing-based broker that investigators say was a crucial conduit for the Panama poison.

In this environment, Wang Guiping, a tailor with a ninth-grade education and access to a chemistry book, found it easy to enter the pharmaceutical supply business as a middleman. He quickly discovered what others had before him: that counterfeiting was a simple way to increase profits.

And then people in China began to die.

Cheating the System

Mr. Wang spent years as a tailor in the manufacturing towns of the Yangtze Delta, in eastern China. But he did not want to remain a common craftsman, villagers say. He set his sights on trading chemicals, a business rooted in the many small chemical plants that have sprouted in the region.

"He didn't know what he was doing," Mr. Wang's older brother, Wang Guoping, said in an interview. "He didn't understand chemicals."

But he did understand how to cheat the system.

Wang Guiping, 41, realized he could earn extra money by substituting cheaper, industrial-grade syrup—not approved for human consumption—for pharmaceutical grade syrup. To trick pharmaceutical buyers, he forged his licenses and laboratory analysis reports, records show.

Mr. Wang later told investigators that he figured no harm would come from the substitution, because he initially tested a small quantity. He did it with the expertise of a former tailor.

He swallowed some of it. When nothing happened, he shipped it.

One company that used the syrup beginning in early 2005 was Qiqihar No. 2 Pharmaceutical, about 1,000 miles away in Heilongjiang Province in the northeast. A buyer for the factory had seen a posting for Mr. Wang's syrup on an industry Web site.

After a while, Mr. Wang set out to find an even cheaper substitute syrup so he could increase his profit even more, according to a Chinese investigator. In a chemical book he found what he was looking for: another odorless syrup—diethylene glycol. At the time, it sold for 6,000 to 7,000 yuan a ton, or about $725 to $845, while pharmaceutical-grade syrup cost 15,000 yuan, or about $1,815, according to the investigator.

Mr. Wang did not taste-test this second batch of syrup before shipping it to Qiqihar Pharmaceutical, the government investigator said, adding, "He knew it was dangerous, but he didn't know that it could kill."

The manufacturer used the toxic syrup in five drug products: ampules of Amillarisin A for gall bladder problems; a special enema fluid for children; an injection for blood vessel diseases; an intravenous pain reliever; and an arthritis treatment.

In April 2006, one of southern China's finest hospitals, in Guangzhou, Guangdong Province, began administering Amillarisin A. Within a month or so, at least 18 people had died after taking the medicine, though some had already been quite sick.

Renwick McLean and
Brent McDonald contributed reporting.

Selection 10.3

This story is what is often referred to in business reporting as a "fly on the wall." Readers become observers to events as they unfold. In fact, the reporters were not present for these events, but they did a marvelous job of reconstructing scenes by using court documents and conducting detailed interviews. (Notice that the eighth paragraph details how this work was done, to reassure readers that the facts have been checked.) The story's use of these details keeps readers moving through what is a complex set of events. The result is a gripping narrative that the reader can't put down.

ENRON'S MANY STRANDS: THE COMPANY UNRAVELS
Enron Buffed Image to a Shine Even as It Rotted From Within
By KURT EICHENWALD with DIANA B. HENRIQUES

Kenneth L. Lay strode onto a ballroom stage at the Hyatt Regency Hill Country Resort in San Antonio, walking between two giant screens that displayed his projected image. Before him, bright

Published: February 10, 2002. Full text available at: www.nytimes.com/2002/02/10/business/enron-s-many-strands-company-unravels-enron-buffed-image-shine-even-it-rotted.html

light from the ballroom's chandeliers spilled across scores of round tables where executives from the Enron Corporation waited to hear the words of Mr. Lay, their longtime chairman and chief executive.

This meeting of hundreds of Enron executives in the first week of January 2001 was a time of revelry, a chance to celebrate a year when business seemed good—even better than good. At night, according to executives who attended, Champagne and liquor flowed from the open bar, while fistfuls of free cigars were available for the taking. Executives could belly up to temporary gambling tables for high-stakes games of poker. Others found their excitement in the company-sponsored car race; one executive had even hired a truck to transport his three Ferraris from Houston for the event.

Now, as waiters wearing bolo ties scurried about, the executives listened eagerly to Mr. Lay's descriptions of Enron's recent year of success, and the new successes that were within reach. Already, Enron was near the top of the Fortune 500, a multibillion-dollar behemoth that had moved beyond its roots in the natural gas business to blaze new trails in Internet commerce. For 2001, Mr. Lay said, the company would take on a new mission, one that would define everything it did in the months to come: Enron would become "the world's greatest company." The words replaced his image on one of the screens.

But it was not to be. For, unknown to almost everyone there, Enron was secretly falling apart. Even as the celebrations unfolded, accountants and trading experts at the company's Houston head-quarters were desperately working to contain a financial disaster, one that threatened—and ultimately would destroy—everything Enron had become. A handful of executives were struggling to sound the alarm, but with Enron's confidence in its destiny, the warnings went unheeded.

"We were so sure of what we were doing and where we were going," one executive who attended the San Antonio meeting said. "We didn't know we were living on borrowed time."

Investigators picking through the wreckage of Enron, seeking to understand what caused its collapse in December, have explored its byzantine partnerships and financial strategies. From these details, a clearer picture has begun to emerge about what happened inside the thick walls of Enron during its last 11 months. It is two completely different tales—the public image, polished by its most senior officers, of an innovative powerhouse on the verge of reshaping the world, and the hidden truth of a company plagued by secrets, whose executives were struggling to hold it together. It was like a gleaming ocean liner seemingly powering forward, its passengers dining in luxury, while, below the waterline, its sweaty crew frantically bails against the force of an in-rushing sea.

By the final days, the sea had won. Attempts by Enron executives to seek a rescue from their powerful friends in Washington and last-ditch efforts to save the company through a merger had ended in failure. When the company finally sought bankruptcy protection, it marked the biggest, fastest corporate collapse in American history.

Details of Enron's last year were pieced together from internal records of the company and its auditor, audio and video tapes, court documents, partnership records, Congressional testimony and information from a report by a special committee of the company's board and from interviews with current and former executives, government officials and lawyers involved in the case.

With the speed in which they traveled from confidence to collapse, executives who once thought they could see their futures clearly and who believed in their employer have found their faith fundamentally shaken. "Given the events at Enron, given the short time period in which it happened, given the economic disaster, it fundamentally challenges everything I think about the way companies work," said Allan Sommer, former vice president for corporate systems at Enron. "If Enron was able to hide this the way they did, why couldn't other companies do it, too?"

Riding High

Power on Parade At Bush Inauguration

As a chilly rain soaked the streets of Washington on Jan. 20, 2001, the motorcade of President George W. Bush moved past the reviewing stand, near where he had just taken the oath of office. As the new president headed toward Pennsylvania Avenue, the cheers of supporters mixed gamely with the boos of protesters, an aural reminder of the divisions that had split the country during one of its most disputed elections ever.

Nearby, in the exclusive "Pioneers" box on the parade route, Ken Lay watched the festivities. He was there amidst an elite group of about 200 men and women who had each raised $100,000 for Mr. Bush's campaign. Nearby, other Enron executives watched the parade from the elegant Willard hotel and office complex, two blocks from the White House, where the company's law firm, Vinson & Elkins, has its Washington office.

It had been a weekend to savor. Enron and its top two executives had kicked in $300,000 for the inauguration, and the company was one of the few to donate $50,000 for the Texas State Society's 2001 Black Tie and Boots Inaugural Ball, where Mr. Bush and the first lady stopped by to salute their Texan friends, including Mr. Lay.

The day after the inauguration, Mr. Lay attended a private luncheon at the White House, where he was able to spend a few minutes with the new president, a luncheon guest said. That night, Enron hosted a private dinner for several congressmen. Mr. Lay did not attend, but his second in command, Jeffrey K. Skilling, did.

Enron's sharp elbows had already been noticed in Washington. Curtis L. Hébert Jr., then chairman of the Federal Energy Regulatory Commission, had gotten a call from Mr. Lay early in the year. As Mr. Hébert recalled the incident, Mr. Lay said that Enron would continue to support him in his new job if he dropped his reservations about electricity deregulation. Mr. Hébert said he had refused. In an interview earlier this year, Mr. Lay remembered the events differently, saying that Mr. Hébert sought Enron's support at the White House. Either way, the message was clear: Enron, a generous contributor to the Bush campaign, would use its White House access to advance its interests.

Its power base in Houston seemed secure. Its stock price was hovering around $80 a share—not its high, but not far from it. And on Feb. 5, scores of special bonus checks were cut for Enron executives, who would collect tens of millions of dollars because of the company's strong reported profits.

The mood that same day was far less jubilant in the nearby offices of Arthur Andersen, Enron's outside accounting firm. There, David B. Duncan and Thomas H. Bauer—two of the firm's lead accountants on the Enron account—joined a group of six colleagues in a conference room for a meeting. Six more Andersen executives were patched in by speakerphone.

For a significant amount of time, according to notes of the meeting, the Andersen accountants debated a critical point: What should they do about two partnerships—called LJM1 and LJM2—that had been set up 18 months earlier by Enron's chief financial officer, Andrew S. Fastow?

Since mid-1999, Enron had engaged in a score of transactions with the Fastow partnerships. It sold the LJM1 partnership a stake in a Brazilian power project and, later, purchased it back. It sold the same partnership a stake in any future gains on one of its technology investments, a complex arrangement that allowed it to report a paper profit on the deal.

On its face, this arrangement partly reflected a common financing technique: decreasing the company's risk by moving its holdings into separate partnerships that could be sold to outside investors more willing to assume those risks. And Enron's board, which had approved Mr. Fastow's dual role in 1999, had ordered that top management—Richard A. Causey, the chief accounting officer; Richard B. Buy, the chief risk officer; and Mr. Skilling—carefully monitor these deals.

Later, the board's special investigators concluded that these partnerships, and others they spawned, had been twisted at Enron into a tool for making the company seem far more profitable that it really was.

If those allegations are true, there is no sign from the notes of the Feb. 5 meeting at Andersen's Houston office that anyone there knew it. Still, the accountants seemed uncomfortable with the LJM arrangement. To solve that, they drew up a "to do" list, which included suggesting that a special committee of the Enron board be set up to review the fairness of the LJM deals, according to the notes. They also decided to make sure with Enron that LJM met accounting tests that allowed it to be treated as a separate entity, rather than as a subsidiary whose financial results would have to be shown on Enron's books.

The opportunity to cross to-do's off the list came just one week later, on Feb. 12. That day, the Enron board's audit and compliance committee held a meeting, and both Mr. Duncan and Mr. Bauer from Andersen attended. At one point, all Enron executives were excused from the room, and the two Andersen accountants were asked by directors if they had any concerns they wished to express, documents show.

Subsequent testimony by board members suggests the accountants raised nothing from their to-do list. "There is no evidence of any discussion by either Andersen representative about the problems or concerns they apparently had discussed internally just one week earlier," said the special committee report released last weekend.

That same day, though, Enron's board approved a big decision: Mr. Skilling, long the second in command at Enron, would be taking over as chief executive. Mr. Lay would remain as chairman.

In stepping aside, Mr. Lay left to Mr. Skilling—whose manner was seen by many as far more abrasive and abrupt—the delicate task of explaining Enron to its critics. By the time Mr. Skilling was named chief executive, the company had become a lightning rod for political outrage over the electric power crisis in California, which was experiencing brownouts and price spikes. Enron's traders bought and sold electric power, and California utility officials were accusing it and other national power companies of manipulating that esoteric market to reap windfall profits at consumers' expense. Enron and other major trading companies denied the accusation, but there were demands for a full-scale investigation.

In late March, a television crew from "Frontline," the PBS news magazine, visited Enron's sleek office towers in Houston as they prepared a documentary on the power crisis. Mr. Skilling responded to the company's critics on camera. "We are doing the right thing," he said during an interview in a fishbowl room at the edge of Enron's busy trading floor, where traders were buying kilowatt-hours in one part of the country to sell at higher prices elsewhere. "We are looking to create open, competitive, fair markets. And in open, competitive, fair markets, prices are lower and customers get better service."

He added: "We are the good guys. We are on the side of the angels."

After the interview, as Mr. Skilling led the film crew out onto the trading floor, he was asked what his top priority would be as chief executive. His answer came lightning-fast: "To get the stock price up," he said.

Few people outside Enron knew how important that single goal was.

Seeking a Quick Fix

Struggling to Avoid Posting Huge Losses

What made Enron's stock price so important was the fact that some of the company's most important deals with the partnerships run by Mr. Fastow—deals that had allowed Enron to keep hundreds of millions of dollars of potential losses off its books—were financed, in effect, with Enron stock. Those transactions could fall apart if the stock price fell too far.

Indeed, Enron's contracts with some of these partnerships had provisions, called triggers, that required Enron's stock price to stay above certain specific levels. If it did not, and if Enron's own credit rating fell, Enron faced a variety of consequences, all of them damaging to its reported profits.

When Enron's stock was trading as high as $90, the stock prices attached to these triggers—$57.78 a share in one case, $47 a share in another, $28 in a third—no doubt seemed absurdly low. But as Enron's share price hovered around $70 a share in early March, the risk these trigger provisions would be activated grew. Enron's deals with a quartet of Fastow partnerships known as the Raptors—deals that were keeping roughly $504 million in red ink off Enron's books—were especially worrisome.

For months, Enron's accountants had been struggling to keep the Raptors afloat. Like many of the Fastow partnerships, they were financed, directly or indirectly, with Enron stock. They had been formed to assume the risks of future losses on Enron's portfolio of volatile technology stocks, so that Enron could erase those risks from its own financial statements.

But under accounting rules, Enron could only keep those losses off its books if the Raptors remained financially healthy enough to fulfill their obligations. As the Nasdaq boom in technology stocks fizzled, the losses that the Raptors had promised to cover were ballooning. At the same time, Enron's stock was falling in value, reducing the Raptors' ability to cover those losses. The Raptor structure was in peril, and if it failed, Enron would have had to accept that $504 million write-off.

One reason the Raptors were so shaky may have been the fact that, according to the board report, they had already paid out more than $160 million to Mr. Fastow's LJM partnerships, whose investors included Merrill Lynch, J. P. Morgan Chase, Citigroup, the MacArthur Foundation and the Arkansas Teacher Retirement System.

As the March deadline for financial reporting approached, and as Enron's stock continued a slide that brought it below $60 a share, the company's financial experts struggled to find a way to make the Raptors strong enough to meet the accounting tests that allowed Enron to avoid reporting the gargantuan losses. According to the board committee's report, senior Enron employees said Mr. Skilling was "intensely interested" in the Raptor credit problems and called resolving them "one of the company's highest priorities." Mr. Skilling disputes that account, insisting that he was only vaguely aware of the credit problems.

Finally, on March 26, just days before the end of the first quarter, the accountants found a way to refinance the Raptors, using a series of complex and fragile transactions that were still vulnerable to further declines in Enron's stock price. The accountants and financial officers celebrated their ingenuity, according to the board report. But they had merely put off the inevitable.

"Especially after the restructuring," the report says, "the Raptors were little more than a highly complex accounting construct that was destined to collapse."

But while this frantic rescue effort was under way, Enron executives put the final touches on a separate deal that allowed some of them to get millions. The same day the Raptor deal was completed, Enron did another deal, this one with a supposedly unrelated partnership named Chewco.

Chewco owned a stake in yet a third Enron-linked partnership, called JEDI, and wanted to sell that stake to Enron. Enron agreed to buy it for $35 million. What few inside Enron—and almost no one outside Enron—knew was that Chewco was actually controlled by Michael J. Kopper, a managing director on Mr. Fastow's staff. After all the debts and fees were settled, Mr. Kopper and his domestic partner, William D. Dodson, had gotten about $10 million from their Chewco investment, according to the board's report. Neither Mr. Kopper nor Mr. Dodson have returned repeated telephone calls seeking comment.

Two weeks later, on April 17, Enron presented its first-quarter results to investors, and the company's executives were positively giddy. With the huge Raptor losses shuffled away, Enron reported $425 million in earnings, another banner quarter.

That day, the company set up a conference call with Wall Street analysts. As they waited on hold for the executives to come on the line, the analysts listened to faint music. Suddenly, an operator broke in, announcing the arrival of Enron's top brass.

"I hope you all heard that music that was on," Mr. Skilling announced, according to a tape recording of the conversation. "We're all dancing here. It's pretty good stuff."

For about 15 minutes, Mr. Skilling laid out the details of Enron's performance. Nothing was said by any of the Enron executives about the Raptors, the single most important transaction in the quarter.

"So in conclusion, first-quarter results were great," Mr. Skilling said. "We are very optimistic about our new businesses and are confident that our record of growth is sustainable for many years to come."

With that, the executives opened the call for questions. When asked about reserves the company had for its exposure in California—where the state's biggest utility, Pacific Gas and Electric, had filed for bankruptcy protection in the wake of the power crises there—Mr. Skilling almost bristled. Enron had been in the business for 10 years, he said; it analyzed the credit quality of every trading partner it had—some 5,000 in total—every day. There was no reason for anyone to worry about credit exposures; Enron knew everything it needed to know.

Later in the call, Richard Grubman from Highfields Capital Management was called on to speak. Mr. Grubman was not a booster of Enron stock—indeed, he had made investments that would have allowed him to profit if the stock declined—and he questioned why Enron did not release its balance sheet, listing its assets and liabilities, at the same time it reported its profits.

Mr. Skilling said that was not Enron's policy, but Mr. Grubman pressed the issue.

"You're the only financial institution that can't produce a balance sheet or a cash flow statement with their earnings," Mr. Grubman said, at last.

Mr. Skilling paused. "Well, thank you very much," he said. "We appreciate it."

Then Mr. Skilling turned to his colleagues in Houston, and muttered a vulgarity. The group in Houston laughed; some of the analysts on the line, who had heard everything, were stunned.

*   *   *

Jeff Gerth, Richard A. Oppel Jr.,
Richard W. Stevenson and Don Van Natta Jr.
also contributed to this article.

Selection 10.4

Financial scams are some of the best-read stories. Readers identify with the victim. But for the story to work, it needs to contain several elements. First, there needs to be a clear sense of the victim and the perpetrator. Next, there must be a motive and a plot. Who profited, at whose expense, and how did they do it? Who suffered, and how? The story needs real people so the reader can identify with the victims. This story is a little like the Tyler Pipe story in that we get a feel for who these people are and what happened to them. This was part of a series of stories on deceptive sales practices involving military personnel that had big results: refunds to thousands of service members and changes in Pentagon regulations and federal and state laws.

Needing Cash, Veterans Sign Over Pensions

By DIANA B. HENRIQUES

Kevin D. Jones, a retired Army veteran, was desperate for money. He wanted to get his wife out of the Philippines quickly after her home had been destroyed in a bombing. But she was being delayed as she waited for immigration papers to come through that would allow her to join him in North Carolina.

His military contacts, cultivated during a 25-year career that included duty in Bosnia and Kosovo, helped speed the paperwork. And a Florida financial services company that he had found through an advertisement in The Army Times helped him raise the money to fly to Manila, resettle his in-laws and return home with his wife.

He was too frantic, he said, to consider the cost of that money. But it was steep. In exchange for $19,980 after fees and insurance, Mr. Jones signed over his $1,000-a-month military pension for the next five years, a total of $60,000. That is the equivalent of paying interest at a rate of 56 percent a year.

Federal law prohibits retired military people from signing over their future pension payments to others. The companies offering these deals say they are arranged to avoid that restriction. But two federal bankruptcy judges ruled this year that deals like Mr. Jones's, in which veterans in need of quick cash give up their future pensions for a small fraction of their value, do in fact violate that law.

But the law has not been enforced or consistently interpreted. Indeed, the Defense Department's payroll centers routinely handle the paperwork that diverts the pension payments, even though veterans are warned "to exercise caution in these arrangements," a Pentagon spokeswoman said.

As a result, a small but persistent band of financial companies using military-sounding names continue to offer these so-called pension advances to retired military people over the Internet and in military newspapers.

Consumer lawyers are getting calls from people facing lawsuits and bankruptcy after signing over future pension payments to these companies. No one is certain how many veterans have been affected, but the potential market is substantial. In the last year, roughly 1.7 million military retirees received about $33 billion in pension payments from the Pentagon.

None of these practices are a surprise to either the Pentagon or to Congress. In September 2002, the Senate passed a bill that would have penalized companies offering military pension advances, but the effort stalled in the House. Veterans' groups have warned members about these deals. And in May 2003, the National Consumer

Published: December 29, 2004.

Law Center, a nonprofit group in Boston that has worked on consumer protection issues for more than 35 years, condemned the cash advances as illegally disguised loans that do not comply with federal truth-in-lending laws.

Despite these warnings, neither the Pentagon nor Congress has clearly defined these deals or decided which laws apply to them.

The Pentagon does not see pension advances as examples of retirees signing away their future pensions, which it acknowledged would be illegal. Instead, to the Pentagon, "these agreements appear to be loans based on retired pay as collateral," said Lt. Col. Ellen Krenke, a spokeswoman for the Defense Department.

The companies making the pension advances, however, flatly deny that they are loans of any kind.

In contrast to the enforcement gap that arises from these dueling definitions, Congress adopted rules a year ago to protect veterans' disability payments from deals like these. Now, Senator Bill Nelson, the Florida Democrat who co-sponsored that law, is "shaking the tree" at the Defense Department "to get some idea of what's going on," a senior aide to Senator Nelson said recently.

In October, the National Consumer Law Center organized a band of lawyers, including the former governor of Georgia, to file a suit that seeks to confirm the fundamental illegality of buying out military pensions through arrangements like the one Mr. Jones made.

"It seems like this practice falls between the cracks of what the military and the veterans' organizations normally deal with," said Steve Tripoli, a consumer advocate with the Boston group.

The group's class action on behalf of three plaintiffs, filed in federal court in Atlanta, names as defendants C & A Financial Programs of Stuart, Fla., and Advanced Funding Inc., a Maryland company that acted as a broker for C & A.

Those were the companies Mr. Jones dealt with during his family crisis in July 2001, when his in-laws were caught in the cross-fire of sectarian violence that had plagued their hometown in the Mindanao province in the Philippines. In August 2003, after repaying $26,000, he directed the Pentagon to stop sending his pension to the Florida company because, he said, he needed the money to support his wife and newborn son. C & A responded by going to court in its hometown in Florida to sue him and a number of other veterans.

Like Mr. Jones, the plaintiffs in the consumer law center's case signed on for pension advances whose repayment terms, expressed as annual interest rates, ranged from 45 percent to 76 percent.

The suit argues that these deals are actually disguised loans that failed to comply with federal truth-in-lending laws and state interest-rate caps, said Stuart Rossman, the litigation director at the center. "But if I'm wrong," he added, "then it's an assignment of a military pension, and that violates the law, too."

Teri Belcher, a lawyer for Advanced Funding, of Glen Burnie, Md., said the company would not comment on the case.

Leif J. Grazi, a lawyer for C & A in Stuart, said that the company had not offered any new military pension deals for several years because it did not find them profitable. But its existing deals are neither improper loans nor illegal pension assignments, he said. "We are just purchasing a stream of payments," he said, adding that other companies were probably handling the business C & A had turned away.

"If the sale of these assets is improper, why is it that the United States allows them to advertise on the Internet and in the military newspapers?" Mr. Grazi said. "You'll see a million ads every month."

Roy Barnes, the former Georgia governor who has joined the suit against C & A, also wonders why the Defense Department allows pensions to be diverted to third parties—and, in fact, handles the paperwork for the payroll deductions, called allotments.

"The easiest way to cut off these companies is for the Defense Department to stop those allotments," Mr. Barnes said. "That would get their attention."

The fundamental issues raised in the suit against C & A and Advanced Funding have not deterred other companies engaged in this business.

Carl Bachmann founded and runs Veterans First Financial Services in Battery Park, Va., which also offers military pension advances. The suit would not affect his business, he said, because his company offered better terms and clearer disclosure than did the companies cited in court. "There is a right way to do this business, and a wrong way to do this business," Mr. Bachmann said. But there is no doubt, he said, that the business itself is not prohibited by military pension laws.

Executives at Structured Investments Company, which offers pension advances through a unit called Retired Military Financial Services, said they were not familiar with the consumer law center's case. But Steven P. Covey, a managing member of Structured Investments, said that Retired Military's business model was legal and that its rates were reasonable.

"Firms that charge outrageous interest rates and take advantage of financially unstable pensioners are completely at the other end of the spectrum from our company," he said. "We look for a long-term relationship with our pensioners."

Some bankruptcy judges have upheld the right of Structured Investments to claim future military pension payments. But none of those judges addressed how their decision squared with federal statutes—Sections 701 and 101 of Chapter 37 of the United States Code—that prohibit assignments of future military pensions.

Judge Arthur B. Federman of Bankruptcy Court in Kansas City, Mo., observed in a footnote to a July 2002 decision that there were "limitations on an individual's ability to assign his or her right to receive monthly pension benefits," citing the law governing military pensions. But the debtor did not raise the argument, the judge said, "and the court will not address it."

Two other bankruptcy judges, in cases decided this year, did address the special nature of military pensions, and in those cases Mr. Covey's company lost.

Judge James G. Mixon in Little Rock, Ark., ruled in July that the sale of future military pension payments was "specifically prohibited by federal law," which, he said, "unambiguously provides" that any such assignment is invalid.

And in August, Judge Philip H. Brandt in Tacoma, Wash., ruled that the company's claim on a retired Navy enlisted man's pension violated the federal pension statutes. While the company's contracts say the deal is not an assignment, Judge Brandt wrote, "in the words of Gabby Hayes, 'Sayin' it don't make it so.' "

But most veterans cannot afford to challenge the companies' claims in court, especially when the court is far from their homes, said Lynn Drysdale, a member of the plaintiffs' team suing C & A and a staff lawyer at Jacksonville Area Legal Aid. Instead, they wind up paying default judgments without ever making the argument that the debts were illegal and therefore uncollectible, she said.

That is what happened to Edgar J. Basford III, known as Jack, who retired from the Navy as a senior chief petty officer in 1993. In May 2001, facing divorce expenses, he got $26,000 from C & A, after fees and insurance, in exchange for signing over his $1,242-a-month Navy pension for five years, a total of $74,520. After repaying almost $35,000, he fell behind on the debt and was sued for the rest of the money.

"I didn't have the money to fly down to Florida to defend myself," Mr. Basford said. The $46,000 judgment the company obtained was the sole reason he filed for bankruptcy last June, he said. But he did not challenge the legality of the debt and wound up agreeing to pay $500 a month to C & A for more than seven years.

Mr. Jones, who now lives in Eldridge, Iowa, said newly retired veterans like himself were especially vulnerable to a marketing approach that relies on reassuring names like Retired Military Financial Services and advertisements in publications that veterans trust, like The Army Times.

Moreover, said Mr. Jones, who joined the Army at age 18, "you spend your whole life in a culture where everything is grounded in clear procedures and high standards," and where instructions are followed without question. "But in the civilian world, you have to question everything—everything."

Now, he added, "I'm learning that."

A Conversation with . . . **Diana B. Henriques**

SENIOR FINANCIAL WRITER

© The New York Times

Diana B. Henriques is an investigative reporter who has covered business governance and regulatory issues for The New York Times since 1989. She previously worked for Barron's magazine, the Trenton Times and The Philadelphia Inquirer. She was a 2005 Pulitzer Prize finalist for her stories exposing deceptive sales practices of insurance, mutual funds and other financial products to young military personnel. Henriques has chronicled the Bernie Madoff and Enron scandals, and reported extensively about how secular nonprofits receive hundreds of special exemptions from laws, taxes and regulations. Her most recent book is "The White Sharks of Wall Street: Thomas Mellon Evans and the Original Corporate Raiders." The following is an edited transcript of a telephone interview.

What do you cover for The New York Times?
More generally, you could say that I cover finance. The areas that I have spent the most time on over the years are white-collar crime, regulatory developments and corporate governance. I write about the application of regulations in the real world: Are they effective? Are they well understood, and are there changes that need to be made? Then there is the basic financial investigative reporting—it ranges from what this crappy little company is doing to how the Pentagon allowed life insurers to rip off soldiers.

How did you gain your expertise in business reporting?
I learned it on the job, with one caveat. I had a grounding in economics at the undergraduate level and I enjoyed it. While working as a copy editor out in California, I took nine or 12 hours toward a masters in business at the University of Santa Clara. They took one look at my undergraduate transcripts and said, "You have not had math." So they required me to take a sort of remedial math for liberal arts, which to my surprise I really enjoyed. I had not taken any math since high school algebra. It wasn't as bad as I feared. I kind of conquered my numbers phobia along the way.

Do people in today's world need a formal business degree or education?
I certainly think it would be helpful. Finance has become increasingly complicated. Corporate life hasn't changed that much in my career, but the world of finance has changed dramatically. What is more important than a formal undergraduate degree in finance or economics is a willingness to become financially literate. I think that is critical for a reporter covering anything today.

Explain what you mean by financial literacy.
The need for financial knowledge has seeped into every area of reportage. Sports stadiums are built with tax-exempt municipal bonds. Citicorp is dispensing welfare benefits through ATMs. The culture scene is dominated by corporate giants. It is almost impossible to cover anything from arts to sciences to criminology to immigration without a grasp of the world of business. I think it is essential for every reporter to conquer the notion that "I don't do numbers, I don't do economics, I don't do finance." The real world is numbers, finance and economics. The day of the generalist who couldn't tell an income statement from a balance sheet or a stock from a bond but could still manage the demands of today's world are long gone.

Why is this so? Is it because the world is so complicated?
No. It is because business has become so dominant. It is the world that we live in. What determines what a neighborhood looks like? Where the shopping centers are built? What films or TV shows we can see? Once you take your blinders off, it is hard to look at any corner of the world and not see the influence and power of business. To say that business is some segregated area of coverage is ignorant. It does not reflect reality.

Where do you come up with your ideas for stories?
Apart from the event-driven ideas and ideas from tipsters, I am always intrigued by anomalies, inconsistencies, things that don't go according to plan. I try to train myself to ask, "Why did this zig when everything else zagged? Why is someone doing better in a sector that everyone else is faltering in?" I try to keep attuned to what people think is going to happen or should be happening. And then I look at what really is happening. I look for deviations. The law of unintended consequences has produced an enormous flow of ideas for me—the perversities of life.

Do you have a thesis that you set out to prove or disprove?
Yes, I do try to start out with a thesis, although I always stand ready to revise it as my reporting demands. I like to plan. I began as an investigative reporter, when I had beat reporting obligations and the notion of taking two months off to pursue an idea was nonsense. I had a grand jury that was going to meet every week and motion days at the courthouse and so forth. I had to squeeze in investigative reporting projects amongst my daily reporting assignments. There is no way to do that if you don't plan. After I do enough fishing, I frame a thesis and ask myself what I need to learn to prove that thesis—or, as important, disprove or revise it.

At this early stage, I also try to look ahead to articulate why you, the general public, should care whether my thesis is true or not. This part of the planning process helps me formulate the nut graf I must have in the final story—the graf that tells the reader why this story matters.

In the military series about financial product sales, what I came up with in terms of why it mattered was that the American public cared so deeply about these kids we were sending off to Iraq, possibly to die, that it would want to know if people were extracting a financial pound of flesh from them before we sent them off. It seemed like something the public would see as morally offensive. Knowing that, I knew I had to find the kids. I couldn't tell this story in an abstract way. I had to find particular people, young service members who had been affected.

So it is a four-step process—framing a thesis, identifying what I already know, identifying what I need to know and then being clear about why it matters. It enables me to come up with a reporting plan that is pretty concise and persuasive. Moreover, I wind up with a clear idea of how big the gap is between what I know and what I need to learn—which gives me some idea about how long it is going to take and how hard it is going to be.

What story are you most proud of in the past decade?

Without a doubt it is the military insurance story. The series ran in 2004. It focused on a variety of financial exploitations ranging from deceptive sales of life insurance to deceptive sales of very high-cost mutual funds. It looked at how service members were being financially exploited and led to very gratifying changes in law and awareness within the military and within the Congress. There was an enormous outpouring of thanks from the families.

Why does business seem to be plagued by so many scandals?

The crooks are always with you. There are cycles in regulatory rigor and cycles of economic booms and busts. When regulatory rigor ebbs and economic activity booms, it is a very ripe breeding ground for fraud. Then regulatory rigor tightens or the economy falters and these frauds come to light. So we have cycles in public tolerance and regulatory attention to fraud. We are now in 2009, a boom time for regulation. The day will come when the good times are rolling again and no one is concerned about their 401(k) and we will become complacent about the risks of financial fraud again. The profit motive unleashed and unregulated is little better than the law of the jungle. For all the benefits it offers mankind, democratic capitalism functions best in a well-regulated environment. If we go through these cycles where people are less interested in regulation and more interested in profit, more fraud is likely to occur. I don't worry that the journalists who come after me are not going to have any crime to write about because we have tackled it all in the post-Enron, post-Madoff era.

What advice do you have for young journalists?

If you have a fear of numbers, and you are reluctant to tackle the more rigorous financial literacy requirement, get over it. Ground yourself firmly in financial literacy either through formal academic training or through self-education. There are a number of ways to acquire it, but you just have to have it. Step two is to remember your audience. You must know something far better to explain it to a general audience than to a sophisticated audience. That sounds counterintuitive. When you are trying to explain a topic to a sophisticated audience you can quote the experts and your audience will understand them. But when you are trying to translate that expertise into commonly understood language, you have to know it down to the ground. You can't describe a credit default swap in a way that is understood by a general reader if you don't thoroughly understand how a credit default swap works. So the notion that someone writing for a general audience can get away with a weaker grasp of the information than someone writing for a sophisticated audience is exactly wrong. It is completely 180-degrees wrong. You must master your topic to keep it simple.

MAKING**CONNECTIONS**

1

Discuss the challenges reporters might have faced covering the story about the deaths and injuries at Tyler Pipe. How would you approach a story about workplace injuries if the company refuses to talk to you? Read the entire story online and list all the sources, people and documents the reporters used. Can you think of any other sources you'd try?

2

The use of a prime ingredient found in antifreeze—diethylene glycol—in food and drug products is a bizarre development that led reporters on a chase covering several continents. This story also has a technical, scientific hurdle. List some sources where you could learn about diethylene glycol and its effects on the human body.

3

The reporters writing the Enron story use passages in a narrative style, with description and dialogue, to tell the story. Yet this narration is based on interviews and court documents. Discuss the reporting, sourcing and ethical challenges a reporter would face in relying on court documents and interviews to reconstruct scenes.

4

One major source for the Henriques story is military personnel. List a couple other places you might find a treasure trove of documents relating to people who have been bilked by unscrupulous sellers of insurance and other financial services.

5

BUSINESS CONCEPTS REVIEW

Anonymous source	A person who agrees to exchange information with a reporter on the condition that his or her name not be disclosed. Courts have held that promises of confidentially are legally binding.
Computer-assisted reporting	The use of computers to analyze data and public records that can then be used to write news stories.
Food and Drug Administration	Federal agency responsible for regulating the safety of foods, drugs, cosmetics, medical devices, veterinary drugs and biological products.
Freedom of Information Act	Law ensuring public access to federal records. The law defines the records subject to disclosure and outlines procedures governing the records released to the public.
Investigative Reporters and Editors, Inc.	Nonprofit organization dedicated to improving the quality of investigative reporting in journalism.
Occupational Safety and Health Administration	Federal agency that enforces rules for governing safety and health in the workplace.
Shield laws	Law that provides a news reporter with protection against having to divulge information and sources obtained during the news-reporting process.
Truth in Lending Act	Federal act that requires full disclosure of the terms and costs of a lending arrangement.

notes

introduction

1. Harris Interactive Inc., Public Relations Research, "The 2009 Consumer Financial Literacy Survey Final Report," 2: www.nfcc.org/Newsroom/Financial Literacy/files/2009FinancialLiteracySurveyFINAL.pdf

chapter 3

1. Joseph Weber, "Boeing to Rein in Dreamliner Outsourcing," Business Week, January 16, 2009: http://bx.businessweek.com/boeing-787/view?url=http%3 A%2F%2Fwww.businessweek.com%2Fbwdaily%2Fdnflash%2Fcontent%2 Fjan2009%2Fdb20090116_971202.htm%3Fchan%3Dtop%2Bnews_top%2 Bnews%2Bindex%2B-%2Btemp_companies
2. Mark Tatge, "Global Gamble—Boeing Is Soaring on Orders for Its New 787— A Plane Assembled from Across the World. That's Part of the Problem," Forbes, April 17, 2006: www.forbes.com/forbes/2006/0417/078.html
3. Telephone interview with Louis Uchitelle, The New York Times, June 2009.
4. Series available at: http://projects.nytimes.com/immigration/

chapter 4

1. Jon Hilsenrath and Deborah Solomon, "Job Cuts Outpace Economic Decline," The Wall Street Journal, July 23, 2009, A1.
2. "Where the Jobs Are," The New York Times, July 24, 2009, A18.

chapter 5

1. TreasuryDirect: www.treasurydirect.gov/NP/BPDLogin?application=np
2. TreasuryDirect: www.treasurydirect.gov/govt/reports/ir/ir_expense.htm
3. David Walker, president and chief executive officer, Peter G. Peterson Foundation: www.pgpf.org/about/faq/#ournationsdebts
4. Ibid.
5. Wikipedia: http://en.wikipedia.org/wiki/Los_Angeles_class_submarine

chapter 6

1. Jennifer 8. Lee, "Cigarettes Top $9 a Pack in City," The New York Times, April 1, 2008.

chapter 8

1. Nicholas J. Mastracchio Jr. and Victoria M. Zunitch, "Difference Between Mergers and Acquisitions," Journal of Accountancy (November 2002): www .journalofaccountancy.com/Issues/2002/Nov/DifferenceBetweenMergers AndAcquisitions.htm

chapter 9

1. William E. Blundell, "The Art and Craft of Feature Writing: Based on The Wall Street Journal Guide" (New York: Penguin Books, 1988).